Capable to Match (CTM) with SAP® APO

SAP® Essentials

Expert SAP knowledge for your day-to-day work

Whether you wish to expand your SAP knowledge, deepen it, or master a use case, SAP Essentials provide you with targeted expert knowledge that helps support you in your day-to-day work. To the point, detailed, and ready to use.

SAP PRESS is a joint initiative of SAP and Galileo Press. The know-how offered by SAP specialists combined with the expertise of the Galileo Press publishing house offers the reader expert books in the field. SAP PRESS features first-hand information and expert advice, and provides useful skills for professional decision-making.

SAP PRESS offers a variety of books on technical and business related topics for the SAP user. For further information, please visit our website: *www.sap-press.com.*

Martin Murray
Discover Logistics with SAP ERP
2008, 385 pp.
978-1-59229-230-1

Sachin Sethi
Enhancing Supplier Relationship Management Using SAP SRM
2007, 695 pp.
978-1-59229-068-0

Martin Murray
SAP Warehouse Management: Functionality and Technical Configuration
2007, 504 pp.
978-1-59229-133-5

Eduard Gerhardt, Kai Krüger, Oliver Schipp
Efficient E-Procurement with SAP
2008, 200 pp.
978-1-59229-209-7

Balaji Gaddam

Capable to Match (CTM) with SAP® APO

Bonn • Boston

ISBN 978-1-59229-244-8
© 2009 by Galileo Press Inc., Boston (MA)
1st Edition 2009

Galileo Press is named after the Italian physicist, mathematician and philosopher Galileo Galilei (1564–1642). He is known as one of the founders of modern science and an advocate of our contemporary, heliocentric worldview. His words *Eppur si muove* (And yet it moves) have become legendary. The Galileo Press logo depicts Jupiter orbited by the four Galilean moons, which were discovered by Galileo in 1610.

Editor   Jenifer Niles/Erik Herman
Copy Editor   Julie McNamee
Cover Design   Jill Winitzer
Photo Credit   Image Copyright Kevin Davidson, 2008. Used under license from Shutterstock.com.
Layout Design   Vera Brauner
Production Editor   Kelly O'Callaghan
Typesetting   Publishers' Design and Production Services, Inc.
Printed and bound in Canada

All rights reserved. Neither this publication nor any part of it may be copied or reproduced in any form or by any means or translated into another language, without the prior consent of Galileo Press GmbH, Rheinwerkallee 4, 53227 Bonn, Germany.

Galileo Press makes no warranties or representations with respect to the content hereof and specifically disclaims any implied warranties of merchantability or fitness for any particular purpose. Galileo Press assumes no responsibility for any errors that may appear in this publication.

"Galileo Press" and the Galileo Press logo are registered trademarks of Galileo Press GmbH, Bonn, Germany. SAP PRESS is an imprint of Galileo Press.

All of the screenshots and graphics reproduced in this book are subject to copyright © SAP AG, Dietmar-Hopp-Allee 16, 69190 Walldorf, Germany.

SAP, the SAP-Logo, mySAP, mySAP.com, mySAP Business Suite, SAP NetWeaver, SAP R/3, SAP R/2, SAP B2B, SAPtronic, SAPscript, SAP BW, SAP CRM, SAP Early Watch, SAP ArchiveLink, SAP GUI, SAP Business Workflow, SAP Business Engineer, SAP Business Navigator, SAP Business Framework, SAP Business Information Warehouse, SAP inter-enterprise solutions, SAP APO, AcceleratedSAP, InterSAP, SAPoffice, SAPfind, SAPfile, SAPtime, SAPmail, SAP¬access, SAP-EDI, R/3 Retail, Accelerated HR, Accelerated HiTech, Accelerated Consumer Products, ABAP, ABAP/4, ALE/WEB, BAPI, Business Framework, BW Explorer, Enjoy-SAP, mySAP.com e-business platform, mySAP Enterprise Portals, RIVA, SAP-PHIRE, TeamSAP, Webflow und SAP PRESS are registered or unregistered trademarks of SAP AG, Walldorf, Germany.

All other products mentioned in this book are registered or unregistered trademarks of their respective companies.

Contents

Acknowledgments 11

1 Overview of SAP SCM 13

    1.1   SAP SCM Overview 14
            1.1.1   SAP Advanced Planner and Optimizer (SAP APO) 15
            1.1.2   Supply Chain Event Management (SCEM) 17
            1.1.3   SAP Supply Network Collaboration 18
    1.2   Supply Network Planning Methods in SAP SCM 18
    1.3   CTM Planning Overview 21
            1.3.1   CTM Planning Process Steps 22
            1.3.2   System Landscape Requirement for CTM Planning 26
            1.3.3   CTM Planning Run — Complete Overview 27
    1.4   Configuration Using CTM Planning Parameters 31
    1.5   Executing the CTM Planning Run 32
    1.6   Summary 33

2 CTM Planning Scope 35

    2.1   SAP SCM Master Data 36
    2.2   CTM Master Data Selection 38
            2.2.1   Master Data Selection Options 39
            2.2.2   Automatic Master Data Selection 40
    2.3   Master Data Attributes for CTM Planning 45
            2.3.1   Location 46
            2.3.2   Location Product 47
            2.3.3   Resource 48
            2.3.4   External Procurement 50
            2.3.5   In-House Production 53
            2.3.6   Product Substitution 57
    2.4   Transactional Data Selection 58
    2.5   Planning and Deletion Modes 59
            2.5.1   Regenerative Planning with CTM 63
            2.5.2   Net Change Planning with CTM 63
    2.6   Planning Strategy with CTM 64

Contents

	2.6.1	CTM Time Stream	65
	2.6.2	Capacity Planning	66
	2.6.3	Planning Type	67
	2.6.4	Late Demand Strategies	68
	2.6.5	Scheduling Direction	69
	2.6.6	Pegging Type	70
2.7	Summary		70

3 CTM Demand and Supply Processing ... 71

3.1	CTM Demand and Supply Attributes		72
	3.1.1	CTM Demand Attributes	73
	3.1.2	CTM Supply Attributes	75
3.2	CTM Demand Aggregation		76
	3.2.1	Demand Aggregation by Time Bucket	77
	3.2.2	Demand Aggregation by Rounding Value	79
	3.2.3	Demand Aggregation by Hierarchy	80
3.3	Demand Prioritization		82
	3.3.1	Demand Prioritization Using Demand Attributes	82
	3.3.2	Demand Prioritization Using Descriptive Characteristics	87
3.4	Supply Aggregation		90
	3.4.1	Supply Aggregation by Time Buckets	90
	3.4.2	Supply Aggregation by Hierarchies	91
3.5	Supply Categorization		92
	3.5.1	Supply Categorization by ATP Categories	93
	3.5.2	Supply Categorization by Supply Limits	95
	3.5.3	CTM Search Strategy for Source Selection	97
3.6	Summary		99

4 CTM Planning Algorithm ... 101

4.1	CTM Planning Algorithm		103
4.2	CTM Search Tree Generation		103
4.3	CTM Decision Criteria for Source Selection		106
	4.3.1	CTM Supply Selection	106
	4.3.2	CTM Source of Supply Selection	107
	4.3.3	Source Selection with Procurement Type	108
	4.3.4	Source Selection with Inbound Quota	110

		4.3.5	Source Selection with Procurement Priorities and Costs ..	113
		4.3.6	Source Selection with Validity Date	114
		4.3.7	Source Selection with PPM/PDS Lot Size	114
	4.4	CTM Order Scheduling		115
		4.4.1	Scheduling Planned Order	116
		4.4.2	Scheduling Stock Transfer Order	126
		4.4.3	Scheduling Purchase Requisitions	129
		4.4.4	Scheduling Substitution Order	129
	4.5	Scheduling Techniques for Late Demands		130
		4.5.1	Late Demand Scheduling Modes	132
	4.6	Additional Parameters Influencing CTM Scheduling		134
		4.6.1	Scheduling Horizons	135
		4.6.2	Order Creation and Deletion Start	135
		4.6.3	Demand Selection Horizon	136
		4.6.4	Order Creation Frame	136
		4.6.5	Maximum Earliness for Planned Orders	138
		4.6.6	Maximum Earliness for Dependent Demands (MPL)	139
	4.7	CTM Planning Results Analysis		142
	4.8	Explanation of CTM Planning Results		142
	4.9	CTM Planning Result Indicators		147
	4.10	Common Scheduling Issues with CTM Planning		148
		4.10.1	CTM Planning with Multilevel Fixed Lot Sizes	148
		4.10.2	CTM Planning with Local Search Strategy	150
		4.10.3	Bucket Planning with Fixed Lot Size and Resource Underutilization	150
		4.10.4	Fair Share Planning with CTM	153
	4.11	Summary		155

5   Supply Control with CTM Planning 157

	5.1	CTM Planning for Safety Stock Quantity		161
		5.1.1	Safety Stock Requirement in SAP liveCache	163
		5.1.2	Safety Stock Requirements as Virtual Demands in CTM	163
		5.1.3	Safety Stock Virtual Demand Generation in CTM	165
		5.1.4	Interval Planning with CTM for Reducing Time-Phased Safety Stock	172
		5.1.5	Additional Planning Parameters for CTM SS Planning	176
	5.2	CTM Planning with Safety Days of Supply		178
		5.2.1	Safety Lead Time Calculation for Constant SDS	179

Contents

		5.2.2 Safety Lead Time Calculation for Time-Phased SDS	180
		5.2.3 CTM Scheduling of Demands Using Safety Lead Time	181
	5.3	Additional CTM Supply Control Techniques	184
		5.3.1 Store Transport at Destination Location	185
		5.3.2 Supply Distribution	187
		5.3.3 Minimum Build of Supply	188
	5.4	Summary	189

6 Advanced Planning Techniques with CTM 191

	6.1	CTM Planning with Requirement Strategies	193
		6.1.1 Make-to-Stock Production (10)	194
		6.1.2 Planning with Final Assembly (20)	195
		6.1.3 Planning Without Final Assembly (30)	196
		6.1.4 Planning with Planning Product (40)	199
	6.2	Make to Order Production with CTM	199
	6.3	Production in Alternative Location	203
	6.4	Supply Chain Planning in the Plant	205
		6.4.1 Component Withdrawal in Another Location	207
	6.5	Subcontracting Planning with CTM	209
	6.6	CTM Planning with Product Interchangeability	212
		6.6.1 Supersession	213
		6.6.2 Form-Fit-Function (FFF) Class	216
	6.7	CTM Planning with Substitution Rules	218
		6.7.1 Product Substitution Procedure	219
		6.7.2 Location Substitution Procedure	219
		6.7.3 Product Location Substitution Procedure	219
		6.7.4 Production Substitution for Supply	221
		6.7.5 Production Substitution for Production (Down Binning)	222
	6.8	Aggregated Planning with CTM	223
		6.8.1 Hierarchy Definitions Used in CTM Planning	224
		6.8.2 Master Data Selection for Aggregated Planning in CTM	227
		6.8.3 Process Steps for Aggregated Planning in CTM	228
		6.8.4 Aggregated Planning with Safety Stock	235
	6.9	CTM Planning in Distribution Networks	237
	6.10	Summary	238

7 Technical Details of CTM Planning 239

- 7.1 CTM Planning Performance Optimization 239
  - 7.1.1 STEP 1: Read Data and Delete Order 242
  - 7.1.2 STEP 2: CTM Engine Planning for Demands 245
  - 7.1.3 STEP 3: Write the CTM Planning Result in liveCache 253
  - 7.1.4 STEP 4: Publish CTM Results to SAP ERP 255
- 7.2 Using Parallel Processing for CTM Planning 257
- 7.3 CTM Planning Business Add-Ins 260
- 7.4 Summary 261

Glossary 263

The Author 269

Index 271

Acknowledgments

This project draws inspiration from the efforts and support of many individuals. Without these friends and colleagues, this book would not have been possible. I would like to extend my sincere thanks to my CTM Development colleagues at SAP Ag, Germany — Michael Wachter, Stefan Merker, Christian Werner, Thomas Dehoust, Markus Riepp and Joachim Altmeyer. I would also like to thank John Larkin, Director, SAP America for his guidance and motivation.

Thank you to our friends at Galileo Press — for their guidance, patience, and support. I would especially like to thank Jenifer Niles, who made this book possible and has encouraged me to get the words onto the printed page (again).

I owe the utmost gratitude to my family, who supported me during the writing of this book. My wife Bindu as well as my daughter's Shreya and Shruthi — thank you for your love and patience throughout this project.

I hope you find this book informative and easy to read. I am hopeful that I will provide you with detailed functions and practical examples as you embark on your CTM implementation projects.

This chapter provides a basic overview of the SAP SCM application. Multilevel Supply Demand Matching (SDM) or more commonly known as Capable-to-Match (CTM) is a constraints-based, finite, multilevel supply planning solution available in SAP SCM. The key components and process steps of the CTM planning solution are explained in this chapter.

1   Overview of SAP SCM

Supply Chain Management (SCM) has evolved over the years but fundamentally SCM is based on two key aspects. The first is that practically every product that reaches an end user represents the cumulative effort of multiple organizations. These organizations are referred to collectively as the supply chain. The second aspect is that while supply chains have existed for a long time, most organizations have only paid attention to what was happening within their "four walls."

Few businesses understood, much less managed, the entire chain of activities that ultimately delivered products to the final customer. A key barrier was the cost of communicating with and coordinating among the many independent suppliers in each supply chain. The result was disjointed and often ineffective supply chains. SCM is the active management of supply chain activities to maximize customer value and achieve a sustainable competitive advantage. It represents a conscious effort by the supply chain firms to develop and run supply chains in the most effective and efficient ways possible. Supply chain activities cover everything from product development, sourcing, production, and logistics, as well as the information systems needed to coordinate these activities. The organizations that make up the supply chain are "linked" together through physical flows and information flows. Physical flows involve the transformation, movement, and storage of goods and materials. They are the most visible piece of the supply chain. But information flows are just as important. *Information flows* allow the various supply chain partners to coordinate their long-term plans and to control the day-to-day flow of goods and material up and down the supply chain. The following are five basic components of SCM:

- **Plan**

  This is the strategic portion of SCM. You need a strategy for managing all of the resources that go toward meeting customer demand for your product or service. A big piece of planning is developing a set of metrics to monitor the supply chain so that it's efficient, costs less, and delivers high quality and value to customers.

- **Source**

  This is the step in which you choose the suppliers that will deliver the goods and services you need to create your product. Develop a set of pricing, delivery, and payment processes with suppliers, and create metrics for monitoring and improving the relationships. Put together processes for managing the inventory of goods and services you receive from suppliers, including receiving shipments, verifying them, transferring them to your manufacturing facilities, and authorizing supplier payments.

- **Make**

  This is the manufacturing step. Schedule the activities necessary for production, testing, packaging, and preparation for delivery. As the most metric-intensive portion of the supply chain, measure quality levels, production output, and worker productivity.

- **Deliver**

  This is the part that many insiders refer to as logistics. Coordinate the receipt of orders from customers, develop a network of warehouses, pick carriers to get products to customers, and set up an invoicing system to receive payments.

- **Return**

  This is the problem part of the supply chain. Create a network for receiving defective and excess products back from customers and supporting customers who have problems with delivered products.

1.1 SAP SCM Overview

SCM is possible today mainly due to advancement in technology that has simplified communication and coordination across the supply chain. Companies recognize that costs can be reduced while customer satisfaction is increased when production and inventory decisions are based on analysis of the total system of delivering products and services.

The SAP SCM application provides comprehensive, industry-specific SCM capabilities and offers a standard interface for SAP ERP for seamless integration of the supply chain planning and supply chain execution functions. SAP SCM contains solutions for the following:

- Supply chain planning
- Supply chain execution
- Supply chain coordination
- Supply chain collaboration

1.1.1 SAP Advanced Planner and Optimizer (SAP APO)

SAP Advanced Planner and Optimizer (SAP APO) provides a robust and scalable solution for real-time collaborative decision support, advanced planning, simulation, and optimization. The powerful memory resident analytical engine (SAP liveCache) and highly flexible and configurable SAP BW technology support strategic, tactical, and operational planning. SAP APO contains several advanced optimization algorithms to support supply network, production, distribution, and transportation planning and optimization.

The core components of SAP APO are listed here:

- **Demand Planning**
  SAP APO Demand Planning (DP) creates a forecast of market demand for the finished products. DP allows you to take into consideration many different causal factors that affect demand. The result of SAP APO DP is the demand plan. DP offers several user-specific planning layouts and interactive planning books to enable you to integrate people from different departments, and even different companies, into the forecasting process. Using the DP library of statistical forecasting and advanced macro techniques, you can create forecasts based on demand history as well as any number of causal factors, carry out predefined and self-defined tests on forecast models and forecast results, and adopt a consensus-based approach to reconcile the demand plans of different departments.

- **Supply Network Planning**
  The seamless integration of DP with *Supply Network Planning* (SNP) supports an efficient SAP Sales and Operations Planning (SAP SOP) process. Using the demand plan, the supply planner uses SNP to create a feasible, synchronized,

and optimized supply plan in a mid-term horizon. SNP offers three main planning options:

SNP Heuristics provides an infinite supply planning function that must be followed by capacity leveling to generate a feasible plan.

SNP Optimizer is a cost-based finite capacity planning function.

Capable-to-Match (CTM) is a constraints-based, multilevel finite capacity planning function.

- **SNP Deployment**
  The *SNP Deployment* function determines how and when inventory should be deployed to distribution centers, customers, and vendor-managed inventory accounts. It produces optimized distribution plans based on constraints, such as transportation capacities, and business rules, such as minimum cost approach or replenishment strategies. The *Transport Load Builder* (TLB) function maximizes transport capacities by optimizing load building.

- **Production planning and detailed scheduling**
  You use the *production planning and detailed scheduling* (PP/DS) component in SAP APO to create procurement proposals for in-house production or external procurement to cover product requirements. PP/DS Optimization functions help to optimize and plan the resource schedule and the order dates and times in detail.

- **Transportation planning and vehicle scheduling**
  Transportation planning/vehicle scheduling (TP/VS) is available in SAP APO to plan and optimize shipments for orders (sales orders, purchase orders, returns, and stock transport orders) and deliveries. You assign the orders and deliveries for which you plan shipments to vehicles. You can take various restrictions into account, for example, requested delivery dates or transportation capacities when assigning the vehicles. The result of TP/VS planning is the creation of planned shipments. TP/VS also supports various processes such as outbound delivery, inbound delivery, and cross-docking.

- **Global Available to Promise**
  Global-ATP (GATP) contains the functions for the ATP check in SAP APO. This includes transportation and shipment scheduling, which is carried out in SAP APO. The ATP check, also known as the availability check, represents an online search that should ensure that your company can provide the requested product at the requested time in the quantity requested by the customer.

Figure 1.1 shows the core components of SAP SCM.

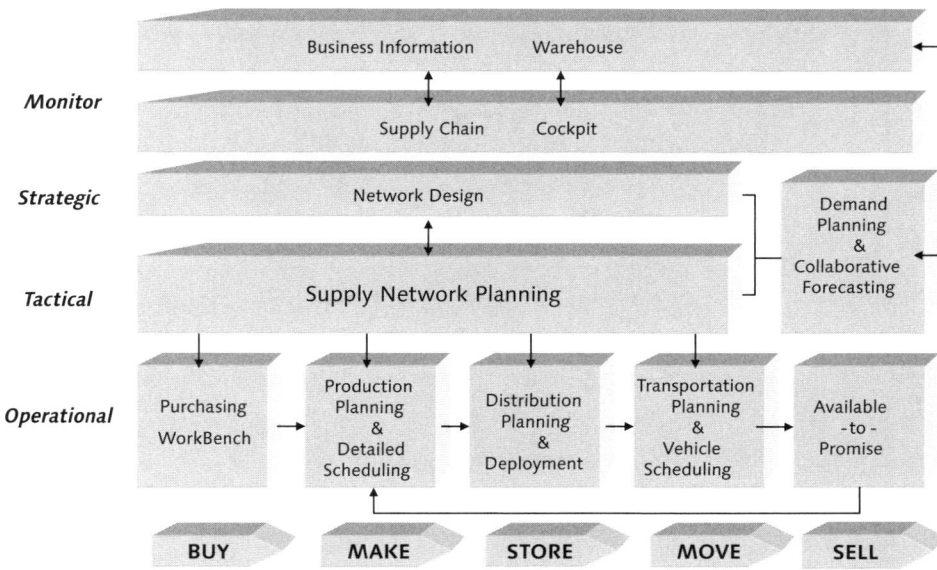

Figure 1.1 Overview of SAP APO

Supply Chain Execution functions such as material management, manufacturing, warehouse management, and transportation execution are done in SAP ECC.

1.1.2   Supply Chain Event Management (SCEM)

SAP SCM provides advanced solutions for *supply chain coordination.* The *Supply Chain Event Management* (SCEM) component provides or improves visibility within your logistics processes for both planning and execution. Due to the flexibility of the solution, you can map, control, and check all required business processes. A role-based approach makes it possible to view the same business process from various points of view.

You can use SAP SCEM to process messages about the events in business processes and thereby notify in various ways those involved in the supply chain network about business events that have occurred. By actively notifying the responsible persons and making them aware of critical situations or exceptions, you can optimize reaction times and improve quality and customer satisfaction.

1.1.3 SAP Supply Network Collaboration

SAP Supply Network Collaboration is one of the core capabilities of adaptive supply chain networks, a fundamental principle for the networked and outsourced enterprise of today and tomorrow. Through SAP Supply Network Collaboration, customers and suppliers can simultaneously eliminate inefficiencies in their supply chains by synchronizing the flow of information between them. SAP Supply Network Collaboration offers a 360-degree view on supply chain collaboration, offering firms different ways to effectively collaborate with customers, suppliers, third-party logistics providers, and outsourced manufacturing partners.

For *supplier collaboration*, SAP Supply Network Collaboration offers upstream business processes such as supplier managed inventory (SMI), discrete purchase order management, scheduling agreement release handling, and web-based kanban signals.

For *customer collaboration*, SAP Supply Network Collaboration offers comprehensive downstream business processes such as responsive replenishment, which represents the next generation in demand-driven replenishment and collaboration.

SAP Supply Network Collaboration also offers market-leading capabilities for collaborating and monitoring contract manufacturing relationships. For outsourced manufacturing, the main capabilities include cross-tier visibility of inventory, supply and demand, and a collaborative work order process that tracks work-in-progress, material consumption, and BOM changes at the outsourced manufacturing partner.

1.2 Supply Network Planning Methods in SAP SCM

SNP integrates purchasing, manufacturing, distribution, and transportation so that comprehensive tactical planning and sourcing decisions can be simulated and implemented on the basis of a single, consistent global model (see Figure 1.2). SNP uses advanced optimization techniques, based on constraints and penalties, to plan product flow along the supply chain. The result is optimal purchasing, production, and distribution decisions; reduced order fulfillment times and inventory levels; and improved customer service.

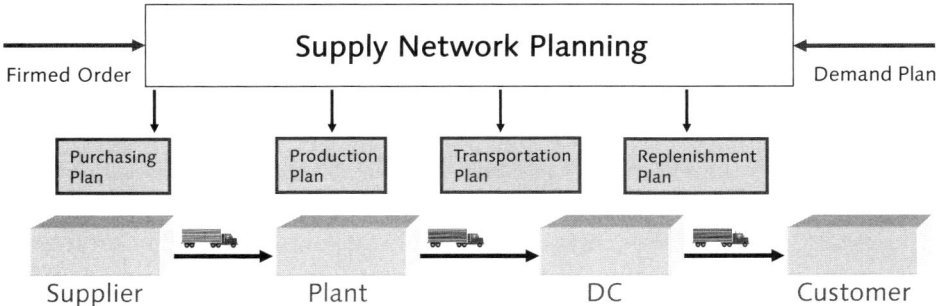

Figure 1.2 SAP APO Supply Network Planning Overview

Starting from a demand plan, SNP determines a permissible short- to medium-term plan for fulfilling the estimated sales volumes. This plan covers both the quantities that must be transported between two locations (e.g., distribution center to customer or production plant to distribution center), and the quantities to be produced and procured. When making a recommendation, SNP compares all logistical activities to the available capacity.

SNP can be executed finitely. In this way, the production, warehouse, or transport resources of your network can already be taken into account in rough-cut planning. In principle, planning in SNP takes place based on so-called time buckets, that is, on the basis of freely defined time bucket profiles. The smallest unit in SNP is one day. In terms of performance, bucket-oriented planning is much better than detailed scheduling in SAP APO PP/DS, so that planning of more complex networks is also possible. Network planning within SNP generally takes place in two steps. In the first step, the stock transfer orders are created to optimally distribute and meet the requirements in the network. After production has taken place in the production plants, planned orders are deployed to meet the requirements at the distribution centers of the network.

In SNP, different planning strategies are available to generate an optimal and feasible supply plan for the entire supply chain network. Supply planning in SAP APO can be performed using the following:

- SNP Heuristics
- SNP Optimizer
- Multilevel Supply Demand Matching (SDM)

SNP Heuristics is a repair- or alerts-based planning strategy where no capacity checks are considered for planning. The sourcing decisions are influenced by the quota arrangements. Capacity leveling must be used to generate a feasible production plan to cover the requirements.

SNP Optimizer on the other hand uses cost-based optimization strategy. The finite supply plan is created with the primary objective of reducing production cost, transport cost, nondelivery cost, storage cost, and so on while considering the production, transport, and handling capacity constraints. SNP Optimizer searches through all feasible plans in an attempt to find the most cost-effective supply plan. The optimizer uses the linear programming method to consider all planning-related factors simultaneously within one optimal solution. As more constraints are activated, the optimization problem becomes more complex, which usually increases the time required to solve the problem. The optimizer makes a distinction between continuous linear optimization problems and discrete optimization problems.

In contrast, Multilevel Supply Demand Matching (SDM), more commonly known as *Capable-to-Match* (*CTM*), creates a multilevel supply plan for the complete supply chain network. The supply plan is created for each of the prioritized demands. Any supply or resource constraints identified at each of the intermediate planning levels are propagated to the finished product demand. CTM uses all available procurement alternatives to create an in-time solution for the demand. Available resources and supplies are allocated in sequence to each of the prioritized demands selected for planning.

Figure 1.3 shows the differences among the three SNP planning strategies. The key difference among the SNP planning methods is process flow. Heuristics uses the low-level code planning approach; that is, the complete supply chain network is resolved into the linear supply chain for planning. The planning levels are identified using the low-level code determination function. The planning is then executed level by level.

The main focus of this book is to explain the CTM planning process in detail, including the key process steps, configurations, functions, master data and transactional data relevant for CTM planning.

The next section provides the overview of the CTM planning process and the key steps involved in CTM planning.

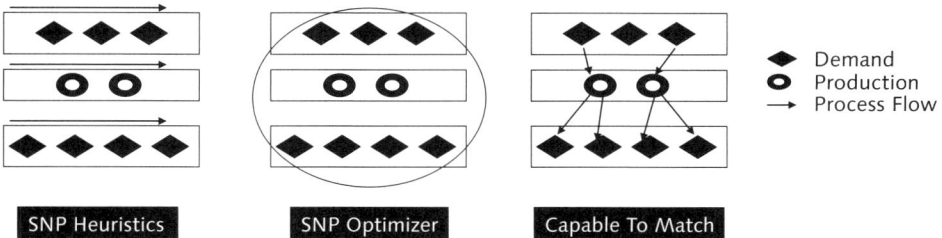

Figure 1.3 Comparison of SNP Strategies

1.3 CTM Planning Overview

CTM planning uses a *constraints-based, multilevel, finite, top-down* planning approach for cross-location checks of supplies, production, and transport capacities. CTM does that on the basis of predefined supply categories and demand priorities. The goal of CTM planning is to calculate a feasible solution for fulfilling all demands and match the demands to the available sourcing alternatives. All sourcing alternatives are checked first for *in-time* demand fulfillment before switching to *late demand* fulfillment. CTM first prioritizes the demands and then schedules them in sequence based on the unique prioritization sequence. CTM then matches the supplies and demands on a first-come, first-served basis while taking the production capacities, means of transports, and existing supplies into consideration. In the standard SAP APO solution, the term and menu option *Multilevel Supply Demand Matching* is used to refer to the CTM planning and supply distribution functions. Due to the limitations of the supply distribution function in CTM, this function has seen very limited adoption by SAP APO customers. As a result, the terms SDM and CTM are used interchangeably. In SAP SCM 5.1, the supply distribution function is significantly developed to overcome the limitations and can be used to finitely plan transporting and handling resource capacities.

Historically, the CTM planning solution was developed in close cooperation with several high technology companies during the late 1990s. Due to its flexibility and scalability, CTM has been implemented in several other industry segments as well. The CTM planning solution isn't only used for SNP but also, in some cases, has been successfully used for near-term production planning. This is possibly due to the generic planning algorithm used by CTM. The planning engine uses the same data model for both time series- (bucket oriented) and order- (time continuous) based planning. The CTM engine is capable of scheduling both bucket and time continuous resources to provide daily and up-to-the-second scheduling results.

The CTM planning results are closely integrated with the SNP planning book and PP/DS planning board for interactive planning. CTM can use both the SNP and PP/DS master data, so the CTM planning results can be seamlessly integrated with either of the interactive planning tools for further processing. CTM can also create both SNP and PP/DS order types. The main advantage of CTM planning is the creation of fixed pegging relationships. The planning solution can be easily traced using the fixed pegging created by CTM. SNP Heuristics and SNP Optimizer lack this capability because they work mainly in the bucket-oriented planning mode.

Because CTM offers both bucket-oriented SNP and time continuous PP/DS planning functions, it's important to understand the key differences and limitation of CTM planning in both of these planning modes.

1.3.1 CTM Planning Process Steps

The complete CTM planning process flow is shown in Figure 1.4. As a first step, you must define the scope of CTM planning. The scope of CTM planning includes the master and transactional data. The CTM planning process contains several parameters — which can be maintained using CTM global customization — and strategies.

The CTM profile is the most fundamental setting required to start the CTM planning process and is supplemented using CTM global customization. The CTM profile contains additional attributes such as planning horizon, capacity planning strategies, and late demand strategies.

The CTM planning process can be optionally followed by the supply distribution function. Using supply distribution, you can create stock transfer orders for the excess supplies. The planning results can be analyzed using the SNP planning books or PP/DS product or receipt view. The constrained supply plan created by CTM can be used to provide input to the demand plan or to propose product allocation data for GATP checks.

To use the CTM planning function, the data selection and planning strategies are combined and configured using the CTM profile. A CTM profile can be created using SAP APO Transaction /SAPAPO/CTM or the SAP Easy Access menu ADVANCED PLANNING AND OPTIMIZATION • MULTILEVEL SUPPLY AND DEMAND MATCHING • PLANNING • CAPABLE TO MATCH PLANNING.

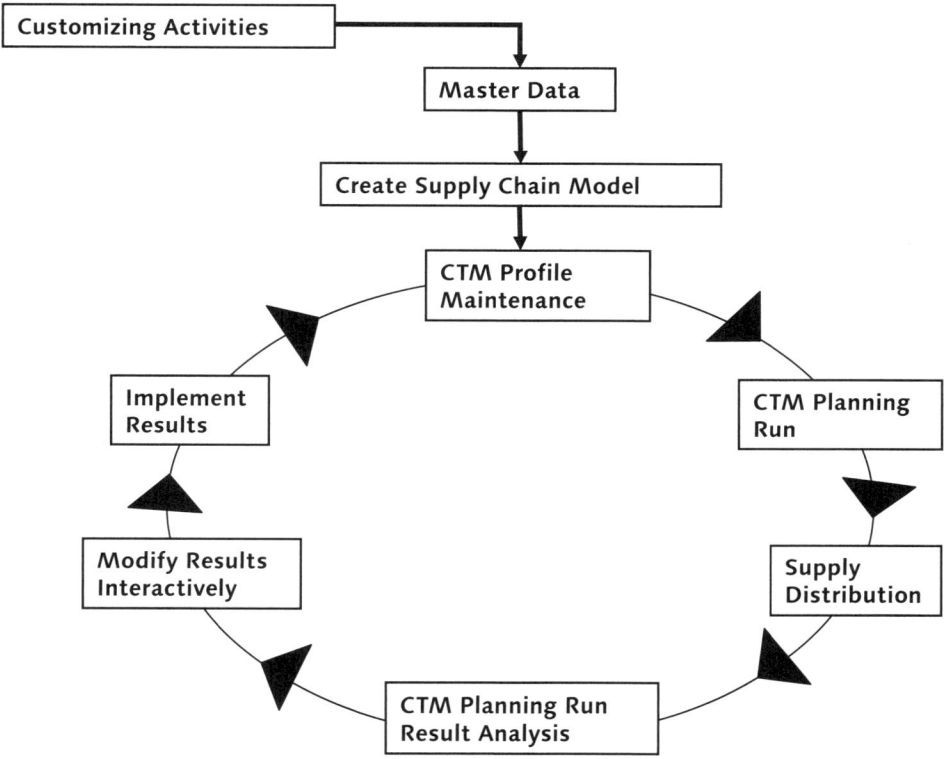

Figure 1.4 CTM Planning Process Steps

As the central access point for working with CTM, the planning profile offers several settings to configure and model the planning requirements. The key configuration settings available in the CTM profile are explained in detail in later chapters. The planning run can be executed online using the CTM profile.

The CTM planning configuration in the profile is divided into multiple tabs as shown in Figure 1.5. The key profile sections are listed here:

- Planning Scope
- Planning Strategies
- Demand and Supply Aggregation
- Demand Prioritization
- Supply Categorization
- Settings

1 | Overview of SAP SCM

Figure 1.5 CTM Planning Profile Overview, SAP APO Transaction /SAPAPO/CTM

Online interactive planning using a CTM profile can be used for smaller models. You can create a smaller master data selection to check the demands and supplies used for planning using the demand and supply simulation list. Using the demand and supply simulation function in the CTM profile, you can select the demand and supplies that will be selected for CTM planning. The master data check function in the CTM profile can be used to display the planning attributes of master data objects selected for planning. CTM profile configuration can be transported using the standard SAP transport request to ensure a robust change management process in the production system. This is important because the CTM planning run is very sensitive to the configuration. The CTM planning run can be negatively influenced by incorrect or unintentional changes in the production system.

In addition to the CTM profile, the CTM global customization shown in Figure 1.6 contains the parameters relevant for CTM planning. The planning process starts with identifying the key requirements for the planning mode in the global customization. This can be accessed using the SAP APO Transaction /SAPAPO/CTMCUST or in the SAP IMG under ADVANCED PLANNING AND OPTIMIZATION • SUPPLY CHAIN PLANNING • MULTILEVEL SUPPLY AND DEMAND MATCHING • CAPABLE TO MATCH • DEFINE GLOBAL VALUES AND DEFAULT VALUES.

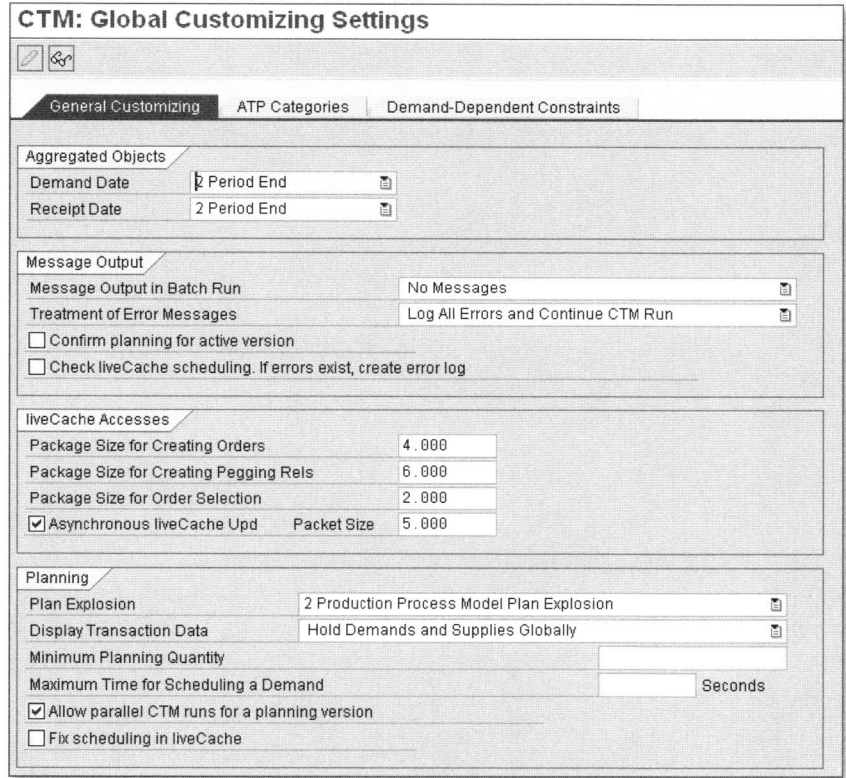

Figure 1.6 CTM Global Customization Settings

Global settings that will be applied to all product locations and across all CTM profiles are Late Demand Fulfillment, Order Creation Frame, and Allow Shortage Setting for the Demands. Performance-related configuration parameters for reading and writing data to liveCache are also maintained under CTM global customization.

Supply distribution is an optional step that is available with multilevel SDM. By using the CTM supply distribution function, excess supply can be distributed to the next location in the supply chain identified by the transport lanes. The distribution quantities are derived using outbound quotas for the source location. The CTM supply distribution functionality is very limited in comparison to the standard SNP Deployment function. It can be started using the SAP APO Transaction /SAPAPO/CTM10 or via the SAP Easy Access menu ADVANCED PLANNING AND OPTIMIZATION • MULTILEVEL SUPPLY AND DEMAND MATCHING • PLANNING • SUPPLY DISTRIBUTION.

Supply planning requirements can be very complex and can't be accomplished using a single CTM planning run or CTM planning profile. To accomplish overall planning requirements, several CTM profiles are required in sequence, which can be combined with other planning steps (PP/DS, SNP Optimizer, SNP Deployment, etc). After all CTM planning jobs are finished, the results can be validated and modified using the SAP SCM interactive planning tools such as the SNP planning book and PP/DS planning board. You can also use exception-based results analysis using the SAP SCM Alert Monitor.

1.3.2 System Landscape Requirement for CTM Planning

The SAP APO system is used for real-time supply chain planning and simulation for the complete supply chain network. In SAP APO, large volumes of data must be permanently available and changeable. For this reason, the relational database system in SAP APO is extended to enable actual data structures and data flows (such as networks and relationships) to be mapped more easily and effectively. All of the transactional data is saved in the additional database called SAP liveCache.

The SAP liveCache object-oriented database is an enhancement of the MaxDB database system. SAP liveCache operates with its data in the main memory of the database system, if configured optimally. SAP liveCache is a memory-resident database capable of providing fast access to the data and contains analytical functions for real-time scheduling of production resources.

The traditional database in the SAP SCM system contains all of the master data required for planning, and liveCache contains the transactional data.

In addition to SAP liveCache, both SNP Optimizer and CTM require a special optimizer server to execute the respective planning engines. Figure 1.7 shows the minimal SAP APO system landscape required for CTM planning.

1.3 CTM Planning Overview

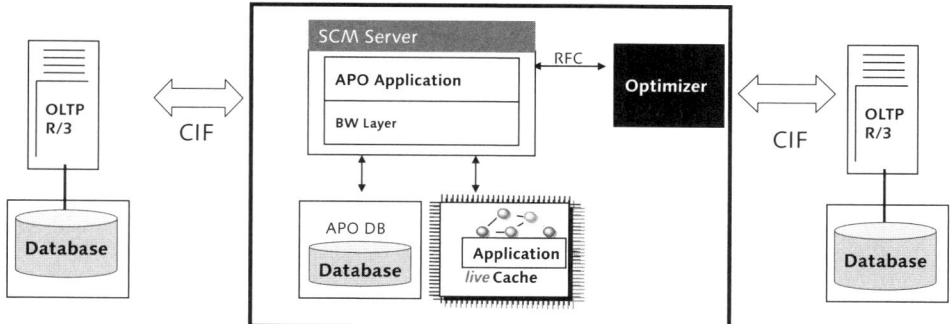

Figure 1.7 SAP APO Minimal Landscape for CTM Planning

The CTM planning engine as of SAP SCM 5.0 is only supported for the Windows operating system. The CTM planning engine is the core of CTM planning, which provides advanced constraint-based planning algorithms and is implemented in C++ to provide a scalable and high-performance planning solution for managing large data models. The SAP APO system is the primary source of master and transaction data for the CTM engine. The communication between the SAP SCM system and the CTM engine is established using standard RFCs. The SAP APO planning system can be connected with one or more R/3 systems for order execution, with communication between the two managed by Core Interface (CIF). To use the CIF function in SAP ERP, you must import a suitable SAP R/3 plug in up to and including SAP ECC 5.0. As of SAP ECC 6.0, CIF is an integrated part of SAP ERP. CIF is also an integrated part of SAP APO.

1.3.3 CTM Planning Run — Complete Overview

A CTM planning run consists of several steps as shown in Figure 1.8. Steps 1-4 are required for CTM planning data preparation. CTM planning is generally executed in the complete replan mode. For example, the previously created supply plan is deleted, and a new plan is recreated. The deletion step can be combined with the planning run, although the deletion can be done independent of the planning step.

Order data in SAP APO can be deleted using the SAP APO Transaction /SAPAPO/RLCDEL. We recommend using the CTM planning profile to delete the current plan to ensure that the orders are deleted consistently with respect to CTM planning strategies.

1 | Overview of SAP SCM

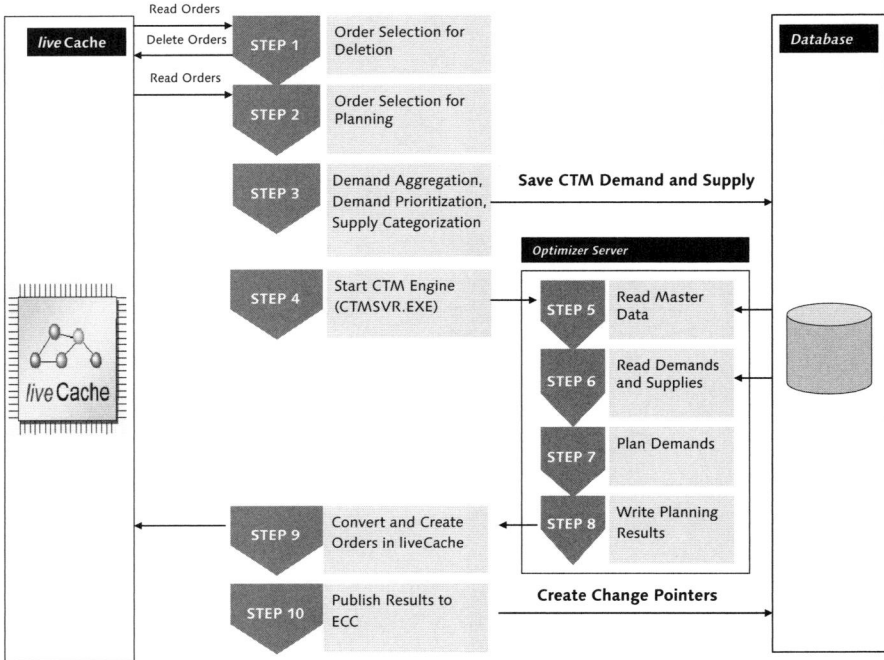

Figure 1.8 Complete CTM Planning Overview

After order deletion, the next planning steps involve selecting master and transaction data. The master data model must be complete and consistent to ensure that the planning results are correct. The CTM master data consistency check function can be used to validate the consistency of the master data used by the planning engine. Depending on the planning option, the master data objects typically consist of products, locations, transport lanes, production process mode/production data structure (PPM/PDS), and resources. In special cases, master data objects may also be ATP rules, super session chains, FFF (Form-Fit-Function) classes, and hierarchy definitions.

The transactional data relevant for planning is also selected in the CTM profile. When a complete regenerative planning is used with CTM, all of the unfirmed orders are selected for deletion. During this step, not only are the unfirmed orders deleted but so is the fixed pegging across firmed orders. This ensures that the open supply will be reallocated to the demand using the latest prioritization sequence. After the unfirmed orders are deleted, the open orders are selected and converted to CTM demand and supplies.

> **CTM Demand and CTM Supply: Defined**
>
> It's important to understand the definition of the CTM demand and CTM supply. CTM demand is similar to any requirement element in SAP SCM with additional planning constraints and planning parameters assigned to them, for example, Late Demand Frame, Early Fulfillment Frame, Pegging type and so on. More detailed description of CTM demand is provided in later chapters. Similarly, CTM supply is a receipt element with additional parameters for CTM planning, for example, Supply Category. This is an important aspect because some of the core CTM functions are applicable only for the CTM demands and supplies and not for the dependent demands and supplies created during the planning run.

Step 3 corresponds to the aggregation step and is used to aggregate the demands and supplies across a given product location and ATP category. For example, if there are multiple sales orders for a given product location, then all of the sales orders can be virtually aggregated to a single sales order for planning using demand aggregation.

The aggregation time buckets can be selected as daily, weekly, monthly, quarterly, or yearly. The main advantage with CTM demand aggregation is that the CTM engine has to plan fewer demands, and the supply plan consists of fewer orders, thus reducing the overall runtime of the planning run. Although aggregation offers many advantages, it's important to understand that aggregation loses the detailed level attribute information required for planning.

If there are several sales orders with different priorities, the aggregated sales order won't have the priority assigned to it mainly because it's not possible to aggregate multiple priorities to a single priority. This is critical if the demand prioritization is based on sales order priority.

Demand aggregation is optional and is followed by demand prioritization where the CTM demands are prioritized using the sort sequence. Demand prioritization is followed by the supply categorization.

Steps 5-8 correspond to CTM engine planning steps. The selected master data, prioritized demands, and categorized supplies are uploaded to the CTM engine. The

CTM engine then uses the input data to generate a feasible supply plan considering the sourcing rules and capacity constraints.

As shown earlier in Figure 1.7, the CTM engine is executed in a separate optimization server. Chapter 4 provides a more detailed description of the planning algorithm and planning parameters that can be configured to achieve the desired planning results.

The CTM planning algorithm is very flexible and generic in terms of the input parameters that can be configured. After the input parameters are selected, the planning logic is fairly constant — the results depend on a set of key rules. CTM planning rules are fixed and consistent and can't be modified by customers using any user exits or Business Add-Ins (BAdIs). On the other hand, several extension points (BAdIs, user exits) are available in the planning data preprocessing and postprocessing steps. Stable core CTM logic also ensures that the planning results are much more explainable and understandable. As shown in Figure 1.9, the core CTM algorithm executes multilevel finite planning using the prioritized demands and categorized supplies. Each source is selected using the priority to generate an in-time feasible plan. Constraints that are detected for any of the assemblies and raw materials are propagated to the finished product demand. As a result, the dependent demands are always satisfied in-time. Late solution is allowed only for the finished product demands that are selected for CTM planning.

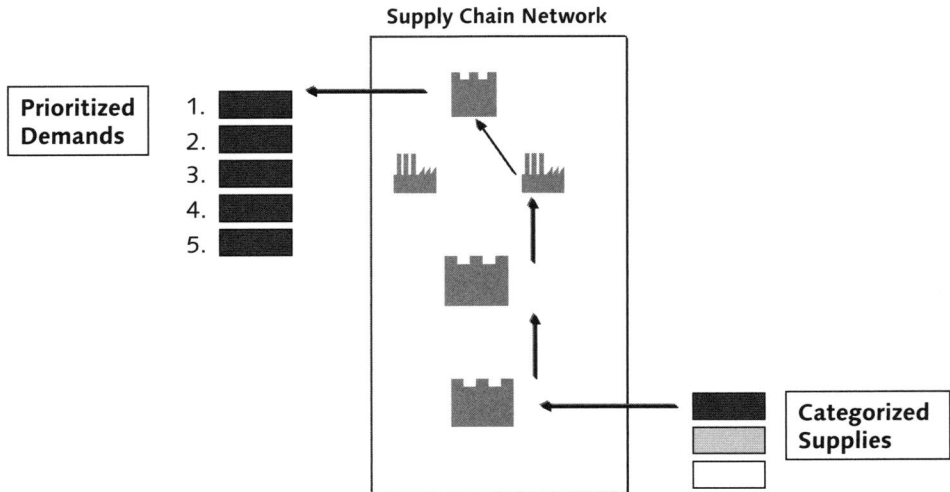

Figure 1.9 Multilevel SDM Using CTM

After the CTM engine generates the supply plan, the results are persistently saved in SAP liveCache in Step 9. In Step 10, CTM planning results are published to the ECC system. Publication of the planning results in SAP SCM is allowed when the planning data is created in the active version (000). The publication is done using the CIF delivered with the SAP SCM solution. There are two options for publishing the results. You can choose to publish the results immediately or collect the planning results and publish them in batch mode at periodic intervals. The latter option is recommended for CTM planning to ensure the planning results are published optimally without causing any performance bottleneck in CIF.

In the next section, you'll learn how to enable special planning functions using CTM planning parameters.

1.4 Configuration Using CTM Planning Parameters

CTM planning parameters can be used to implement a specific behavior or a new function without changing the interface to the planning engine in a given SAP SCM release. In customer projects, the interface often has to be extended to implement a new functionality that can be switched on or off. By using planning parameters, it's not required to extend the interface. The planning parameters provide a generic interface to transfer additional planning attributes to the CTM engine.

You can search the list of all CTM planning parameters in the SAP Service Marketplace in the Notes section. Some parameters must be recommended by SAP because they are available for specific requirements only. Using these parameters in an unsupported function can lead to incorrect results. The parameters follow the naming convention. All parameters names for the CTM engine (C++) are in lowercase, and the rest are in uppercase. CTM planning parameters are profile-specific; that is, you can specify in the CTM profile whether a parameter should be applied or not. The parameters are maintained in a separate screen, but they belong to the profile. The parameters are saved together with the normal profile. The planning parameters can be accessed from the CTM profile and are available under the Control menu item (see Figure 1.10).

1 | Overview of SAP SCM

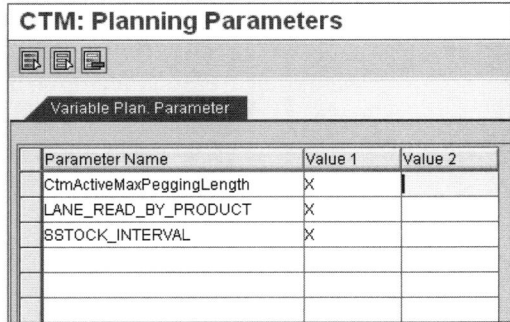

Figure 1.10 CTM Planning Parameters Screen

1.5 Executing the CTM Planning Run

CTM planning can be executed in the online mode using the CTM profile, in the background mode using the SAP APO Transaction /SAPAPO/CTMB, or by scheduling the background job using the SAP APO Report /SAPAPO/CTMPLRUN. The CTM planning process step is also available in the Process Chain central job scheduling tool (see Figure 1.11).

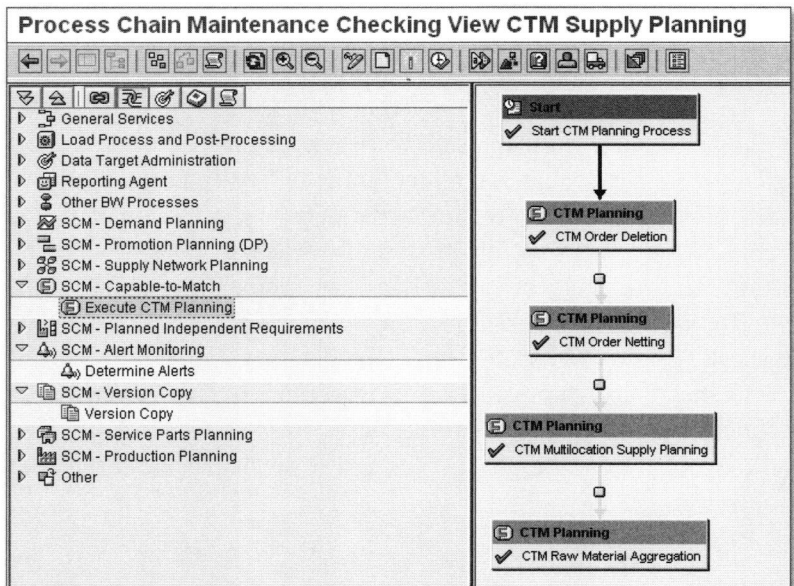

Figure 1.11 CTM Process Chain Definition in the Central Job Scheduling Tool

The CTM process can be easily integrated with other planning steps to implement the complete business process. If you use process chains, you can automate the complex schedules in the SAP SCM system with the help of the event-controlled processing, visualize the schedule by using network applications, and centrally control and monitor the processes.

1.6 Summary

This chapter explained the basics of the SAP SCM solution. We showed you the SAP APO SNP planning functions and the key difference among SNP Heuristics, SNP Optimizer, and CTM planning logic. Now that you understand the CTM planning process steps, you can execute the CTM planning run with basic configuration.

In the next chapter, you'll learn about the CTM planning scope, which includes the master data, transactional data, and detailed planning strategies that are available for CTM planning.

This chapter explains the CTM planning strategies and options available in the CTM profile. The chapter will familiarize you with the key decision points that must be understood and answered when selecting the CTM supply planning function.

2 CTM Planning Scope

Successful planning with CTM requires careful analysis of the key business requirements you need to address. When considering using CTM, it's important to first understand that CTM is a heuristic-based planning method and not an optimization solution. CTM is mostly used for rough-cut capacity planning and determining the optimal sourcing decisions in the medium- to long-term horizon when considering finite material and capacity constraints. Although CTM is considered part of the SNP solution, along with SNP Heuristics and SNP Optimizer, there are several key differences you should understand.

CTM is an order-based planning solution that can operate in both the Supply Network Planning (SNP) bucket planning mode and production planning and detailed scheduling (PP/DS) time-continuous planning mode. Additionally, CTM planning can be used to create fixed pegging relationships between the receipt and requirement elements in both the SNP and PP/DS planning modes.

This chapter explains the key steps you need to perform for executing the CTM planning run. There are several key decision points we'll evaluate in detail, but the main aspects of CTM planning are to understand the master data, transactional data, and strategies applied for planning. Also keep in mind that in many practical situations, the complete planning requirements can't be addressed with one single CTM profile. For instance, in some productive environments, customers have used up to 10 CTM profiles to address the complete CTM planning requirements.

We'll start exploring the CTM planning process with a look at the SAP SCM master data because the CTM planning process provides very flexible master data selection options. There are several master data objects available in the SAP SCM application that are supported in the CTM planning process. In the next section, you'll learn about the SAP SCM master data objects and the attributes that are used for CTM planning.

2.1 SAP SCM Master Data

The master data in SAP Advanced Planner and Optimizer (SAP APO) consists of locations, location products, PPM/PDS, resources, and transport lanes. Most of the master data objects are transferred from the SAP ERP system using the Core Interface (CIF). The Supply Chain Model (SC Model) is the basis for planning in SAP SCM, so you can create the SC Model in SAP SCM using the SAP APO Transaction /SAPAPO/MVM or use the SAP Easy Access menu path ADVANCED PLANNING AND OPTIMIZATION • MASTER DATA • PLANNING VERSION MANAGEMENT • MODEL AND VERSION MANAGEMENT.

The model combines all of the master data and is used and accessible for all planning tools in SAP APO. Model 000 refers to the active model, and the master data is created for the active model when transferred from SAP ERP. The planning version contains all of the transactional data relevant for planning. And each version contains a separate copy of the transactional data and is assigned to the model, so you can create and assign one or more versions to a given model.

Version 000 refers to the active version. Only the planning results generated in the active version can be published to SAP ERP and vice versa. Simulation versions are mostly used for what-if analysis and can be created using the copy from the active version. Some additional master data required for what-if scenarios can also be assigned to a version. After the planning in the simulation version, you can merge the planning data completely or partly into the active version before publishing the results to SAP ERP. Figure 2.1 shows the model and version management transaction in SAP APO.

The key master data elements, such as products and locations, are transferred from SAP ERP or created directly in SAP APO. It's very important to understand that the mere presence of parameters in the master data does not imply that the parameter is supported by all of the planning tools. For example, in the product location master, the Shelf Life parameter is available under the Properties tab but isn't supported by CTM. Similarly the Order Creation Frame parameter available under the SNP2 tab is only supported by CTM and not by SNP Heuristics or SNP Optimizer.

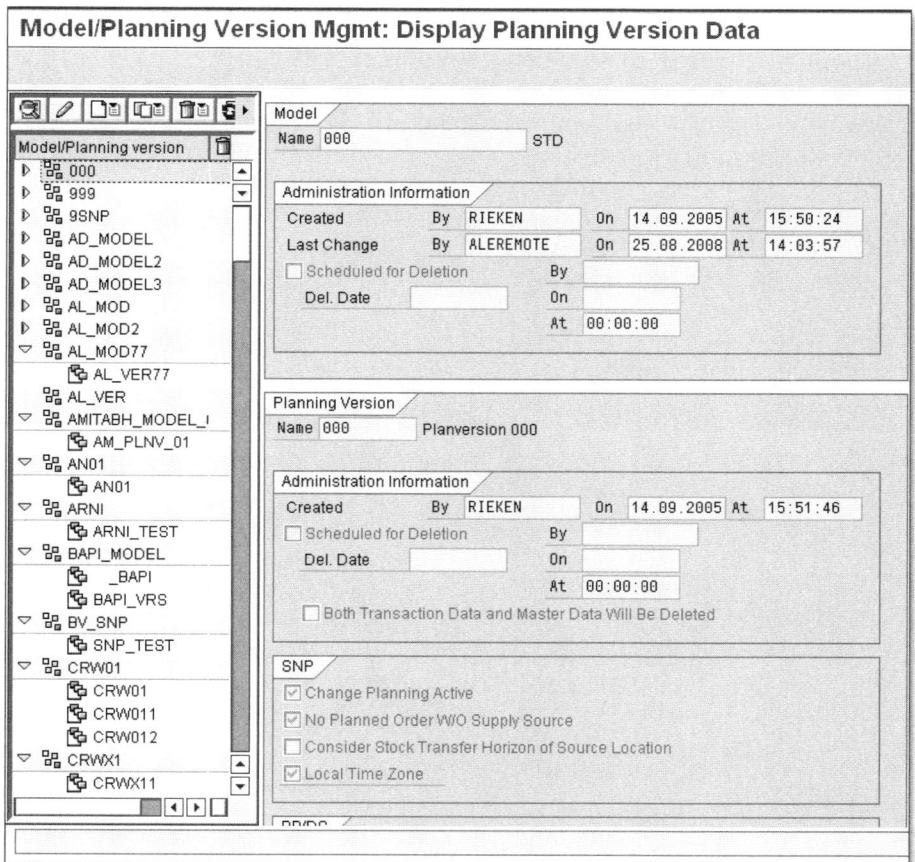

Figure 2.1 SAP SCM Model and Version Management, SAP APO Transaction /SAPAPO/MVM

Now we need to look at how to use the CTM master data selection identifier (ID) to create a subset of the SC Model. During supply network planning for a complex network, it isn't always desirable to use CTM planning for the complete model. CTM master data selection ID provides you with extensive functions to manually and automatically define logical subsets of master data selections for CTM planning.

2.2 CTM Master Data Selection

CTM planning can be executed with reference to the complete SC Model or a small subset of the model using the Master Data Selection ID as shown in Figure 2.2. The CTM master data selection transaction offers flexible data selection functions for selecting a smaller subset of the SC model. For example, you can use master data selection to limit CTM planning to a specific bill of material (BOM) level of your finished product.

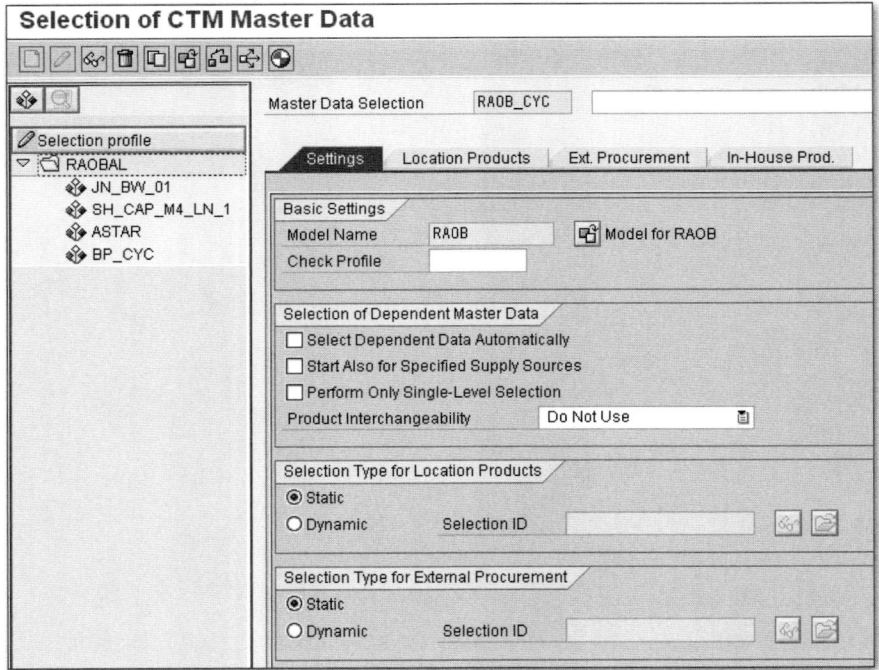

Figure 2.2 CTM Master Data Selection Identifier (ID)

CTM profiles offer two options for master data selection. The complete master data assigned to the model can be used directly in the CTM profile using the All Master Data in Model option available in the Planning Scope section of the CTM profile. For scenarios where CTM must be executed for a subset of the model, it's possible to define the CTM master data selection ID. Once defined, the master data selection ID can be used in multiple CTM profiles.

The CTM master data selection ID can be created and changed using the SAP APO Transaction /SAPAPO/CTMMSEL or can be accessed using SAP Easy Access menu ADVANCED PLANNING AND OPTIMIZATION • MULTILEVEL SUPPLY AND DEMAND MATCHING • ENVIRONMENT • MASTER DATA SELECTION. This function offers very flexible master data selection options. The main planning objects products, transport lanes, and PPM/PDS can be selected individually to create an SC Model suitable for your business requirements.

> **Example**
> If some of the sourcing decisions are predetermined, the corresponding transport lanes can be included in CTM planning. It's also possible to generate the dependent master data automatically using the finished products.

2.2.1 Master Data Selection Options

Each of the planning objects — product locations, transport lanes, and PPM/PDS — can be selected using the Shuffler function in the master data selection ID. Selection of each of the planning objects is supported by several attributes. Table 2.1 shows the attributes available for each of the master data objects.

Object	Selection Attributes
Product	Product and Location
Location	Custom Material Location Attributes (AT101, AT102, AT103, AT104, AT105)
	Custom Material Attributes (ATT01, ATT02, ATT03, ATT04, ATT05)
	SNP and PP/DS Planner
Transport Lane	Source Location
	Destination Location
	Location
In-House Production	Product
	PPM Name
	Resource
	Production Location, Planning Location

Table 2.1 Attributes of Each Master Data Object

The master data selection ID can be created using the following selection options:

- **Static data selection**
  Static data selection is used primarily when the SC Model is very stable, and changes to the model aren't very frequent. In this mode, the master data objects are saved with the selection ID. The selection can be done using the Shuffler function, which is most commonly used in DP and SNP planning books. After the planning objects are selected and saved with the CTM master data selection ID, any changes in the master data model aren't automatically available for CTM planning. Using static selection, it's possible to manually add and delete additional objects to the selection ID. CTM saves the materials and locations required for planning in the master data selection ID. The material and location attributes are selected during the CTM planning run.

- **Dynamic data selection**
  Dynamic data selection is used mainly for SC Models where frequent changes are anticipated. For example, the BOM is changed in SAP ERP. In this case, the CTM planning must adjust the planning scope in real time to reflect the new BOM structure. When using the Dynamic master data selection option, only the selection definition is saved with the master data selection ID. During the planning run, the SC Model is evaluated that meets the selection criteria. And when using Shuffler, you can define and save the selection ID and assign it to the Dynamic selection.

2.2.2 Automatic Master Data Selection

The CTM master data selection function also offers an automatic master data selection option that can be used to automatically select the dependent products, transport lanes, and PPM/PDS for planning. When using this function, only the finished products will be initially selected. However, the dependent objects relevant for planning are evaluated and selected if they are required for planning a demand. Automatic data selection can be used either in Static mode to select the model or in Dynamic mode during the planning run. Figure 2.3 shows the interface between the master data objects in SAP ERP and SAP APO and the usee of automatic master data selection in the CTM profile.

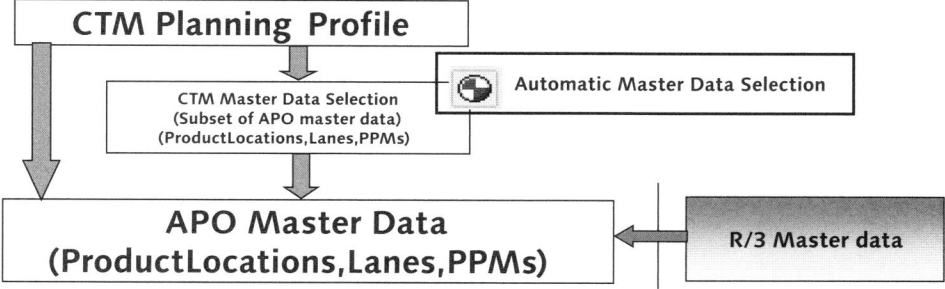

Figure 2.3 Automatic Master Data Selection

The master data is then replicated in the SAP APO system from SAP ERP and is assigned to the SAP APO model 000. The CTM master data selection function selects and saves the master data objects for CTM planning. Using manual selection of dependent data, the master data objects are selected and saved with the CTM profile. Typically, CTM planning is executed as a nightly batch run without any manual intervention because it isn't practical to execute the master data generation function manually before every CTM run. The Select Dependent Data Automatically option can be used in this scenario to generate the master data during the planning run. This step is executed automatically with no manual intervention required. The dependent master data selection uses the finished product locations as input to select dependent master data objects. The relationships are then evaluated using the transport lanes and PPM/PDS. Master data dependencies due to the super session chains and FFF classes are also evaluated for automatic master data selection.

> **Note**
>
> Keep in mind that dependencies due to the ATP rules aren't evaluated during automatic master data selection.

Figure 2.4 shows the SC Model used for all of the examples shown in this book. As you can see in this figure, the automatic master data selection is triggered using the finished product BP_CYC at location BL_FRNK_DC. As a result, all of the products and locations in the plant and supplier locations are also selected (BP_FRM and BP_TYR). Keep in mind that the dependent data selection is based on the direction of material flow, so, for example, using BP_TYR at supplier location BL_FRM_VEND as input for master data selection would not generate any additional objects because no further sourcing options exist for this product location. However, two additional master data selection functions are available for flexible SC Model selection:

- **Start Also for Specified Supply Sources**
  Using this option, the master data selection is generated using the SOS (transport lane and PPM/PDS) selected in the In-House Prod. tab.

- **Perform Only Single Level Selection**
  Using this option, the master data is generated only for the single level of the SC Model using the initial selection of product locations.

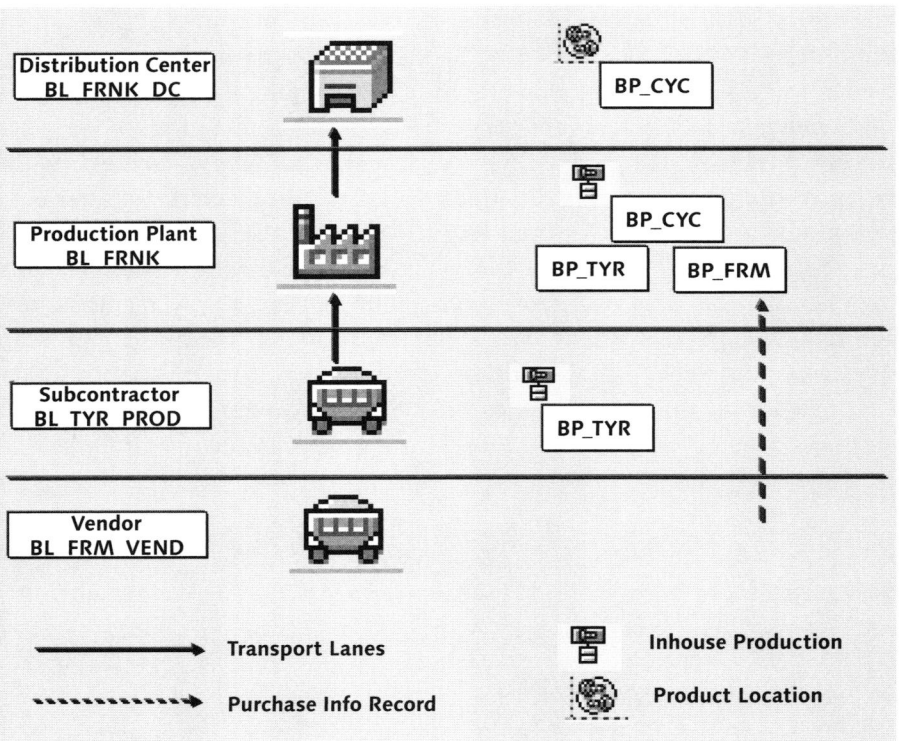

Figure 2.4 Example of CTM Planning Model

Master data parameters used by CTM can be displayed using the master data check function available in the CTM profile or by using the SAP APO Transaction /SAPAPO/CTM01. This function can also be accessed using the SAP Easy Access

CTM Master Data Selection | **2.2**

menu path ADVANCED PLANNING AND OPTIMIZATION • MULTILEVEL SUPPLY AND DEMAND MATCHING • ENVIRONMENT • CONSISTENCY CHECK FOR CTM MASTER DATA. The master data check function shown in Figure 2.5 is very useful in CTM because it provides an overview of the master data parameters used for planning by the CTM engine.

For example, the Production Horizon defined in the number of days is translated to the date time with reference to the CTM planning start date. The consistency of the CTM model used for planning is also verified by the CTM master data check function. So if any of the input components used in a PPM/PDS aren't included in the model, the consistency check displays the error.

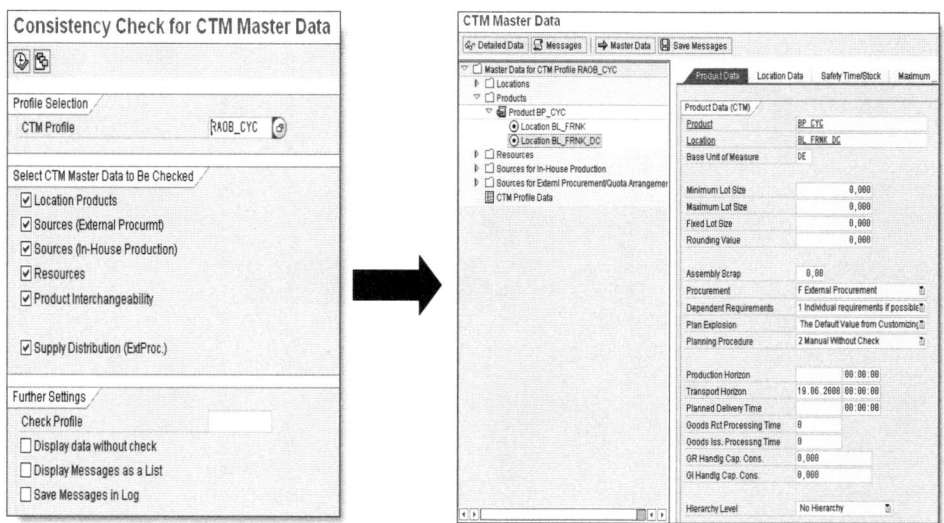

Figure 2.5 CTM Master Data Consistency Check

Note

Keep in mind that with the master data check function, only the syntax of the master data is checked, and an error report is generated. The semantics of the master data, such as lot sizes or cyclical supply networks, aren't detected and reported using the CTM master data check function.

Using the model consistency check profile available in SAP APO, you can configure and apply checks with reference to allowed tolerance limits. For example, you can define a minimum and maximum planned delivery time tolerance. This is very

43

2 | CTM Planning Scope

useful in detecting incorrect planning parameters entered by the planners. The model consistency check profile shown in Figure 2.6 can be started using the SAP APO Transaction /SAPAPO/CONSPRF or using the menu path ADVANCED PLANNING AND OPTIMIZATION • MASTER DATA • MODEL CONSISTENCY CHECK • MAINTAIN PROFILE.

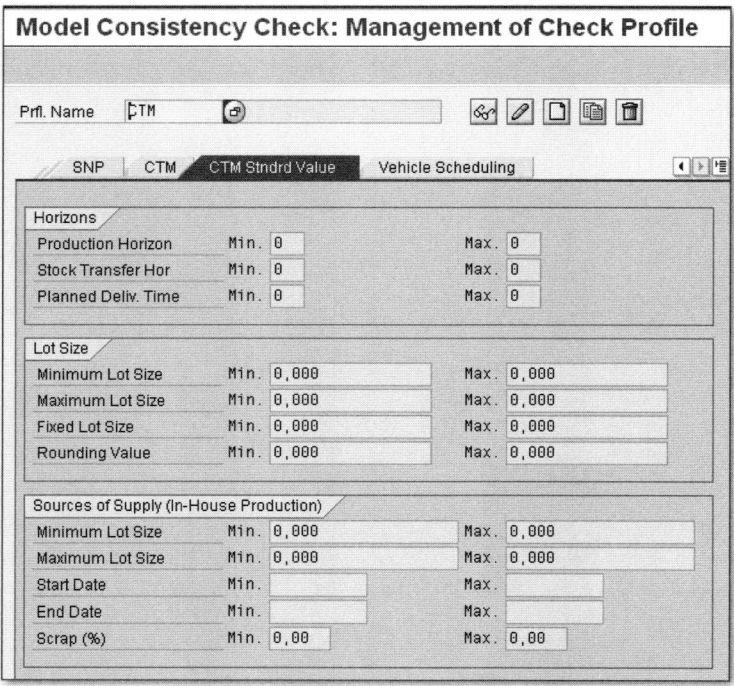

Figure 2.6 CTM Model Consistency Check Profile.

The consistency check profile can be used in the CTM planning profile to check the parameters defined in the check profile. The master data consistency check in CTM is also used to validate all of the master data values assigned to the planning objects. For example, for safety stock planning in CTM, you can display the safety stock parameters used for planning in CTM. Similarly, the hierarchy and FFF classes used in CTM planning can be displayed and validated. This function can also be used to understand and validate all of the parameters available in the master data objects that are supported in CTM.

> **Example**
> In the material master, the Shelf Life parameter is maintained, but in the master data check, the field isn't displayed indicating that the parameter isn't supported in CTM.

Now that you know how to define the master data selections and check the consistency of the model, in the next sections, you'll learn about the master data attributes that are supported for CTM planning.

2.3 Master Data Attributes for CTM Planning

Several master data parameters and attributes are available in SAP SCM for each of the master data objects. But as mentioned earlier, not all parameters are relevant for CTM planning or supported in CTM planning. The CTM master data check function provides an overview of all of the parameters used in CTM planning. In this section, we'll explain all of the master data objects and parameters that are relevant for CTM planning.

The key master data objects supported by CTM planning include the following:

- **Locations**
- **Location products**
- **Resource**
  - Production, transport, and handling
- **External procurement alternatives**
  - Transport lanes, purchasing info records
- **In-house production alternatives**
  - Production process mode (PPM)
  - Production data structure (PDS)
- **Hierarchy**
  - Location product, resource
- **Substitution alternatives**
  - Super session chains, FFF classes, ATP rules

All master data objects can be accessed under the SAP Easy Access menu ADVANCED PLANNING AND OPTIMIZATION • MASTER DATA, and the mass maintenance Transaction MASSD can be used to maintain the values in SAP APO for a large set of product locations.

In the next sections, you'll learn about the master data objects and the attributes that are supported by CTM. We'll start with location master data.

2.3.1 Location

Location in SAP APO represents the central point where all of the physical logistical processes are executed. The location represents the physical place where products or resources are managed. A single location object in SAP APO represents all of the different SAP ERP locations and is differentiated using the location type. For example, the location Production Plant is location type 1001, Vendor is location type 1011, Customer is location type 1010, Transport zone is location type 1005, and so on. The locations are selected for CTM planning based on the selected products.

The following parameters assigned to the location are supported in CTM planning:

- Location Time Zone
- Location Priority
- Receiving Calendar
- Shipping Calendar
- Inbound Handling Resource
- Outbound Handling Resource

The usage and function of each of these parameters in CTM planning is explained in later sections or chapters. Figure 2.7 shows the location master data object in the SAP SCM system that can be maintained using the SAP APO Transaction /SAPAPO/LOC3.

After the location master data object is created, you have to create and extend the products to the appropriate locations of the supply chain to create receipt and requirements during the CTM planning run.

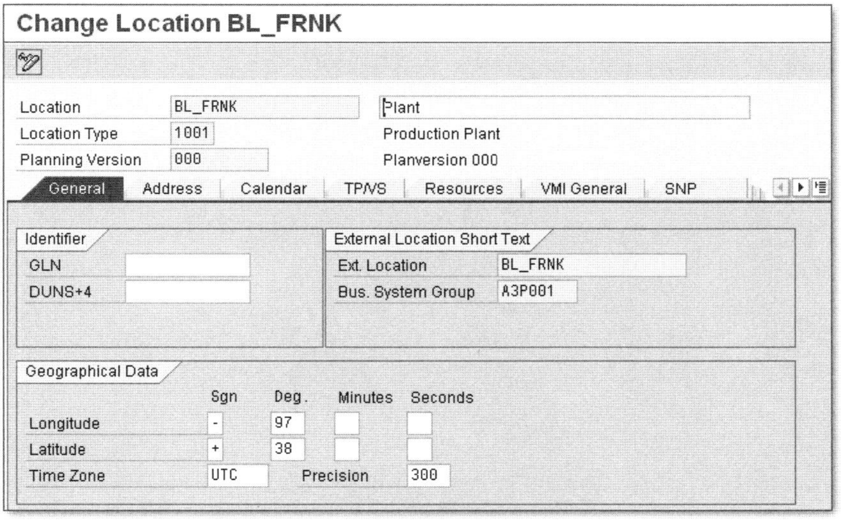

Master Data Attributes for CTM Planning | 2.3

Figure 2.7 Location Master Data Maintenance in SAP APO

2.3.2 Location Product

Product in SAP APO represents the goods or services used in the value chain upon which all business activities are executed. Product parameters can be maintained at the global and location level. Most of the product location parameters are transferred from the SAP ERP system, but it's also possible to maintain SAP APO specific master data for planning. Figure 2.8 shows the product location master data object that can be maintained using the SAP APO Transaction /SAPAPO/MAT1in the SAP SCM system.

The following parameters assigned to a location product are supported in CTM planning:

- Lot Size (Minimum/Maximum/Fixed), Rounding value
- Procurement Type, Assembly Scrap
- Horizons (Production, Stock Transfer)
- Planned Delivery Time
- Safety Days' Supply, Safety Stock and Maximum Earliness
- Order Creation Frame, Product Priority, and Demand Selection Horizon
- GR/GI Times and GR/GI Capacity Consumption

2 | CTM Planning Scope

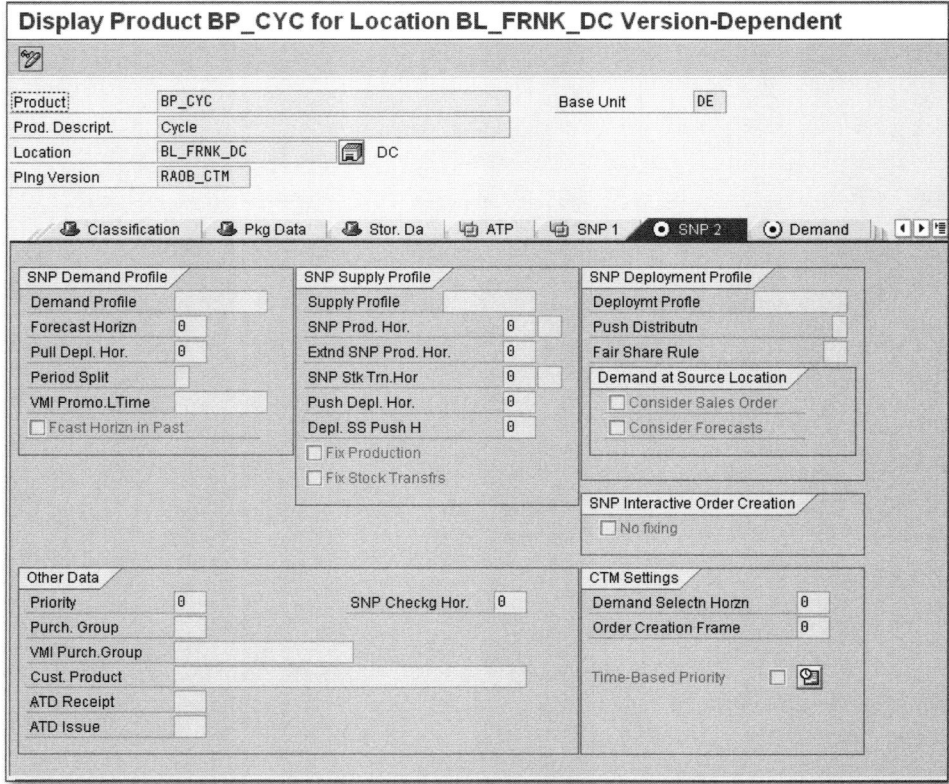

Figure 2.8 Product Location Maintenance in SAP SCM

2.3.3 Resource

Resources in SAP APO are used to represent capacities for machine, labor, and transport modes. Each resource is assigned to a model, and version-specific master data can be maintained for the resources. The work centers in SAP ERP are transferred to SAP APO as resources. And, planning and scheduling with resources depend on the type of the resource.

There are three main types of resources available for CTM planning:

- **Time-continuous resource**
  Time-continuous resources are used mainly for PP/DS planning where the scheduling is done in the time-continuous mode with exact start and end times

up to a second. CTM planning also supports scheduling of time-continuous resources in the PP/DS planning mode. These resources can be either *single activity* or *multi-activity* resources. As the name implies, the single activity resources can be scheduled with one activity at any time without overloading the resource. A multi-activity resource can be scheduled with multiple activities as the same time.

- **Bucket resource**
  Bucket resources are used for SNP bucket planning. Bucket resources are scheduled with a fixed duration of up to a minimum of one-day duration. In the rough capacity planning for mid- to long-term horizons, the exact times smaller than one day aren't important. So, the bucket resource offers the flexibility to schedule such activities on an aggregated level. CTM planning supports scheduling of bucket resources when planning in SNP mode. Bucket resource capacity can be defined as quantity or rate of production.

- **Mixed resource**
  Mixed resources have both the SNP bucket and PP/DS time-continuous capacity definition. CTM planning can use mixed (single mixed, multi-mixed) resources for planning. When planning in PP/DS mode, CTM uses the time-continuous capacity as the primary capacity for finite planning. The bucket capacity is calculated for the scheduled activity to keep the time-continuous and bucket capacity requirements consistent. On the other hand, when planning in SNP mode using mixed resources, the bucket capacity is used for finite planning, but the time-continuous capacity isn't calculated.

Resources are also categorized according to the function, for example, production, transport, handling, and storage resources. CTM planning supports production, handling, and transport resources. All of these resources can be defined as bucket or time continuous based on the SNP or PP/DS planning mode. There are also important scheduling differences between production and transport resources that will be explained in later chapters. For now, keep in mind that the Unscheduled breaks parameter and the Utilization Factor parameter aren't supported by CTM when planning in PP/DS planning mode.

CTM only supports the active capacity variant. For production activities, the production resource capacity is adjusted according to the factory calendar. For GR/GI (goods received/goods issued) activities, it's possible to define both the handling resources and receiving/issuing calendars. In this case when both calendars and resources are defined, only the resources are considered for scheduling in CTM

49

planning. Figure 2.9 shows the resource master data object in the SAP SCM system that can be maintained using the SAP APO Transaction /SAPAPO/RES01.

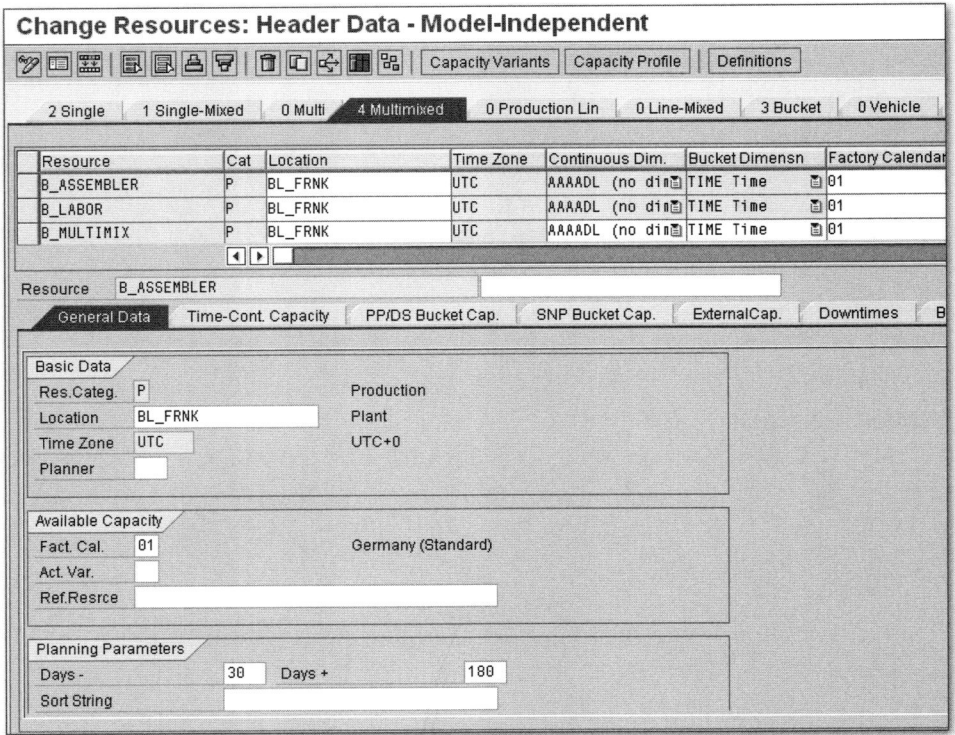

Figure 2.9 Resource Master Data Maintenance in SAP SCM

To execute cross-location network planning in CTM, you require the master data object that contains the procurement relationships and the means of transports used for procurement. In the next section, you'll learn about the external procurement alternatives available in SAP SCM that are supported by CTM planning.

2.3.4 External Procurement

External procurement relationships for distribution and procurement in SAP APO are defined using the transport lanes. For example, a stock transfer order can be created across two locations only if the transport lanes are valid and defined between the two locations. Transport lanes can be manually created in SAP APO or can be automatically transferred to SAP APO from the SAP ERP system. For automatic creation of transport lanes, you must have maintained purchasing info records, contracts, or scheduling agreements. CTM planning only supports the transport lanes created using the info records, and scheduling agreements and contracts aren't supported in CTM. Figure 2.10 shows the transport lane master data object that can be maintained using the SAP APO Transaction /SAPAPO/SCC_TL1.

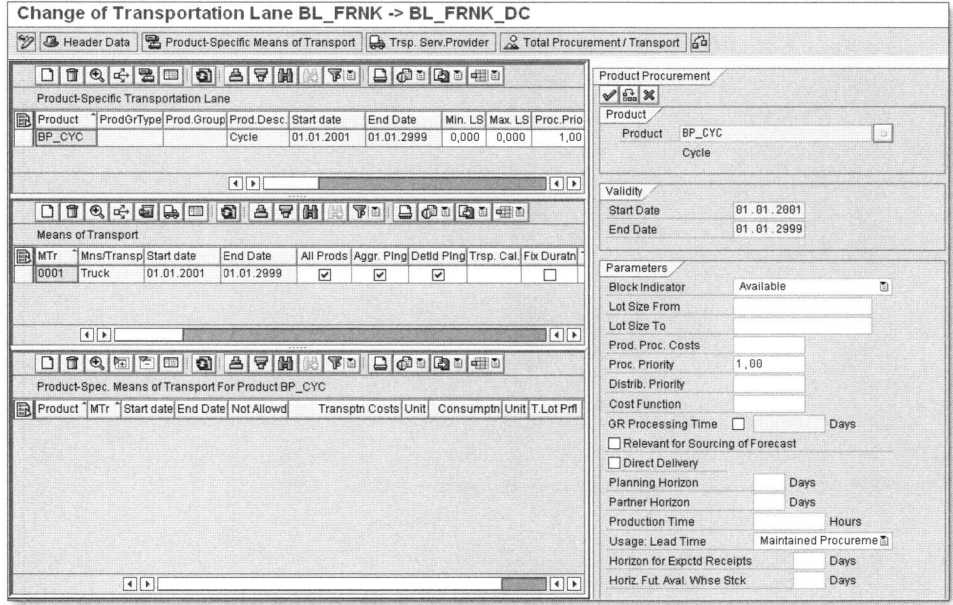

Figure 2.10 Transport Lane Maintenance in SAP SCM

From SAP SCM 5.0 onward, the external procurement relationships created using the info records are also supported in CTM. In earlier CTM versions, you had to model the products at the vendor locations to plan for vendor capacity constraints. Additionally, for CTM planning, both the source and destination location product must be included in the planning scope. This can have a negative impact on the overall system performance due to the high number of vendor location products modeled in SAP SCM.

You can transfer the info records in SAP ERP to the SAP APO system as external procurement relationships. These external procurement relationships are linked to the transport lanes that can be used for planning in CTM. So when you use the transport lanes created with reference to the external procurement relationships, the source location product isn't required anymore for CTM planning. Instead, CTM will select the transport lane for planning, if the source location product is either not created in SAP APO or not assigned to the SAP APO SC Model. Additionally, you can use the planned delivery time assigned to the purchasing info record for CTM order deletion and order creation process steps. Figure 2.11 shows the external procurement relationship master data object in the SAP SCM application.

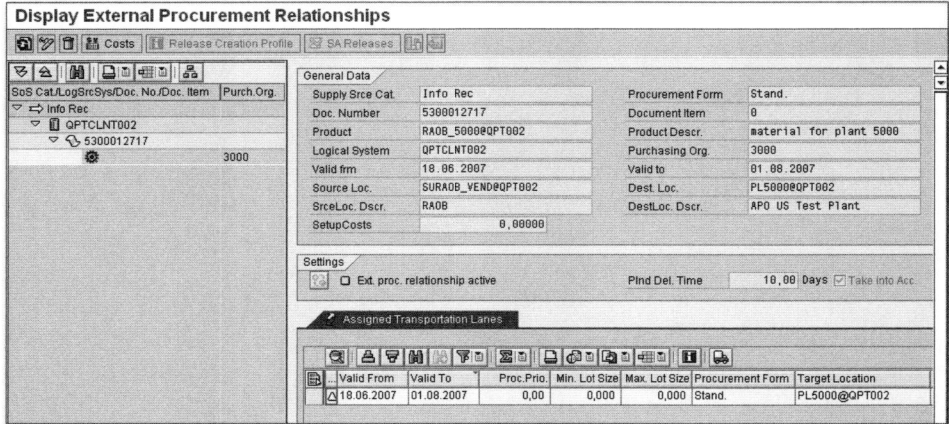

Figure 2.11 External Procurement Relationship Maintenance in SAP SCM

During a CTM planning run, you can use the CTM variable planning parameter LANE_NOSOURCE_IGNORE to exclude the transport lanes created by Info records.

> **Note**
> Refer to SAP Note 993071 for more details about the CTM planning parameter LANE_NOSOURCE_IGNORE.

CTM planning using transport lanes utilizes transport calendars and transport resources for scheduling. Additionally the GR/GI times at the destination and source location are also supported. For planning with the transport lanes, special attention must be paid to the use of the stock transfer horizon. By default, the stock transfer horizon of the destination location is used for planning. The Consider Stock Transfer Horizon of Source Location option in the planning version can be used to consider the stock transfer horizon of the source location.

The following parameters assigned to the transport lanes are supported in CTM planning:

- Procurement Priority and Inbound Quota
- Means of Transport
- Transport Duration and Transport Costs
- Transport Resource and Consumption
- Transport Calendar
- Transport Lot size Profile (Minimum, Maximum, and Rounding Value)
- GR Processing time
- Planned Delivery Time
- Validity Duration
- Subcontracting Transport Lanes

To execute production planning in CTM, you require the master data object that contains the production process activities and components. In the next section, you'll learn about the in-house production alternatives available in the SAP SCM system that are supported by CTM planning.

2.3.5 In-House Production

In-house production in SAP APO is carried out using the production process model (PPM) or production data structures (PDS). Figure 2.12 shows the PPM master data object that can be maintained using the SAP APO Transaction /SAPAPO/SCC03 in the SAP SCM system.

PPM describes the production process for manufacturing one or more products on a non-order-specific basis. A PPM plan consists of BOM and routing data from SAP ERP that is based on the PPM plan. The PPM plan is a location-independent master data object that describes which process steps, activities, and components are required to manufacture the output products. In PPM, you define the validity conditions, lot size margins, and priority for each output product for the usage of PPM. You also describe the planning and production location for the output products defined in the plan.

2 | CTM Planning Scope

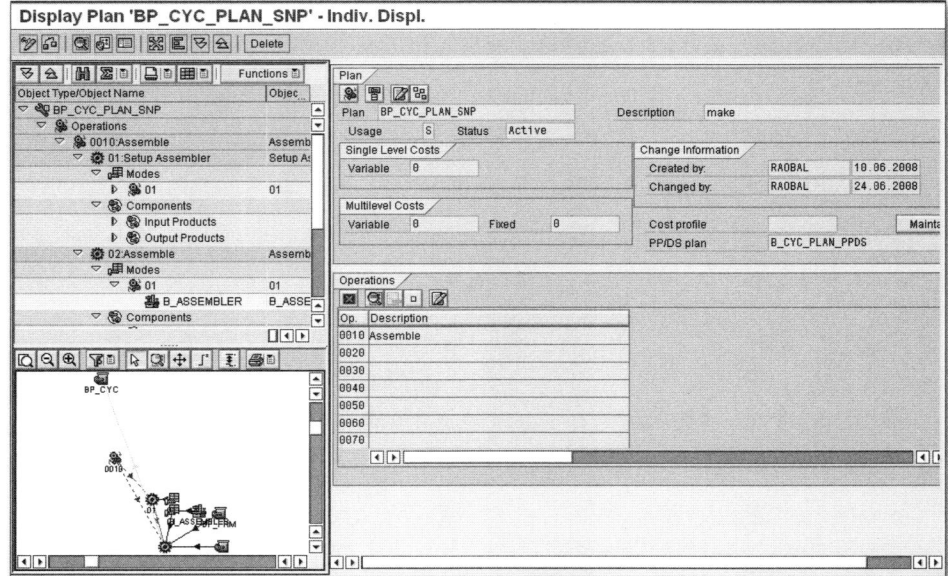

Figure 2.12 Production Process Model Maintenance in SAP SCM

PPM is created in SAP APO using CIF by using the production version in the SAP ERP software. PPM represents the single data structure that combines the BOM and routing parameters required for planned order creation. PPM can be modified in the SAP SCM system using the SAP APO Transaction /SAPAPO/SSC03. For bucket-oriented rough-cut capacity planning, SNP PPM is required, whereas for time-continuous detailed planning, PP/DS PPM is required. Because CTM can plan in both SNP and PP/DS planning mode, both the SNP and PP/DS PPM are supported for CTM planning. CIF is used to create the PP/DS PPM in the SAP SCM system. And using the utility Transaction /SAPAPO/PPM_CONV, you can create an SNP PPM from PP/DS PPM.

In addition to PPM, you can also define a PDS to execute production planning in CTM. PDS is a much newer form of modeling the production alternative in SAP APO compared to PPM. Unlike PPM, there are three kinds of PDS available for capacity planning:

- SNP PP/DS is similar to SNP PPM and can be used in CTM for SNP bucket planning.

- CTM PDS is required for time-continuous PP/DS planning with CTM.

- PDS can be created in SAP SCM from SAP ERP using CIF. PDS is generated in SAP APO from a production version or BOM in SAP ERP, or a production version in the SAP Discrete Industries and Mill Products (DIMP) solution.

PPM and PDS generation options are shown in Figure 2.13.

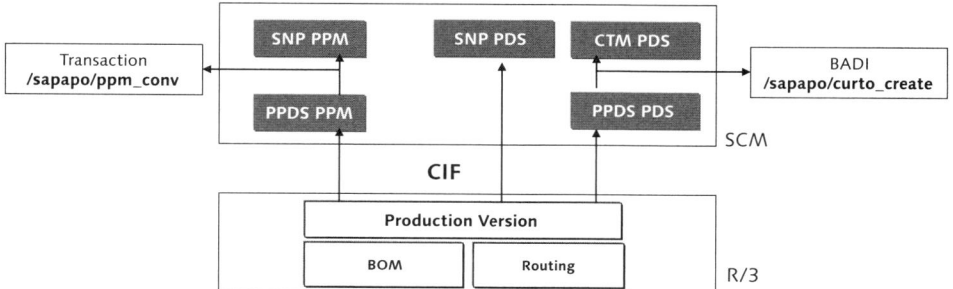

Figure 2.13 PPM and PDS Creation in SAP SCM Using the SAP ERP Production Version

The production data structure contains information about the production cycle and the component assignment for the production of a product. Unlike PPM, PDS parameters can't be modified in SAP SCM. In the SAP SCM application, you can only display and delete the PDS using the SAP APO Transactions /SAPAPO/CURTO_SIMU and /SAPAPO/CULL_RTO_DEL. The transactions can be accessed using the SAP Easy Access menu under ADVANCED PLANNING AND OPTIMIZATION • PRODUCTION DATA STRUCTURE. When planning in bucket-oriented mode, CTM can use the SNP PDS. On the other hand, PP/DS PDS must be converted to a CTM PDS for planning in time-continuous mode. The creation of the CTM PDS for planning can be automated in CIF using the BAdI /SAPAPO/CURTO_CREATE. And the method CREATE_CTM_PDS can be implemented to create the CTM PDS along with the PP/DS PDS.

Planning with PPM and PDS can also be combined. For example, it's possible to define PDS for one set of products and PPMs for another set of products. SAP APO uses the Plan Explosion setting from the product location master to determine the allowed production alternatives (PPM/PDS) for planning. As shown in Figure 2.14, option "2" indicates PPM selection and option "5" indicates PDS selection. The default option for plan explosion can be set in the CTM global customization using Transaction /SAPAPO/CTMCUST.

2 | CTM Planning Scope

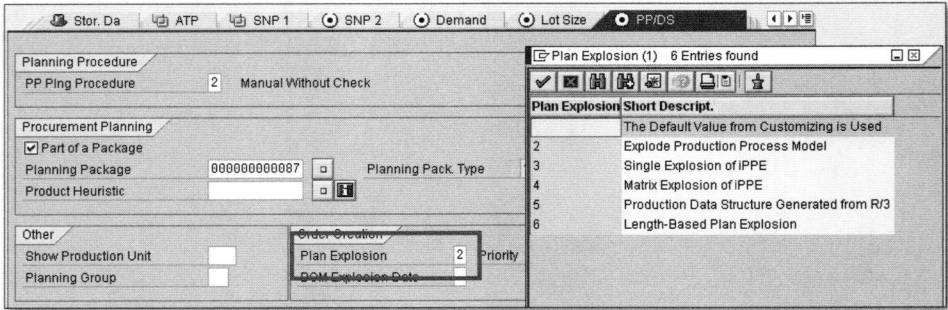

Figure 2.14 Plan Explosion for Product Location

The following parameters assigned to the production sources (PPM, PDS) are supported in CTM planning:

- Validity Period, Lot Size Interval, Procurement Priority
- Activity Relationships and Precedence Constraints (minimum, maximum intervals between activities)
- Activity Scrap (time-dependent)
- Co-production
- Fixed/Variable (time-dependent) Material Consumption
- Fixed/Variable (time-dependent) Mode Duration
- Fixed/Variable (time-dependent) Resource Consumption
- Quota Values and Component Validity

When using PPM or PDS with CTM planning, it's important to understand the following requirements:

- The main output component in PPM must be assigned to the last activity. The input components can be assigned to any activity, including the setup activity.
- All activities in PPM/PDS must have end-start relationships.
- Queue and tear down activities are only considered for planning if the output components are reassigned to the last activity using CTM planning parameter COMP_REASSIGN.

The options shown in Table 2.2 are available for the planning parameter COMP_REASSIGN.

Value1	Value2	Description
I		All input components are assigned to the first activity; setup activities aren't deleted.
O		All output components are assigned to the last activity; setup activities aren't deleted.
X		All input or output components are assigned to the first or last activity; setup activities aren't deleted.
	X	Setup activities aren't deleted.

Table 2.2 Planning Parameter COMP_REASSIGN Options

▶ Master data selection must contain all components used in PPM/PDS. PPM without main output product in the planning scope can be ignored with planning parameter PPM_CHECK_PRODUCT with Value1 = X.

Note

For more details about the planning parameter PPM_CHECK_PRODUCT, refer to SAP Note 934892.

2.3.6 Product Substitution

Product interchangeability and ATP rules provide options for using product substitution in CTM planning. The product substitution rule is a linear chain that defines the source location product and target location product that can be used for substitution during planning. The substitution definition in CTM can be used in multiple business processes. The three key business processes that CTM supports using the substitution definition are the following:

▶ Planning with product discontinuation
▶ Planning with FFF classes
▶ Planning with ATP rules

Now that we've defined all of the master data required for CTM planning, you'll learn about the transactional data used in CTM planning. Similar to master data selection, CTM offers several flexible options to define transaction data selection as described in detail in the next section.

2.4 Transactional Data Selection

CTM provides a flexible transactional data selection and control function using CTM order selection. The transactional data is selected for planning in CTM using the location product master data object. By default, only the orders that belong to the location products selected in the CTM master data selection ID are selected for planning. In some scenarios, if you only want to plan specific order types of a given location product, then you can use CTM order selection for demands. The order selection ID can be defined using the SAP APO Transaction /SAPAPO/CTMORDSEL or using the SAP Easy Access menu ADVANCED PLANNING AND OPTIMIZATION • SUPPLY CHAIN PLANNING • MULTILEVEL SUPPLY AND DEMAND MATCHING • CAPABLE TO MATCH • ENVIRONMENT • ORDER SELECTION.

The order selection ID can be used to restrict either the demand or supplies used in CTM planning. For example, if you want to plan only the sales orders of a given product location and exclude all forecast orders in the CTM profile, then you define the order selection ID and use it for demand selection in the CTM profile. Figure 2.15 shows the CTM order selection ID definition. Order selection in CTM can be based on the following criteria:

- **Location products based**
  You'll use location products order selection to select only the demands and supplies for planning instead of selecting all of the location products selected in the master data selection.

- **Time based**
  Time-based order selection is used to select the demands and supplies in a given time frame instead of the complete planning horizon. Order selection using a time frame is only applicable for initial demand and supply selection for planning. CTM planning can create orders outside the selection time frame for the selected demands.

- **ATP category based**
  Selection by ATP categories is the most useful and widely used selection method. Using this option, only the demands and supplies of a given ATP category are selected for planning. For example, you can choose to plan only the sales orders instead of forecast orders in a given CTM run. The ATP categories used for order creation during the CTM run aren't influenced by this setting.

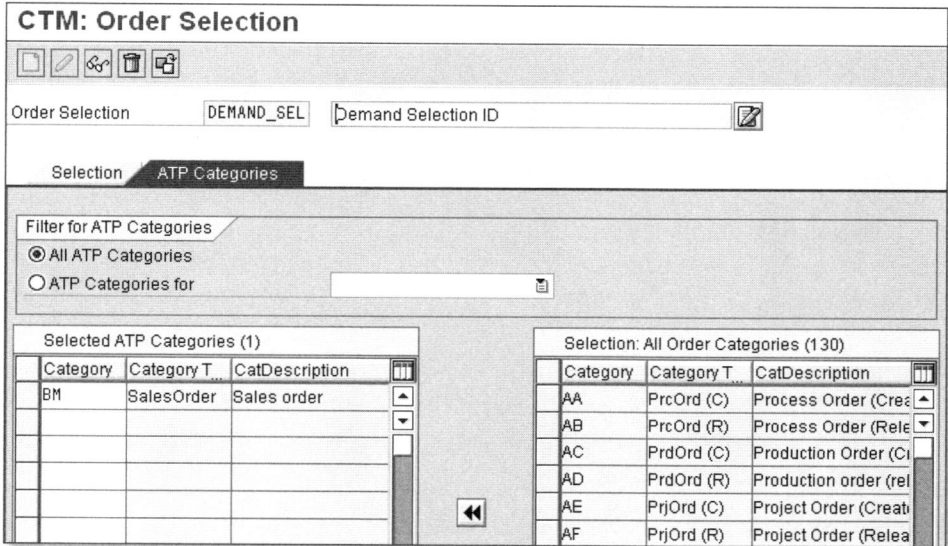

Figure 2.15 CTM Demand Selection by ATP Categories

2.5 Planning and Deletion Modes

CTM planning prioritizes the demands and matches them with the existing supplies by considering the resource capacity constraints. In many cases, CTM is used for mid-term planning and for complete regenerative planning. In this scenario, the current supply plan is deleted, and the new plan is generated considering the new master and transactional data. On the other hand, some scenarios require you to plan for only open demands without deleting the current plan. In either case, CTM offers flexible configuration options for planning and deleting existing transaction data as shown in Figure 2.16.

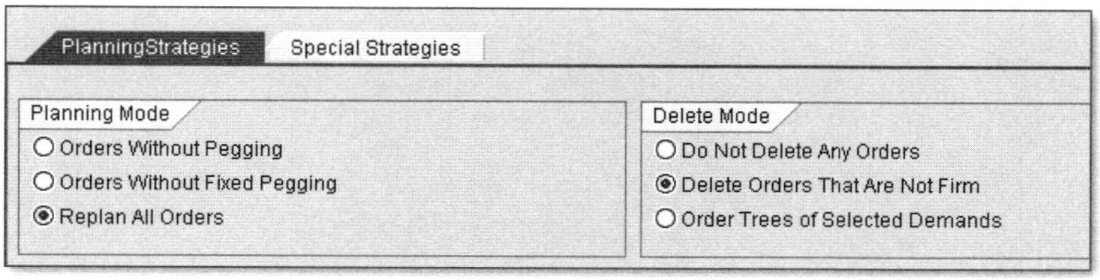

Figure 2.16 CTM Planning and Deletion Mode

2 | CTM Planning Scope

To better understand the usage and significance of the options, note that *pegging* is a procedure used in SAP APO that establishes the relationship between the receipt elements and requirements elements of a product within a location. By using pegging, the corresponding receipt elements are assigned to the requirements.

Two types of pegging are available in SAP SCM:

- **Fixed pegging**
  Fixed pegging is used to create fixed relationships between a receipt and requirement element during planning. Any change in the new receipt of requirement elements for the given product does not influence the fixed pegging. CTM can create fixed pegging during planning. Fixed pegging improves the traceability of the CTM planning results. In constrained planning mode, fixed pegging is very useful for understanding the supply consumption and demand prioritization sequence used by CTM.

- **Dynamic pegging**
  Dynamic pegging, as the name indicates, is changing based on the current receipt and requirement elements. Dynamic pegging is evaluated by SAP liveCache for a given product location using up-to-date receipt and requirement elements in SAP SCM. Planning tools such as CTM don't create dynamic pegging in SAP liveCache because dynamic pegging doesn't exist persistently in liveCache. However, you can convert the dynamic pegging results to fixed pegging to store the pegging relationships persistently in SAP liveCache. As shown in Figure 2.17, dynamic pegging by SAP liveCache can be disabled using the Deactivate Dynamic Pegging option on the Dynamic Pegging tab in the product master.

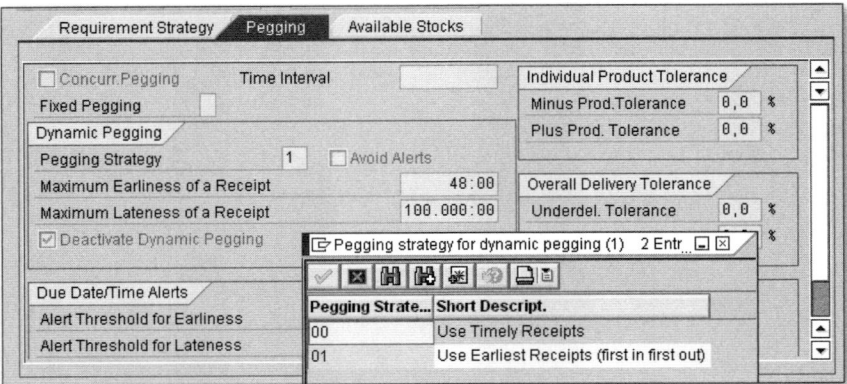

Figure 2.17 Dynamic Pegging Option in SAP SCM

Planning modes in CTM are used to select the orders relevant for planning. So, you can choose to replan all of the existing orders (as shown in Figure 2.18) to determine the new demand prioritization sequence and assign the resources and supplies accordingly.

The options available for planning modes are shown in Table 2.3.

Planning Mode	Description
Orders Without Pegging	All orders (input and output nodes) that are linked by either fixed or dynamic pegging relationships are selected for planning.
Orders Without Fixed Pegging	All orders (input and output nodes) that aren't linked by fixed pegging relationships are selected for planning.
Replan All Orders	All orders (input and output nodes) are selected for planning.

Table 2.3 Planning Mode Options

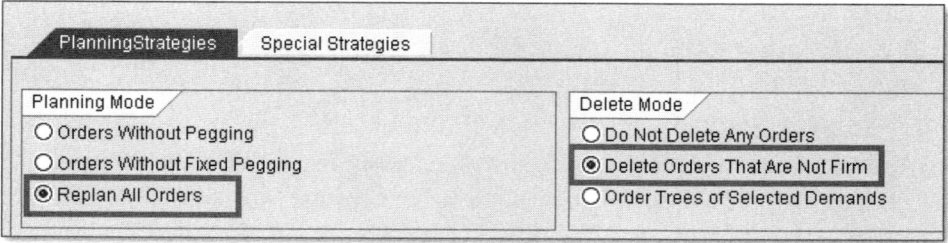

Figure 2.18 CTM Regenerative Planning Mode

Deletion modes in the CTM profile can be used to select the orders for deletion. You can choose to delete all of the unfirmed orders, or select only the orders that are pegged to the demands selected for CTM planning. CTM can only delete the unfirmed orders existing in the CTM planning horizon. All of the firmed orders such as sales orders, forecast orders, firmed production orders, and so on can't be deleted by CTM planning. In addition, unfirmed orders inside the production and transport horizon aren't deleted by the CTM planning run.

61

2 | CTM Planning Scope

Table 2.4 shows the options available for deletion modes.

Deletion Mode	Description
Do Not Delete Any Orders	Don't delete any orders.
Delete Orders That Are Not Firm	All orders that aren't firmed are deleted. An order can be deleted if it meets the deletion criteria.
Order Trees of Selected Demands	All orders that are linked to the demand using fixed or dynamic pegging relationships are deleted.

Table 2.4 Deletion Mode Options

Using the deletion mode, you can choose to delete the orders in the CTM planning run, however, not all orders can be deleted in the CTM planning run. An order is considered fixed during the CTM order deletion step under the following conditions:

- The CTM planning run can only delete planned orders, purchase requisitions, stock transfer requisitions, and substitute requisitions. All of the other order types, such as forecast, sales order, stock, and so on, can't be deleted at all by the CTM planning run. These orders are always considered as fixed by CTM. Note that the subcontracting scenario is an exception to this rule. If a stock transfer requisition for a subcontractor is deleted, the corresponding subcontractor production order is also deleted, even if it's fixed.

- An order is manually changed in SAP APO using the SNP interactive planning book or product view. Any manual changes to the order by the planner will fix the order status.

- When planning in SNP mode, PP/DS orders can't be deleted. On the other hand, both SNP and PP/DS orders can be deleted when using the PPDS Order Type parameter in the CTM profile.

- An order is considered fixed if it starts before the planning start date or ends after the planning end date. Additionally, product horizons are considered for order deletion. Planned orders inside the production horizon, stock transfer orders inside the transport horizon, and purchase requisitions inside the planned delivery time are considered fixed. Orders are considered fixed if they are pegged (fixed or dynamic) to the demands that lie outside the planning horizon or to the demands that aren't selected for CTM planning.

- Orders are considered fixed if all of the components of the order aren't included in the CTM master data selection. For example, a planned order can only be deleted if all of the output and input components of the planned order are selected in the CTM master data selection.
- When planning in active version 000, the orders that exist in SAP APO and R/3 are considered fixed if you select the Planning Results Not Transferred or the Only New Orders Transferred parameters in the CTM profile.

The planning modes can also be combined with the order deletion modes. And the CTM planning and deletion modes can be used based on the pegging relationships existing for the orders. CTM regenerative planning can be executed using the Replan All Orders and Delete Orders That Are Not Firm options. In this mode, the current plan is completely deleted. CTM deletes the existing unfirmed orders and fixed pegging relationships and regenerates the new supply plan using the current planning parameters.

2.5.1 Regenerative Planning with CTM

The Order Without Pegging and Do Not Delete Any Orders options can be used to plan only open demands and supplies without changing the supply plan for already planned orders. Other combinations between planning and deletion modes must be carefully used. For example, Orders Without Pegging can't be combined with Order Trees of Selected Demands because it's implicit that the order tree represented by pegging can't be determined if orders are selected without pegging relationships.

2.5.2 Net Change Planning with CTM

Planning with CTM can also be used to plan only the net changes in the demand and supply situation from the last planning run. Each order in the SAP SCM system contains the net change attribute stored in SAP liveCache. Any changes in the order or the fixed pegging between the orders create the "net change" indicator for the related orders. The CTM Net Change Planning option can be used to plan only such orders (see Figure 2.19). Note that to use net change planning with CTM, you must use one of the following options for the deletion option:

- Do Not Delete Any Orders
- Order Trees of Selected Demands

By choosing the Delete Orders That Are Not Firmed option, CTM sets the net change flag for all orders that were pegged to the deleted orders.

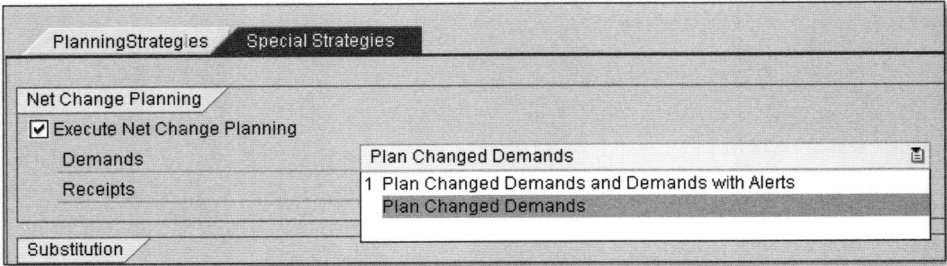

Figure 2.19 CTM Net Change Planning

Net change planning with CTM doesn't use the Planning File Entry option available in SAP SCM. Planning File Entry is available in SNP and PP/DS planning and can be displayed using the SAP APO Transaction /SAPAPO/RRP_NETCH. Planning File Entry is created for all master data and transactional data changes in SAP SCM. Because CTM doesn't use Planning File Entry for net change planning, the master data changes alone don't trigger CTM net change planning.

In the next section, you'll learn about the various planning strategies available in CTM.

2.6 Planning Strategy with CTM

Planning strategies in CTM define the planning horizon and special strategies available in CTM for modeling different planning requirements. CTM offers both bucket and time-continuous planning options using both the SNP and PP/DS master data. Based on the overall supply and production planning strategy used in SAP SCM, careful selection of the planning strategies in CTM must be made. Figure 2.20 shows the planning strategies available in the CTM profile.

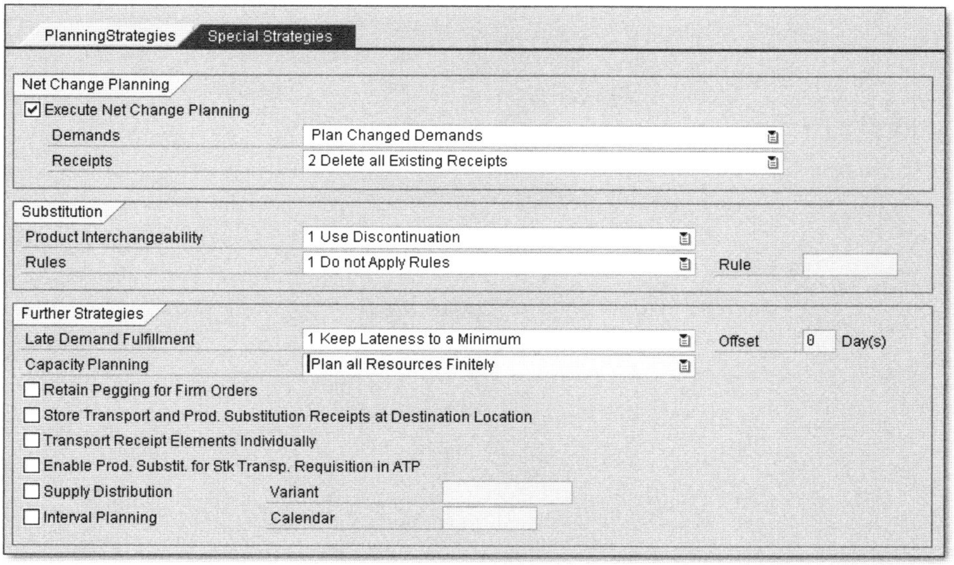

Figure 2.20 CTM Planning Strategies

2.6.1 CTM Time Stream

CTM time stream defines the planning horizon used for planning. The start and end time defined in the time stream defines the time interval for demand selection for planning. As shown in Figure 2.21, CTM time stream can be defined using SAP APO Transaction /SAPAPO/CTMTSTR. The time stream can be defined with reference to the current day as the planning start. It's also possible to define the time stream with respect to a relative or absolute date in the past or future. This provides a lot of flexibility in defining the planning horizon. A planning start date in the past ensures that the demands in the past are also selected for planning. When you select the demands with requirement date in the past, any new supplies to meet the requirement date aren't created in the past. This is because, by default, the order creation in CTM planning starts from the current day. On the other hand, you can select all firmed and open supplies available before the planning start for planning. None of the demands or supplies after the CTM planning end time is selected for planning.

The time stream also contains the planning buckets. Planning buckets are used only for the demand and supply aggregation, which will be discussed in detail in Chapter 4. The planning buckets aren't relevant for bucket planning in CTM SNP planning mode.

2 | CTM Planning Scope

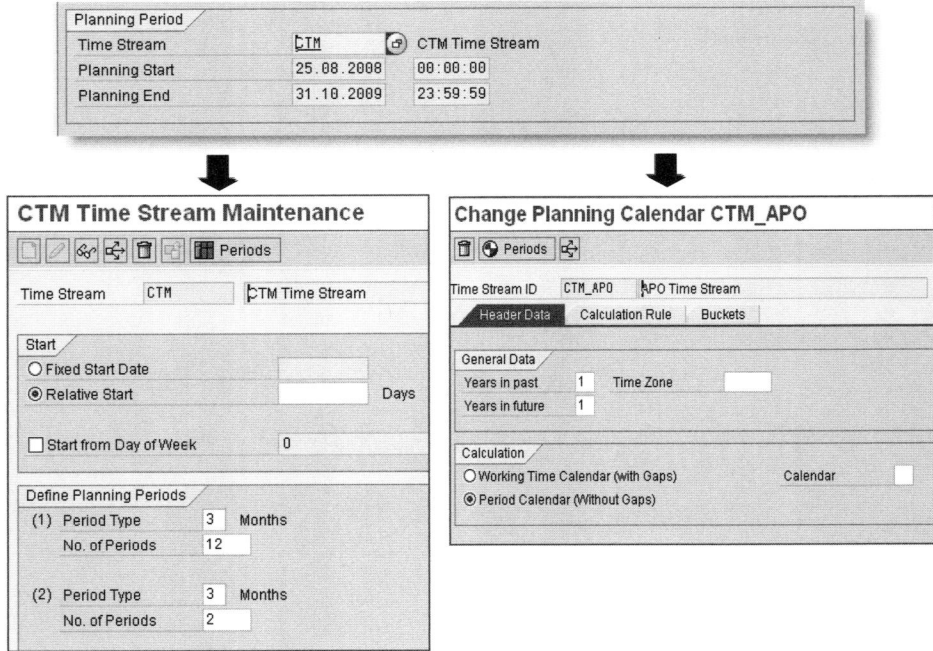

Figure 2.21 CTM Time Stream Maintenance Options in SAP SCM

Time stream used for CTM planning can also be maintained using the SAP APO calendar using SAP APO Transaction /SAPAPO/CALENDAR. Both the options are shown in Figure 2.21. The SAP APO planning calendar must be defined without gaps. The main advantage of using the SAP APO calendar is the ability to define flexible buckets. The CTM time stream can only be defined with daily, weekly, monthly, quarterly, and yearly buckets with bucket start always at the start of the calendar week, month, quarter, or year. With the SAP APO calendar, you can define the buckets with variable durations. You can also use the time zone in SAP APO calendar, whereas the CTM time stream definition is created only for the UTC (Universal Time Coordination) time zone.

2.6.2 Capacity Planning

CTM planning is used for finite capacity planning for the production, transport, and handling of resources. The CTM profile strategy offers the flexibility to select either planning all of the resources finitely or infinitely (see Figure 2.22). It's also possible to select finite planning per resource in the resource master data object.

Using the Use Setting from Resource option, the resources are finitely planned only if the Finite Scheduling flag is set.

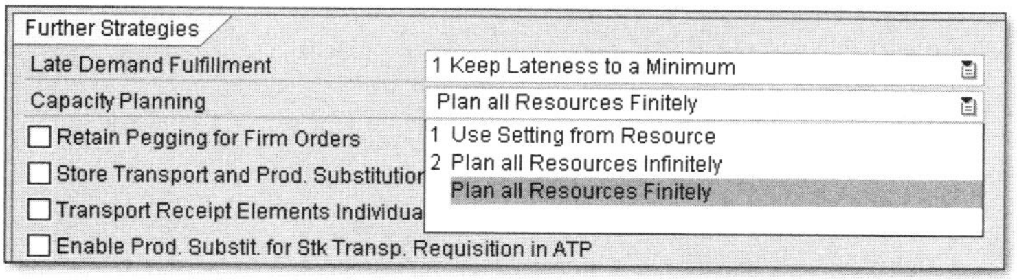

Figure 2.22 CTM Capacity Planning

Keep in mind that when using infinite planning in the CTM profile, only the resource capacity constraints are ignored during CTM planning. Material constraints, calendars, and resource downtimes aren't ignored during infinite planning.

2.6.3 Planning Type

If you're working with long-term, rough-cut finite capacity planning, then using the SNP bucket mode is more appropriate. For short-term production planning, using CTM in PP/DS mode is better because the CTM-created PP/DS orders can be used in PP/DS for setup optimization without order conversion from SNP order type to PP/DS order type. It's important to understand the key difference between the SNP and PP/DS planning modes as described next.

Planning in time-continuous mode requires using PP/DS PPM and CTM PDS with single activity, multi-activity, or mixed resource types. PPM/PDS generally has variable duration of the mode and fixed consumption of the single or multi-activity resource capacity. Time-continuous PP/DS planning is used in CTM for scheduling the resources with exact start and end times up to a second. The order duration varies depending upon the lot size of the planned order. The PP/DS PPM and CTM PDS are required for planning in time-continuous mode. It's also possible to define fixed duration in PPM/PDS when planning in time-continuous mode, but variable resource consumption must not be used in time-continuous planning. In the CTM profile, the following settings must be made for time-continuous planning (see Figure 2.23):

- **Type of Planning:** Continuous Planning
- **Order Category:** PP/DS Order
- **Source of Supply:** PP/DS Type

2 CTM Planning Scope

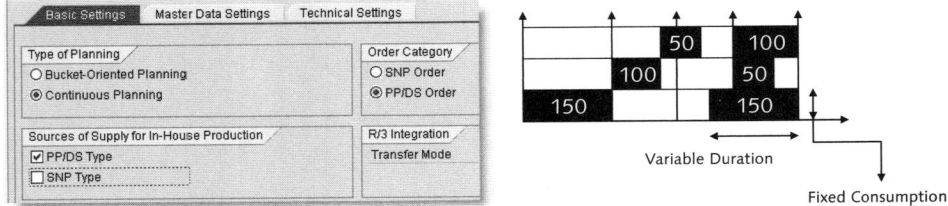

Figure 2.23 CTM Time-Continuous Planning Mode

Planning in the SNP bucket mode requires using SNP PPM/PDS with the bucket or mixed resource type. The PPM/PDS generally has a fixed duration of the mode and variable bucket consumption of the resource. The duration is always defined as multiples of days. Bucket planning mode in CTM is used for planning rough-cut capacity up to a minimum of one day. Resource scheduling times smaller than one day aren't available for SNP orders; that is, the orders always start at the start of the day and end at the end of the day. It's possible to use the fixed resource consumption, but variable mode duration must not be used.

In the CTM profile, the following settings must be made for bucket-oriented planning (as shown in Figure 2.24):

- **Type of Planning:** Bucket-Oriented Planning
- **Order Category:** SNP Order
- **Source of Supply for In-House Production:** SNP Type

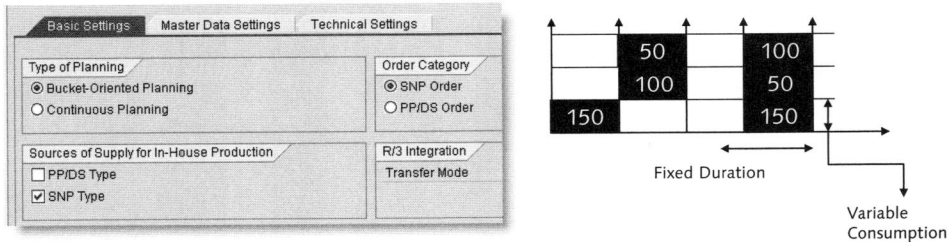

Figure 2.24 CTM Bucket Planning Mode

2.6.4 Late Demand Strategies

CTM planning will propose a feasible plan that is as close as possible to the demand date. All of the alternatives in the supply chain are evaluated to propose an on-time supply plan. If material or capacity constraints keep the demand from being fulfilled on time, CTM tries to create a late supply plan. It's possible to configure the late demand strategy in CTM global customization. The allowed late demand frame for the demands planned in the CTM profile is also maintained in the global customization. In the late demand Airline Strategy option, if the demand can't be fulfilled on time, then the demand is skipped, and the next demand is planned. After all of the demands are planned, the skipped demands are planned again for a late solution. Using the Domino Strategy option (see Figure 2.25), every demand is planned on time first, and then if no on-time solution can be found, a late supply plan is created before planning for the next demand in the demand list.

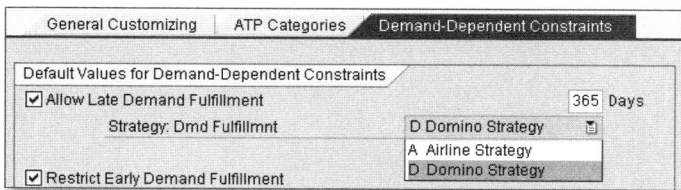

Figure 2.25 CTM Late Demand Strategy

2.6.5 Scheduling Direction

Resource scheduling using backward or forward scheduling mode is also available in CTM (see Figure 2.26). In backward scheduling mode, the orders are created as close to the original demand date as possible; in forward scheduling mode, the orders are created as early as possible. In backward scheduling mode, the supply consumption uses the closest supply for a given demand, whereas in forward scheduling mode, the earliest supply is consumed to fulfill the demand quantity in time. Keep in mind that the late demand strategies used for CTM planning are only applicable in backward scheduling mode.

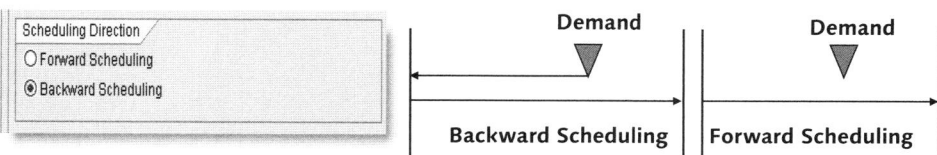

Figure 2.26 CTM Backward and Forward Scheduling Modes

2.6.6 Pegging Type

Pegging in SAP SCM defines the relationship between a receipt and a requirement element (see Figure 2.27). Unlike SNP Heuristics and SNP Optimizer, CTM can create fixed pegging for the demands and supplies planned in CTM. Fixed pegging can be used to trace the CTM supply plan to identify the demand prioritization and supply consumption sequence. During CTM planning, the fixed pegging is automatically created in SAP liveCache. Using fixed pegging could have performance impact on the overall CTM run. If fixed pegging isn't required for CTM planning, always use dynamic pegging. On the other hand, for planning safety stock requirements in CTM, fixed pegging must always be used.

As mentioned earlier, dynamic pegging is evaluated by SAP liveCache for a given product and isn't persistently stored in SAP liveCache.

Figure 2.27 CTM Pegging Type

2.7 Summary

SNP with CTM can be executed in both bucket-oriented and time-continuous planning mode to generate a finite supply plan. Planning with CTM must be preceded by a careful evaluation of planning requirements and strategies such as planning horizon, SNP scope, late demand strategies, pegging type, and integration with SAP ERP.

In the next chapter, we'll talk about CTM demand and supply processing options, including demand aggregation, demand prioritization, and supply categorization.

CTM demand and CTM supply form the main input data for planning. This chapter explains the main attributes of CTM demand and supply, demand prioritization and supply categorization functions, and the CTM search strategy.

3   CTM Demand and Supply Processing

When executing global network planning for your complete supply chain network, you need to balance the demands and supplies across your supply chain. The net demands are then used for generating the production plan. CTM planning matches the prioritized demands to the categorized supplies based on the resource and material constraints. The CTM demands and supplies are determined using the transactional data stored in SAP liveCache, which consists of sales orders, forecast orders, stock, purchase orders, production orders, planned orders, and so on. The orders are selected for CTM planning and converted into CTM demands and supplies. Aggregation and prioritization are the key planning functions available for CTM demands. You'll use demand aggregation to combine multiple demands into a single demand for planning. With demand prioritization, you can determine the criteria to be used in CTM for sorting demands and the sequence in which CTM will cover these demands.

In this chapter, you'll learn about both the basic and advanced methods used for influencing demand prioritization and aggregation. You'll learn about the customer exits and how to implement custom prioritization logic. You'll also learn how CTM supplies can be aggregated before the supply categorization, and how you can group receipts and supplies according to various criteria and assign them to your own supply categories. In addition, this chapter covers the key configurations that are required to implement supply categorization using supply limits by quantity or by using ATP categories.

The most important point to understand about aggregation, prioritization, and categorization is that these functions are applied for the existing demands and supplies before the CTM planning run because the dependent demands and supplies created during the planning run aren't subject to aggregation, prioritization, and categorization.

CTM demands and supplies are processed in the following sequence during CTM planning:

- Demand aggregation
- Demand prioritization
- Supply aggregation
- Supply categorization

3.1 CTM Demand and Supply Attributes

To better understand the key processing function available with demands and supplies in CTM, you should know the definition of the CTM demand and CTM supply. Every order in SAP liveCache that is relevant to planning gets converted to CTM demand and CTM supply. For CTM planning, the demand is represented by the requirement element with negative quantity requirements. Similarly, CTM supply is represented by the receipt element with positive receipt quantity. For example, a sales order gets converted into a CTM demand element, and a stock element gets converted into CTM supply. Some orders such as firmed stock transport orders get converted into a CTM demand and CTM supply in source and target locations.

In addition, production orders get converted into CTM supply for output product and CTM demand for component products. As you can see in Figure 3.1, most of the orders in the SAP SCM system contain the input nodes, output nodes, and activities. The orders (input and output nodes) are connected using fixed or dynamic pegging relationships. The input node of the order is then converted to the CTM demand, and the output node of the order is converted to the CTM supply. You should also keep in mind that the CTM demands and supplies are used for CTM planning after demand prioritization and supply categorization.

In addition, the CTM demand and supply selected for planning can be displayed in the demand and supply simulation list. The selected demands and supplies are referred to as primary demands, and all of the dependent demands generated during multi-level planning are referred to as secondary demands. Be sure to remember this key difference between the primary demands and the secondary demands used for CTM planning. The key demand processing functions such as demand prioritization and aggregation are only applied for the primary demands selected for CTM planning. Similarly, the key demand planning attributes, such as the late demand frame and early demand frame, are applied only for the primary demands. In addition, supply categorization and aggregation functions are applied only for the initial supplies selected for CTM planning.

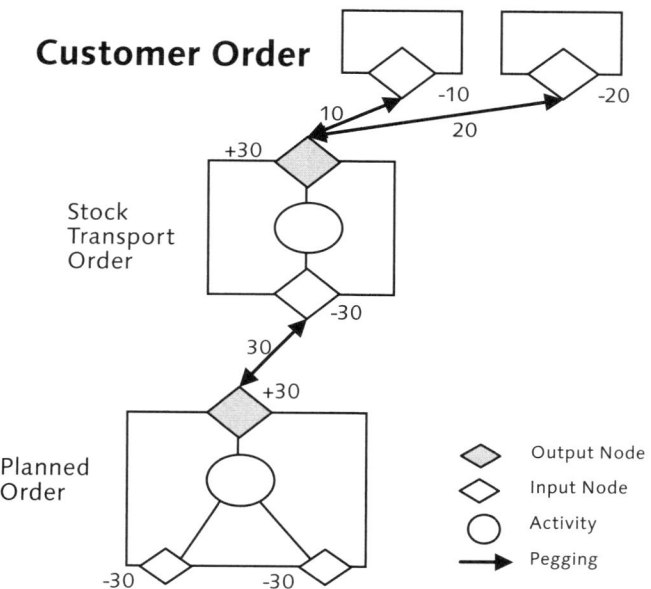

Figure 3.1 Demand and Supply Selection Using SAP liveCache Order Data

3.1.1 CTM Demand Attributes

CTM demand selected for planning contains several planning-relevant attributes and several options to maintain and modify each individual demand attribute using both standard functions and customer exits. The CTM demands and demand attributes can also be displayed using the demand simulation function (see Figure 3.2) available in the CTM profile. However, the demand attributes used for planning in the CTM engine are fixed and can't be extended by customers.

3 | CTM Demand and Supply Processing

Object ID	Product	Location	PlngSegTyp	Acct Assgt	Ct	Date	Time	Quantity	Pr.	Cat	Subloc.	Strategy	Delay	Frame	Earliness	PartFulfil	Part Fulf.	Peggi
1	BP_CYC	BL_FRNK_DC			FC	16.08.2008	12:00:00	10,000-	21	FA				300	999	☑	☑	
2	BP_CYC	BL_FRNK_DC			FC	16.08.2008	12:00:00	10,000-	43	FA				300	999	☑	☑	
3	BP_CYC	BL_FRNK_DC			FC	16.08.2008	12:00:00	10,000-	64	FA				300	999	☑	☑	
4	BP_CYC	BL_FRNK_DC			FC	16.08.2008	12:00:00	10,000-	85	FA				300	999	☑	☑	
5	BP_CYC	BL_FRNK_DC			FC	16.08.2008	12:00:00	10,000-	106	FA				300	999	☑	☑	
6	BP_CYC	BL_FRNK_DC			FC	16.08.2008	12:00:00	10,000-	128	FA				300	999	☑	☑	
7	BP_CYC	BL_FRNK_DC			FC	16.08.2008	12:00:00	10,000-	149	FA				300	999	☑	☑	
8	BP_CYC	BL_FRNK_DC			FC	16.08.2008	12:00:00	10,000-	170	FA				300	999	☑	☑	
9	BP_CYC	BL_FRNK_DC			FC	16.08.2008	12:00:00	10,000-	191	FA				300	999	☑	☑	
10	BP_CYC	BL_FRNK_DC			FC	16.08.2008	12:00:00	10,000-	213	FA				300	999	☑	☑	
11	BP_CYC	BL_FRNK_DC			FC	16.08.2008	12:00:00	10,000-	234	FA				300	999	☑	☑	
12	BP_CYC	BL_FRNK_DC			FC	23.09.2008	12:00:00	10,000-	255	FA				300	999	☑	☑	

Figure 3.2 CTM Demand List

The key CTM demand attributes used for CTM planning are listed here:

- Demand ID
- Product name
- Location name
- Planning segment
- Account assignment
- CTM demand category
- Demand date
- Demand quantity
- Demand priority
- Demand ATP category
- Late demand fulfillment strategy
- Late demand fulfillment frame
- Order creation frame
- Maximum earliness for planned orders
- Partial demand fulfillment
- Pegging type

The demand attributes are mainly derived from the orders, product master, and CTM global customization. These demand attributes can be modified using the user exit. In addition, other demand attributes relevant for CTM planning, such as substitution rules, descriptive characteristics (DCs), sales orders, and aggregation data used for CTM planning, can be displayed in the additional information section of the demand list.

3.1.2 CTM Supply Attributes

CTM supply selected for planning contains the necessary attributes for functions such as supply categorization and search strategy. The stock elements used in CTM planning are always displayed with the date 01.01.1970 to indicate that stock is always available for all CTM demands. This is, however, different from the stock date shown in the product view where the current date is displayed for stock elements. In this case, the CTM supplies and supply attributes can be displayed using the supply simulation function (refer to Figure 3.3) available in the CTM profile.

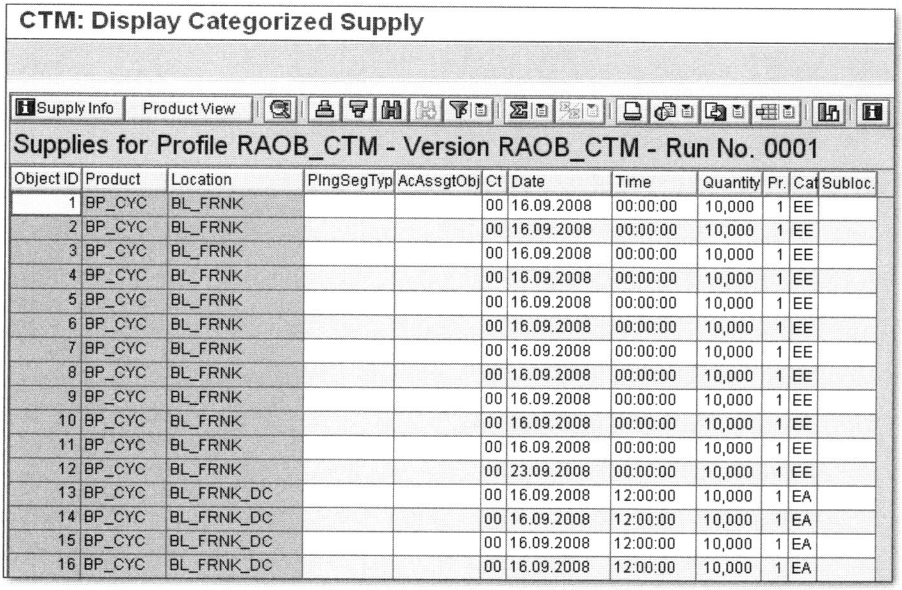

Object ID	Product	Location	PlngSegTyp	AcAssgtObj	Ct	Date	Time	Quantity	Pr.	Cat	Subloc.
1	BP_CYC	BL_FRNK			00	16.09.2008	00:00:00	10,000	1	EE	
2	BP_CYC	BL_FRNK			00	16.09.2008	00:00:00	10,000	1	EE	
3	BP_CYC	BL_FRNK			00	16.09.2008	00:00:00	10,000	1	EE	
4	BP_CYC	BL_FRNK			00	16.09.2008	00:00:00	10,000	1	EE	
5	BP_CYC	BL_FRNK			00	16.09.2008	00:00:00	10,000	1	EE	
6	BP_CYC	BL_FRNK			00	16.09.2008	00:00:00	10,000	1	EE	
7	BP_CYC	BL_FRNK			00	16.09.2008	00:00:00	10,000	1	EE	
8	BP_CYC	BL_FRNK			00	16.09.2008	00:00:00	10,000	1	EE	
9	BP_CYC	BL_FRNK			00	16.09.2008	00:00:00	10,000	1	EE	
10	BP_CYC	BL_FRNK			00	16.09.2008	00:00:00	10,000	1	EE	
11	BP_CYC	BL_FRNK			00	16.09.2008	00:00:00	10,000	1	EE	
12	BP_CYC	BL_FRNK			00	23.09.2008	00:00:00	10,000	1	EE	
13	BP_CYC	BL_FRNK_DC			00	16.09.2008	12:00:00	10,000	1	EA	
14	BP_CYC	BL_FRNK_DC			00	16.09.2008	12:00:00	10,000	1	EA	
15	BP_CYC	BL_FRNK_DC			00	16.09.2008	12:00:00	10,000	1	EA	
16	BP_CYC	BL_FRNK_DC			00	16.09.2008	12:00:00	10,000	1	EA	

Figure 3.3 CTM Supply List

The key CTM supply attributes used for CTM planning include the following:

- Supply ID
- Product name

- Location name
- Planning segment
- Account assignment
- Supply CTM category
- Supply date
- Supply quantity
- Supply priority
- Supply ATP category

In mid- to long-term planning with CTM, you can aggregate the demands in a given location and use CTM to create an aggregated supply. The CTM demand aggregation function is explained in detail in the next section.

3.2 CTM Demand Aggregation

CTM demand aggregation groups CTM Demands for a given location product and ATP category into user-defined time buckets. With CTM demand aggregation, all of the independent demands or primary demands are grouped into a single virtual demand for CTM planning. As a result, during your CTM planning, a single supply is created that corresponds to the aggregated demand if there are no capacity constraints and lot size requirements.

You can also use demand aggregation in CTM planning using the settings under the Aggregation tab in the CTM profile. Keep in mind, however, that demand aggregation is applied on the CTM demands available before the planning run because dependent demands generated during the planning run aren't implicitly aggregated in the same planning run. For this to occur, additional CTM runs for aggregating and planning the dependent requirements are required. Three options are available for demand aggregation in CTM:

- Demand Aggregation by Time Buckets
- Demand Aggregation by Location Product Hierarchy
- Demand Aggregation by Product Lot Size

3.2.1 Demand Aggregation by Time Bucket

Demand aggregation using time buckets is enabled using the Activate Time-Based Aggregation setting in the CTM profile. The time buckets are derived using the CTM time stream. All of the demands of a given location product with the selected ATP category are then aggregated into a single virtual demand for planning. By default, demand aggregation is applied from the start of planning. For example, all of the demands from the planning start are aggregated during demand aggregation. The Start (Days) parameter can be used to enable the aggregation start for a future date. Using the Aggregate Demands and Receipts from Different ATP categories option, CTM aggregates the demands across all of the selected ATP categories. In addition, using the settings displayed in Figure 3.4, forecast and sales orders will be aggregated and planned as a single requirement.

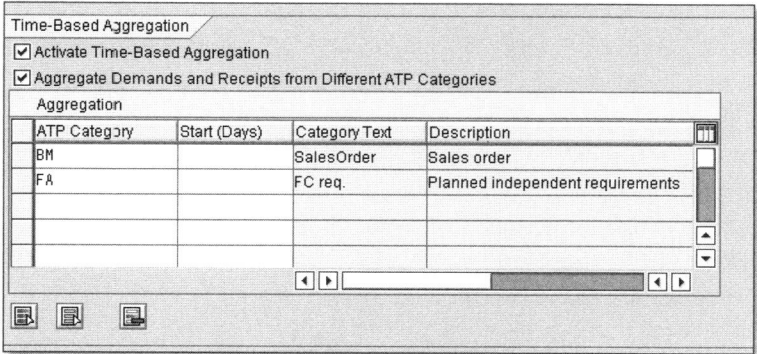

Figure 3.4 CTM Time-Based Demand Aggregation

With demand aggregation, you can aggregate the quantities if the individual demands into a single aggregated virtual demand. The requirement time for the aggregated virtual demand can be configured in the CTM global customization as you can see in Figure 3.5. The following options are available:

- Period Start
- Period End
- Middle of Period
- As Earliest Demand/Supply
- As Latest Demand/Supply

3 | CTM Demand and Supply Processing

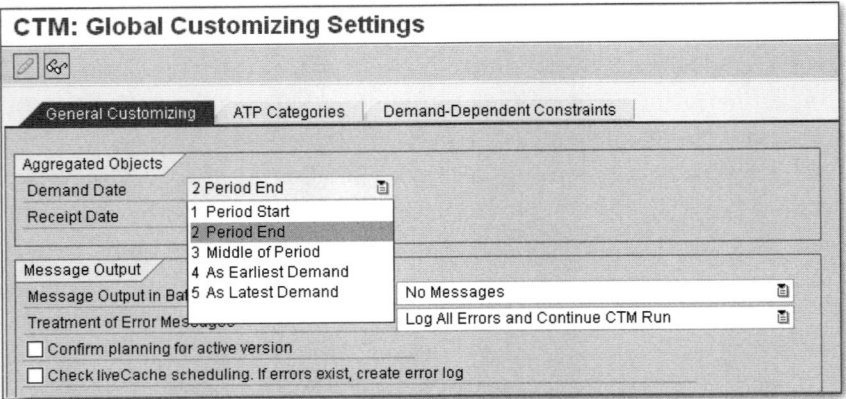

Figure 3.5 Customization for Demand and Supply Aggregation

Figure 3.6 shows the demand simulation list that is the result of demand aggregation. The three individual demands of 75, 50, and 30 units are aggregated into a single demand of 155 units, and the requirement date for the aggregated virtual demand is then selected as the end of the weekly time bucket. Keep in mind that the aggregated demand isn't created in SAP liveCache; rather, the CTM planning engine generates the supply plan corresponding to the aggregated demand date and quantity. Then CTM planning is executed for the virtual demand similar to normal demands, and the supply plan is created to fulfill the complete demand quantity by evaluating all of the procurement alternatives.

The generated supply for the aggregated demand is then pegged to the individual demands that exist in SAP liveCache. As a result, fixed pegging relationships are created for the individual demands and the supplies. In constrained planning scenarios, the supply generated can be less than the aggregated demand quantity. In this scenario, the fixed pegging creation will use the FIFO (First In First Out) logic. For example, CTM will select the first demand of the aggregated demands and create the fixed pegging relationship for the demand quantity before selecting the second demand. Remember that the fixed pegging creation process doesn't use any fair share logic to create fixed pegging relationships across individual demands. For example, for the demand of 155 units, CTM generates a supply of 125 units due to capacity constraints. CTM would allocate 75 to Demand 1, 50 to Demand 2, and Demand 3 will remain unfulfilled. This is because it isn't possible to influence the supply allocation process to individual demands when the demand aggregation process is used in CTM.

3.2 CTM Demand Aggregation

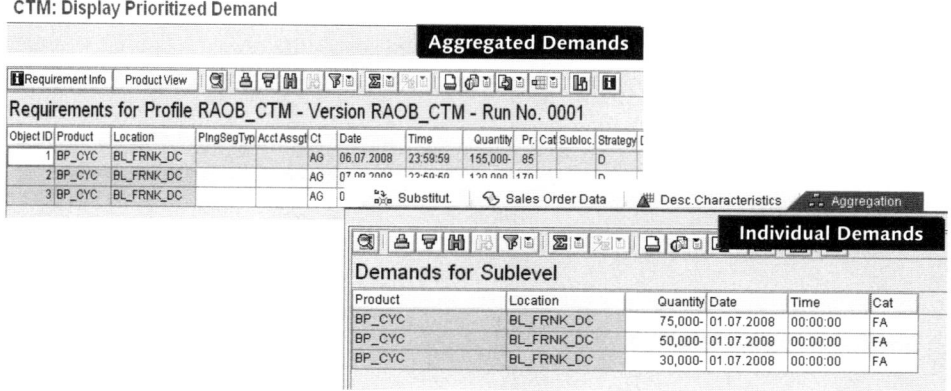

Figure 3.6 CTM Demand Aggregation Using Time Buckets

With demand aggregation, it's imperative that some of the attributes used for individual demands aren't available for aggregated demand. For example, the order priority of the individual demands can't be used for the aggregated demand because during CTM planning with ATP rules, demand aggregation is applied for a given location product, ATP category, and substitution rule. The substitution rule is then evaluated for each demand before demand aggregation. So remember that demands with different substitution rules can't be aggregated during CTM demand aggregation.

3.2.2 Demand Aggregation by Rounding Value

As you know, the CTM supply planning is driven by the demand quantity, demand date, and lot size profile (minimum, maximum lot size, rounding value). When you use CTM planning, CTM always uses the rounding-up logic for the supplies created for the selected demands. As a result, if the demand quantity isn't in the multiples of the rounding value, then an excess supply quantity is created by CTM planning. However, the excess supply created gets consumed for all of the later demands in the demand list. For certain planning scenarios, the excess supply can't be consumed for later demands, or the storage costs will limit the creation and storage of excess supplies. In this case, the supply quantity needs to be in line with the rounding value, and no excess supply will be created for any demand.

The planning parameter DEMAGGBYLOTSIZE with Value1 = X can be used to aggregate the demands as per the rounding value maintained for the location product. As shown in Figure 3.7, a Rounding Value of 50 units is used for the location product BP_CYC at BL_FRNK_DC. The individual demands are aggregated in such a way that the new quantity is always in multiples of 50.

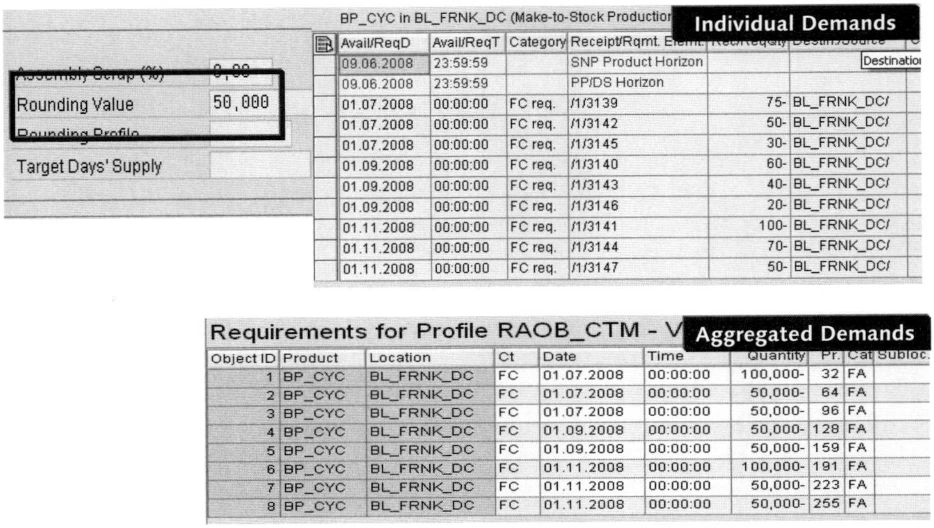

Avail/ReqD	Avail/ReqT	Category	Receipt/Rqmt. Elem.	Rec/ReqQty	Destin./Source
09.06.2008	23:59:59		SNP Product Horizon		
09.06.2008	23:59:59		PP/DS Horizon		
01.07.2008	00:00:00	FC req.	/1/3139	75-	BL_FRNK_DC/
01.07.2008	00:00:00	FC req.	/1/3142	50-	BL_FRNK_DC/
01.07.2008	00:00:00	FC req.	/1/3145	30-	BL_FRNK_DC/
01.09.2008	00:00:00	FC req.	/1/3140	60-	BL_FRNK_DC/
01.09.2008	00:00:00	FC req.	/1/3143	40-	BL_FRNK_DC/
01.09.2008	00:00:00	FC req.	/1/3146	20-	BL_FRNK_DC/
01.11.2008	00:00:00	FC req.	/1/3141	100-	BL_FRNK_DC/
01.11.2008	00:00:00	FC req.	/1/3144	70-	BL_FRNK_DC/
01.11.2008	00:00:00	FC req.	/1/3147	50-	BL_FRNK_DC/

Object ID	Product	Location	Ct	Date	Time	Quantity	Pr.	Cat	Subloc.
1	BP_CYC	BL_FRNK_DC	FC	01.07.2008	00:00:00	100,000-	32	FA	
2	BP_CYC	BL_FRNK_DC	FC	01.07.2008	00:00:00	50,000-	64	FA	
3	BP_CYC	BL_FRNK_DC	FC	01.07.2008	00:00:00	50,000-	96	FA	
4	BP_CYC	BL_FRNK_DC	FC	01.09.2008	00:00:00	50,000-	128	FA	
5	BP_CYC	BL_FRNK_DC	FC	01.09.2008	00:00:00	50,000-	159	FA	
6	BP_CYC	BL_FRNK_DC	FC	01.11.2008	00:00:00	100,000-	191	FA	
7	BP_CYC	BL_FRNK_DC	FC	01.11.2008	00:00:00	50,000-	223	FA	
8	BP_CYC	BL_FRNK_DC	FC	01.11.2008	00:00:00	50,000-	255	FA	

Figure 3.7 CTM Demand Aggregation by Rounding Value

3.2.3 Demand Aggregation by Hierarchy

Aggregated planning with location product hierarchy is supported in CTM with SAP SCM 5.0. The hierarchy structure in SAP SCM represents the hierarchical relationships between the planning objects. CTM planning supports hierarchies for location product, resource, and PPM/PDS. Demand aggregation in CTM uses location product hierarchy to aggregate the demands and supplies from the sublevel products to the header-level product. CTM checks the hierarchy relationships and translates the individual demands for the sublevel products to the header-level products. And as a follow-up process, the aggregated demands using hierarchy can be aggregated using time buckets. In this chapter, we'll explain the use of hierarchy in CTM demand aggregation, and then we'll cover aggregated planning in CTM in greater detail in the next chapter.

You can enable demand aggregation using hierarchy in the CTM profile using the Header Level option in the Aggregated Planning section in the Aggregation tab, as you can see in Figure 3.8.

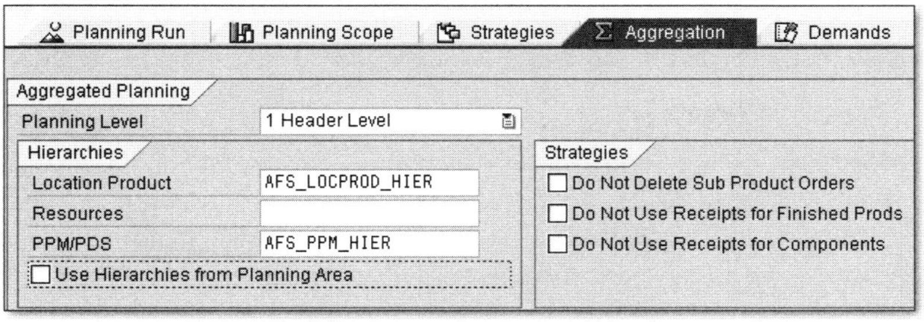

CTM Demand Aggregation | 3.2

Figure 3.8 CTM Demand Aggregation Using Location Product Hierarchy

You can create the master data relevant for the hierarchy using the Transaction /SAPAPO/RELHSHOW or using the SAP Easy Access menu ADVANCED PLANNING AND OPTIMIZATION • MASTER DATA • HIERARCHY. Figure 3.9 represents the location product hierarchy master data. The header product AFS_FIN at the DC location AFS_DC_1 has three components or sublevel product locations. The planning relevant transactional data such as stock, forecast, sales orders, and so on exists for the subproducts. During the CTM demand aggregation, your CTM demands are aggregated to the header product as shown in Figure 3.9.

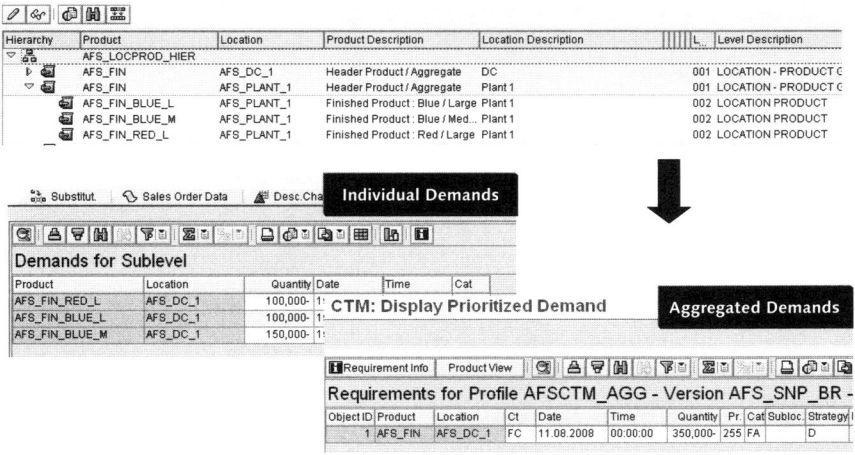

Figure 3.9 CTM Demand Aggregation by Location Product Hierarchy

The aggregated demands aren't created in SAP liveCache but exist only during the planning run. Unlike demand aggregation using time buckets, aggregation with hierarchy can occur across location products. For example, the header product and

81

subproduct are different and represent independent pegging areas in SAP live-Cache. As a result, the aggregated supply created for the header product in CTM planning can't be fixed pegged to the sublevel demands.

The most important advantage with CTM planning is its ability to use demand prioritization. In your supply chain, you can have multiple demand stream and demands for multiple product and customer groups. Each demand stream can have a different priority, and you want to allocate the constrained resources and supplies to the highest priority demands. In the next section, you'll learn about different options that are available for assigning the priority to the demands that are selected for planning.

3.3 Demand Prioritization

The CTM demand prioritization function represents one of the most important functions available with CTM planning. In planning situations where your supply is constrained, you need to allocate the resources and supplies to the most important demands. These demands can be prioritized using several standard attributes available. For example, using DCs, you can define several custom attributes for forecast orders in SAP SCM. And with the demand prioritization function, you can select both the standard and custom attributes to prioritize the demands selected for CTM planning. Another option for demand prioritization in CTM is based on transport lead time.

3.3.1 Demand Prioritization Using Demand Attributes

CTM demands selected for planning contain several attributes that are derived from the sales order data created in SAP ERP. You need to understand that demand aggregation is similar to demand prioritization in that it's also applied only for existing demands or primary demands. The dependent demands generated during the planning run aren't prioritized. The dependent requirements inherit the sort sequence of the independent demand because CTM always plans for the complete supply network. To enable demand prioritization, you must maintain the sort sequence explicitly in the CTM profile using the Define Sequence for This Profile option, or you can use a sort profile maintained in customization. In either case, the sort sequence defines the attributes used for prioritization. Figure 3.10 shows the list of demand attributes available for the demand prioritization.

Demand Prioritization | 3.3

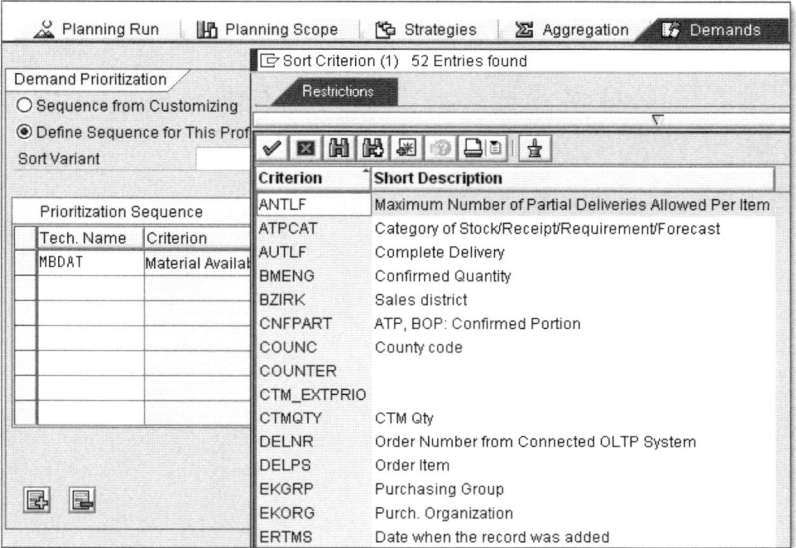

Figure 3.10 CTM Demand Prioritization Attributes

The sort direction assigned to each of the attributes can also be specified in the CTM profile. You have three options available for defining the sort direction:

- Ascending
- Descending
- Special Sorting

For attributes such as material priority and demand date, you can use the ascending and descending sort sequences. Unfortunately, because ATP category is defined with special naming convention, you probably shouldn't use the ascending and descending sort sequence for the ATP category. Instead, you can use special sorting. Other attributes where you should use special sorting include material number, location number, order number, and so on. As you can see in Figure 3.11, the special sort sequence for the attribute Category (ATPCAT) defines the prioritization sequence as Delivery (BR), Sales Order (BM), and Forecast (FA). The special sorting variant can be defined using the SAP APO Transaction /SAPAPO/VASOSORT or using the SAP Easy Access menu ADVANCED PLANNING AND OPTIMIZATION • SUPPLY CHAIN PLANNING • MULTILEVEL SUPPLY AND DEMAND MATCHING • ENVIRONMENT • CURRENT SETTING • DEMAND PRIORITIZATION • VARIANT DEPENDING SPECIAL SORTING.

3 | CTM Demand and Supply Processing

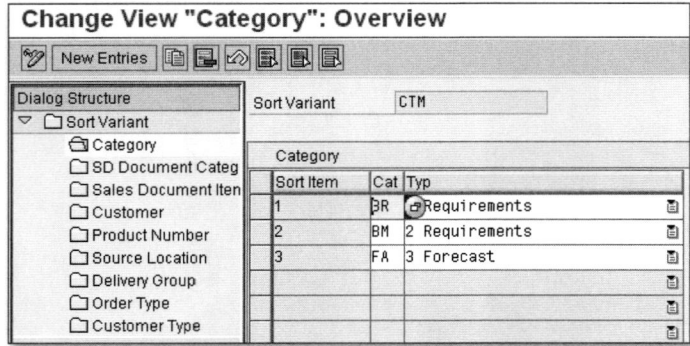

Figure 3.11 Special Sort Sequence for CTM Demand Prioritization

The sort sequence can also be maintained in a sort profile (see Figure 3.12). The sort profile groups the attributes and defines the sequence for each of the attributes, which can be used in multiple CTM profiles.

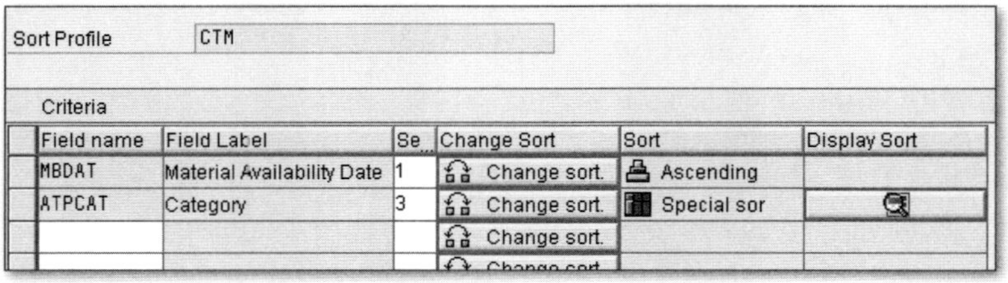

Figure 3.12 Sort Profile for CTM Demand Prioritization

The sort profile can be accessed using the SAP APO Transaction S_AP9_75000206 or by using the SAP Easy Access menu ADVANCED PLANNING AND OPTIMIZATION • SUPPLY CHAIN PLANNING • MULTILEVEL SUPPLY AND DEMAND MATCHING • ENVIRONMENT • CURRENT SETTING • DEMAND PRIORITIZATION • SORT PROFILE.

Based on the sort attributes and the sort sequence used in the CTM profile, CTM demand prioritization selects and prioritizes all of the demands before supply planning. The prioritization sequence can be seen in the demand simulation list in the CTM profile. If multiple attributes are used, CTM applies the sort for each attribute. For example, the sort attributes used in the CTM profile are demand date (MBDAT) and category (ATPCAT). In this case, all of the demands are sorted as per demand date, and then demands with the same dates are sorted with ATP category. If the demands have the same date and category (see Figure 3.13), then the sort isn't unique, and the sequence can't be predetermined. In this scenario, it isn't possible to define the same priority to the demands 1, 2, and 3 because they have the same date and priority. Every demand in CTM planning must be assigned a unique priority for planning. After the demand prioritization using sort attributes, each of the demands is created with a unique demand number or demand ID. The demand ID represents the unique sequence of planning by the CTM engine (see Figure 3.13).

Object ID	Product	Location	Ct	Date	Time	Quantity	Pr.	Cat	Subloc.
1	BP_CYC	BL_FRNK_DC	FC	01.07.2008	00:00:00	75,000-	28	FA	
2	BP_CYC	BL_FRNK_DC	FC	01.07.2008	00:00:00	50,000-	57	FA	
3	BP_CYC	BL_FRNK_DC	FC	01.07.2008	00:00:00	30,000-	85	FA	
4	BP_CYC	BL_FRNK_DC	FC	01.09.2008	00:00:00	60,000-	113	FA	
5	BP_CYC	BL_FRNK_DC	FC	01.09.2008	00:00:00	40,000-	142	FA	
6	BP_CYC	BL_FRNK_DC	FC	01.09.2008	00:00:00	20,000-	170	FA	
7	BP_CYC	BL_FRNK_DC	FC	01.11.2008	00:00:00	100,000-	198	FA	
8	BP_CYC	BL_FRNK_DC	FC	01.11.2008	00:00:00	70,000-	227	FA	
9	BP_CYC	BL_FRNK_DC	FC	01.11.2008	00:00:00	50,000-	255	FA	

Figure 3.13 CTM Demand Prioritization List

The standard sort sequence can be used in conjunction with the user exit APOBO020 to define and implement any customer-specific sort logic that isn't available in the standard CTM solution. The user-exit is called implicitly at the end of the standard demand prioritization. When multiple attributes are used, the user exit for custom demand prioritization can be called explicitly using the attribute USEREXIT as shown in Figure 3.14.

Demand prioritization in CTM is most commonly driven by the material requirement date (MBDAT). Your supply chain network contains demand locations in different time zones, and, by default, CTM uses the demand date with respect to the UTC time zone. As a result, the demand prioritization provides an incorrect prioritization sequence. For example, say you have two locations in the SC network with time zone UTC-6 and UTC+6. The forecast order is released at 15.09.2008 24:00 HRS for both the locations. The demand date in the UTC time zone will be 16.09.2008 06:00 HRS and 15.09.2008 18:00 HRS, respectively, for each of the locations. As a result, the demand location with the UTC+6 time zone is planned before the demand in the location with the UTC-6 time zone. To use the demand prioritization using the location time zone, you can use the CTM planning parameter MBDAT_TZ with Value1 = X.

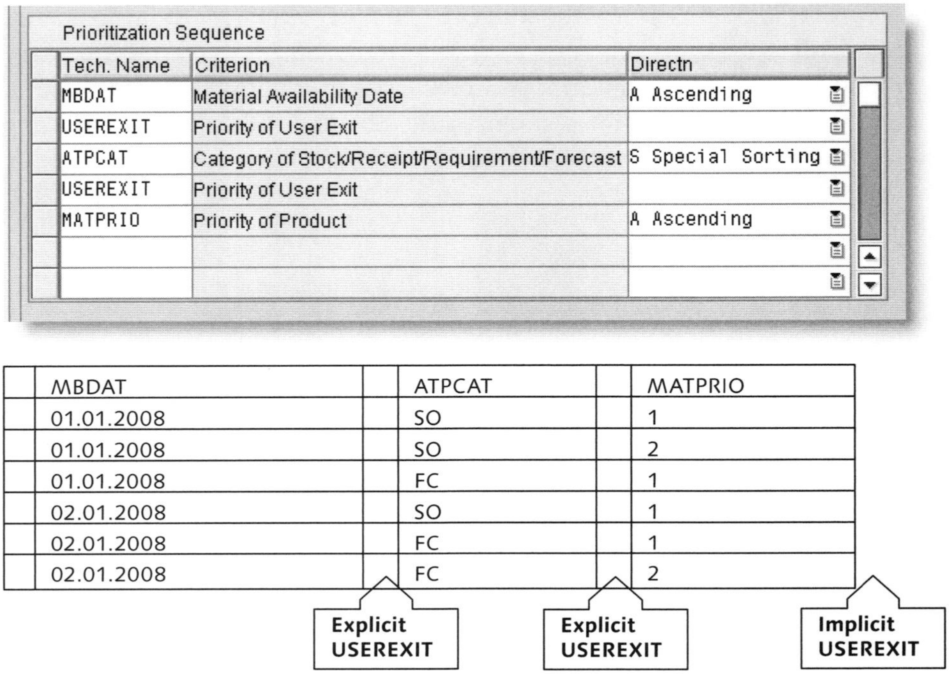

3 | CTM Demand and Supply Processing

Prioritization Sequence			
Tech. Name	Criterion	Directn	
MBDAT	Material Availability Date	A Ascending	
USEREXIT	Priority of User Exit		
ATPCAT	Category of Stock/Receipt/Requirement/Forecast	S Special Sorting	
USEREXIT	Priority of User Exit		
MATPRIO	Priority of Product	A Ascending	

MBDAT	ATPCAT	MATPRIO
01.01.2008	SO	1
01.01.2008	SO	2
01.01.2008	FC	1
02.01.2008	SO	1
02.01.2008	FC	1
02.01.2008	FC	2

Explicit USEREXIT   Explicit USEREXIT   Implicit USEREXIT

Figure 3.14 CTM Demand Prioritization Customer Exit

Demand prioritization by requirement date (MBDAT) considers only the demand date for prioritization, and, by default, the demand requirement time isn't considered for demand prioritization. You can use the demand requirement time for demand prioritization using the CTM planning parameter MBDAT_TZ with Value1 = X and Value2 = X.

When planning with sales orders, you can choose to plan with either the requested or confirmed quantity of the sales order. You make this selection using the Planning Procedure option assigned to individual products and locations. You can define the planning procedure in SAP IMG customization ADVANCED PLANNING AND OPTIMIZATION • SUPPLY CHAIN PLANNING • PRODUCTION PLANNING AND DETAILED SCHEDULING • MAINTAIN PLANNING PROCEDURES. This indicator displays the quantity of a schedule line in a customer requirement that is relevant for pegging; in other words, the quantity that the system takes into consideration in the net requirements calculation and in dynamic pegging. Then if the indicator is set, the *confirmed* quantity is relevant for pegging. If the indicator isn't set, the *desired or requested* quantity is relevant for pegging. If you want to change the setting for a planning method, you use the Convert Pegging-Relevant Quantity of Customer Requirements function. The system copies the desired setting into the planning method and changes the pegging-relevant quantity for existing customer requirements accordingly. Based on this setting, CTM selects the quantity and the date for demand prioritization.

3.3.2 Demand Prioritization Using Descriptive Characteristics

Planning in SNP and PP/DS is based on order data as compared to Demand Planning (DP) where data is in time series. The order data is normally created with reference to location and product characteristics only. You can use DP to forecast at multiple user-defined levels or characteristics, but the forecast must be released to SNP and PP/DS only at the product location level. As of SAP APO 3.1, additional characteristics can be assigned for order data used in SNP and PP/DS planning. The additional attributes are referred to as descriptive characteristics (DCs). In DP, the DCs are similar to any other characteristics. When you use DCs, you can assign additional values to the unconstrained forecast released from DP.

> **Example**
>
> DP can be used to create forecasts for a given location product at the customer level. The unconstrained forecast in SNP is created for a location product and customer. Each of the DCs can be assigned to the sales order attribute to use additional planning functions such as forecast consumption and pegging. For example, the DC CUSTOMER can be assigned to the sales order attribute KUNNR. As a result, the forecast for a given customer can consume only the sales order created for the customer. Without the use of DCs, forecast consumption is only executed at the location product level.

DCs can also be used for releasing the constrained plan from SNP back to DP. Figure 3.15 shows the relationship between the DP characteristics and sales order characteristics. These characteristics are linked together using the consumption group. The consumption group can be individually assigned to each location product. Consumption groups can be maintained using the SAP APO Transaction /SAPAPO/CSP1 or using the SAP IMG customization ADVANCED PLANNING AND OPTIMIZATION • SUPPLY CHAIN PLANNING • DEMAND PLANNING • BASIC SETTINGS • CONSUMPTION • MAINTAIN CONSUMPTION GROUP.

3 | CTM Demand and Supply Processing

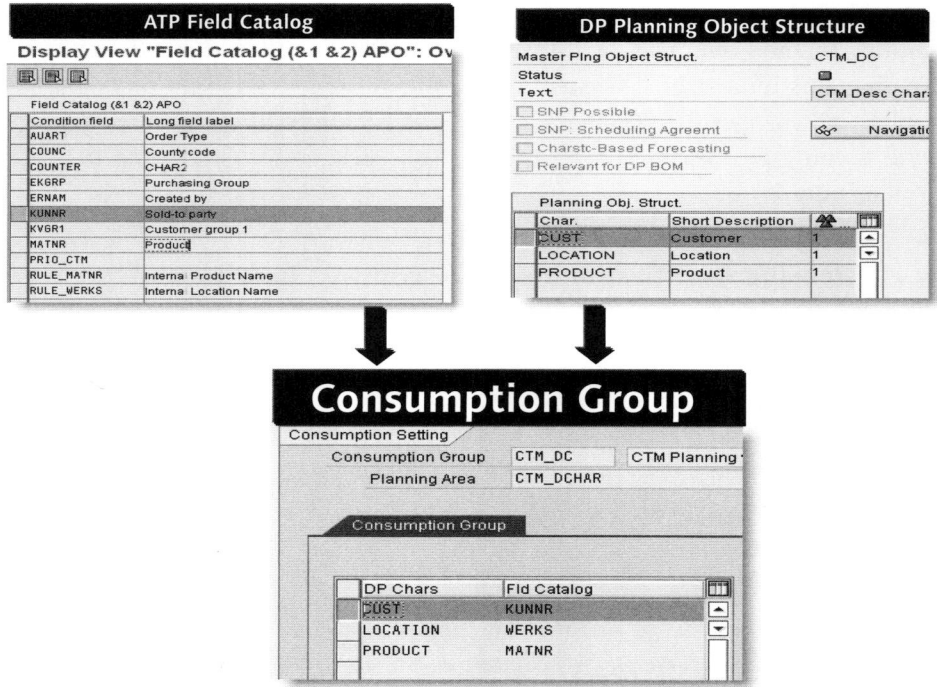

Figure 3.15 Descriptive Characteristics and Consumption Group

CTM supports DCs for demand prioritization and ATP rule evaluation. The DC values aren't used for supply planning, so the supply plan isn't created with the DC of the corresponding demands. However, during demand prioritization, you can use additional attributes defined as DCs for special sorting. For example, forecast orders are released for customers where the customer is defined as a DC. As you can see in Figure 3.16, DP is used to create the unconstrained forecast at each customer level for the product BP_CYC at location BL_FRNK_DC.

Using the consumption group, the customer characteristics are assigned to the ATP field KUNNR. The forecast release from DP to SNP then creates the forecast in liveCache for each individual customer (KMART, TARGET, and WALMART). The DCs assigned to the forecast orders can be displayed using the green triangle icon for each of the orders. The characteristics product and location are also assigned by default.

Demand Prioritization | 3.3

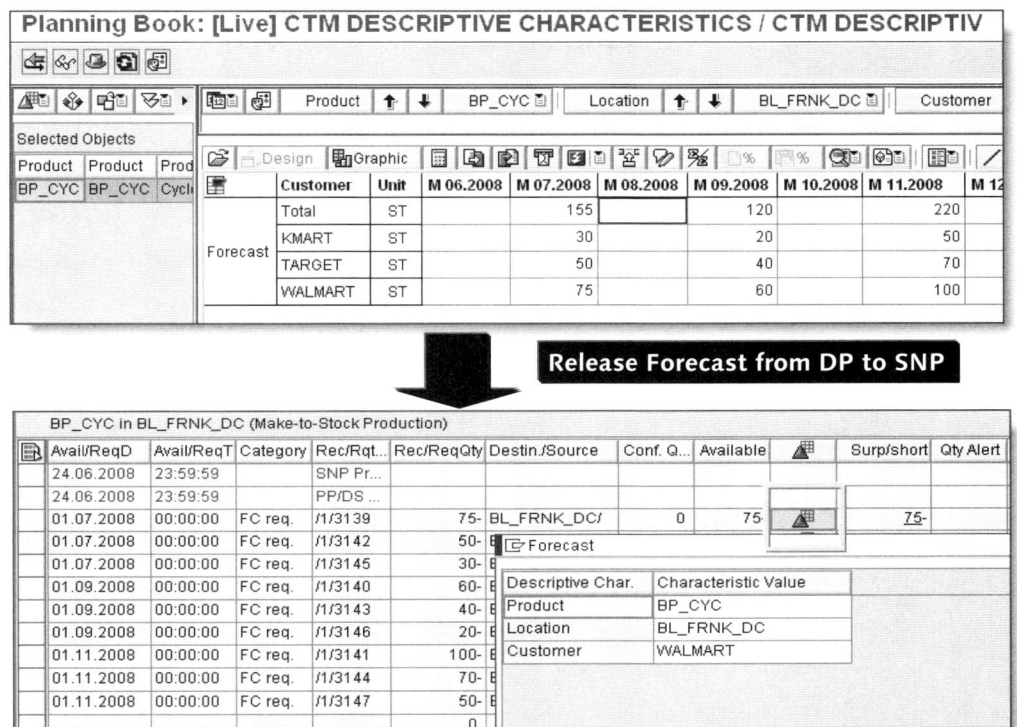

Figure 3.16 Forecast Release Using Descriptive Characteristics

CTM demand prioritization can be used to prioritize the demands for a given customer using the demand prioritization attribute customer ("KUNNR") and defining the special sorting for customer. For example, as shown in Figure 3.17, special sorting is used to prioritize the demands for customer WALMART over other customer demands; as a result, CTM will plan all of the demands for the customer WALMART before demands for other customers are planned.

The DCs in CTM are only used for demand prioritization, so the supplies (planned orders and purchase requisitions) created for a given demand don't inherit the corresponding DC values. If you use the fixed pegging option in CTM planning, the demands and supplies will be fixed pegged by CTM. As a result, you can evaluate and display the DCs assigned to the supply created for a given demand. Similarly, dependent requirements created for planned orders don't inherit the DC values, but using fixed pegging in CTM planning allows you to evaluate DC values easily. The DCs can also be used in ATP rule evaluation in CTM planning.

3 | CTM Demand and Supply Processing

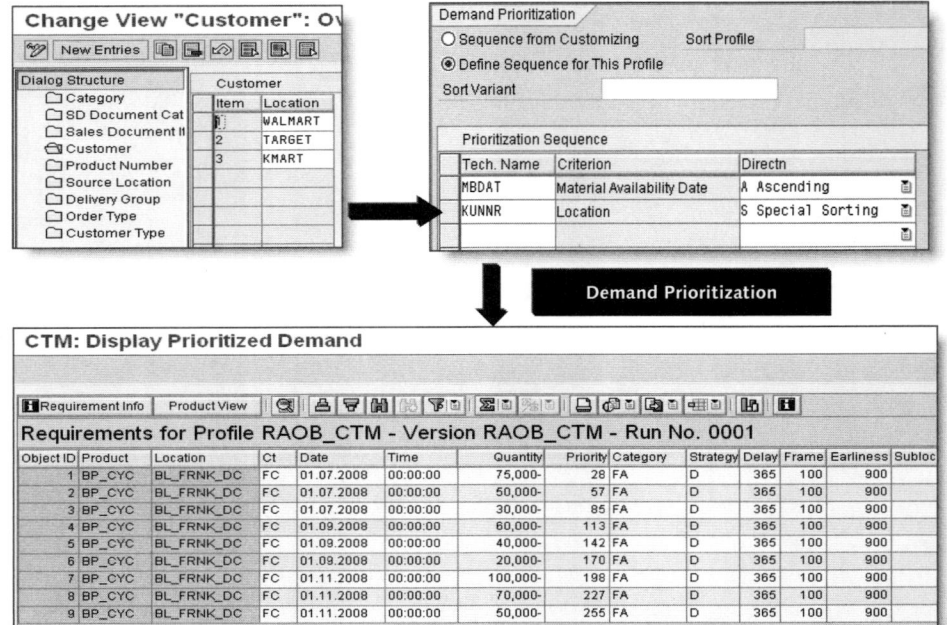

Figure 3.17 CTM Demand Prioritization Using Descriptive Characteristics

3.4 Supply Aggregation

The supply aggregation function in CTM is similar to the demand aggregation. Using supply aggregation, you can aggregate the individual supplies into an aggregated single supply. When you use the CTM supply aggregation, the individual supplies for a given location product and ATP category are grouped in user-defined time buckets. You can define the time buckets using the CTM time stream. You can also use the supply aggregation function with product location hierarchies, which follows the same rules as demand aggregation. Supply aggregation with hierarchies can be used to aggregate supplies across location products that are grouped using product location hierarchy definitions.

3.4.1 Supply Aggregation by Time Buckets

Supply aggregation using time buckets is enabled using the Activate Time-Based Aggregation setting in the CTM profile. The supplies for aggregation are selected based on the ATP category. For example, as shown in Figure 3.18, the planned orders with category "AJ" are selected for aggregation. Three individual planned orders are aggregated into a single planned order with an aggregated quantity. The aggregated supply date is derived using the customization setting as shown earlier in Figure 3.4. For the selected CTM supplies, the aggregation bucket is derived using the material availability date.

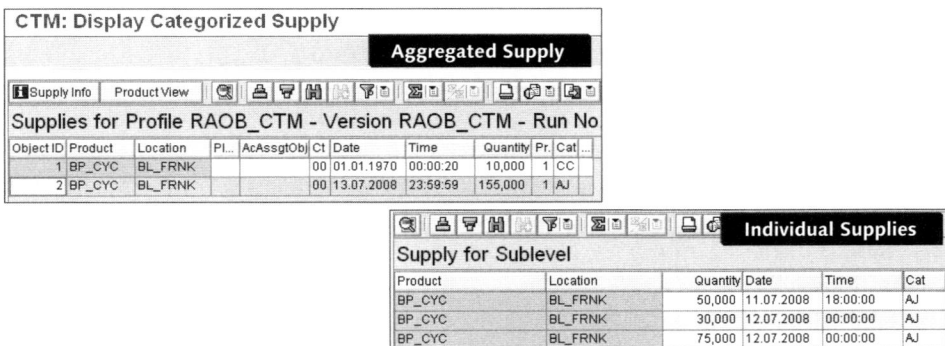

Figure 3.18 CTM Supply Aggregation by Time Buckets

Aggregation of stock elements needs special attention because the CTM supply for stock elements has the available date of 01.01.1970. As a result, the stock elements don't use the time buckets defined in the CTM time stream and hence aren't aggregated.

3.4.2 Supply Aggregation by Hierarchies

The hierarchy structure definition is used to define the hierarchy of location products. Similar to demand aggregation, the CTM supply aggregation function aggregates the supplies of the subproducts of the hierarchy to the header product. Supply aggregation can be enabled using the Header Level option planning under the Aggregation tab of the CTM profile. As you can see in Figure 3.19, the individual supplies at the sublevel products AFS_RAW_BLUE and AFS_RAW_RED are aggregated into a single supply of the header product AFS_RAW when you use hierarchy and time-based aggregation. The aggregated supply date is derived using the customization setting as shown earlier in Figure 3.4 in the global customization.

3 | CTM Demand and Supply Processing

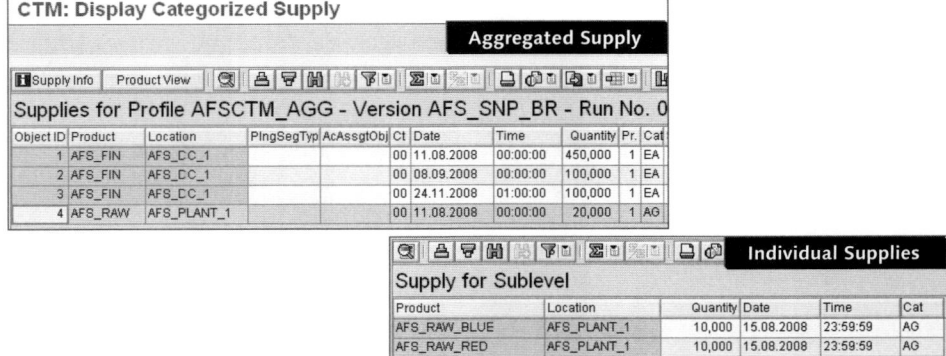

Figure 3.19 CTM Supply Aggregation by Hierarchy

Normally, in aggregated planning using hierarchy, the supplies are netted before the planning run. Only the open demands are planned using the hierarchy. As a result, the supply aggregation function with hierarchy isn't used very often.

3.5 Supply Categorization

CTM supply can be grouped and categorized to influence the sequence in which CTM consumes the supplies. As described earlier, the CTM supply contains the CTM category attribute. The CTM category is a user-defined value that can be defined using the SAP APO Transaction /SAPAPO/CTMSUPCAT or using the SAP Easy Access menu path ADVANCED PLANNING AND OPTIMIZATION • MULTILEVEL SUPPLY AND DEMAND MATCHING • ENVIRONMENT • CURRENT SETTING • SUPPLY CATEGORIZATION · SUPPLY CATEGORIES.

As you see in Figure 3.20, three supply categories are defined. The category 3 C3 is used for defining the reserved supply, which will be used after C1 and C2 category supplies are used by the CTM planning run. The categories are defined independently of the CTM profile and location product and hence exist globally for all of the planning runs. The default supply category used by CTM is 00. The CTM supply can be categorized using supply limits or ATP categories. The main advantage of using the user-defined category is to define a custom search sequence. The CTM engine uses a standard search sequence for creating a feasible plan for a given demand, which involves using all supplies with category 00 before using source determination for creating production or procurement plans. The supply categories are assigned to the supplies using the supply limits or ATP categories, and the supply categorization profile is used to assign the supply category to the CTM supplies selected for planning. You can create the categorization profile using the SAP APO Transaction /SAPAPO/CTMSCPR or using the menu path ADVANCED PLANNING AND OPTIMIZATION • MULTILEVEL SUPPLY AND DEMAND MATCHING • ENVIRONMENT • SUPPLY CATEGORIZATION • CATEGORIZATION PROFILE.

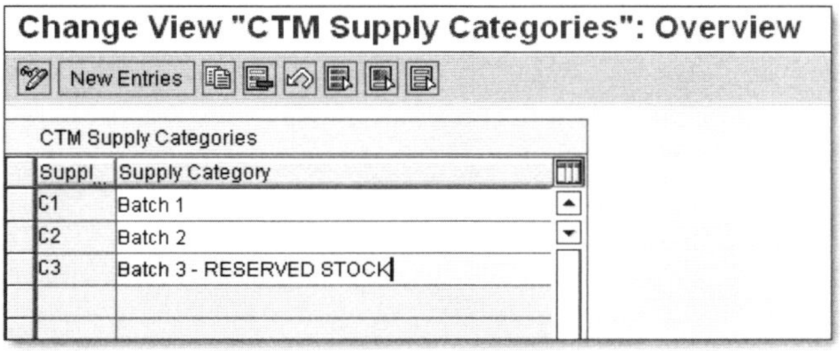

Figure 3.20 CTM Supply Category Definition

Similar to the aggregation and prioritization function in CTM, the supply categorization function is applied only on the independent supplies. Any excess supplies created in the CTM planning run (due to lot size) are created in default category 00. You can modify the default category of the excess supplies created during the CTM planning run using the CTM profile setting Categorization for New Receipts, which is available under the Supplies tab.

3.5.1 Supply Categorization by ATP Categories

For a given location product, multiple supplies can exist with different ATP categories, for example, planned orders, production orders, and stock. Each of the receipt elements in SAP SCM is identified using the corresponding ATP category (AG, AJ, etc.). When you use CTM supply categorization with ATP categories, each individual supply can be assigned CTM categories to create a user-defined search sequence. In the categorization profile, you'll use the Categorization Using ATP Categories option to enable supply categorization using ATP categories.

As shown in Figure 3.21, three supplies exist for the CTM planning run for product BP_CYC at location BL_FRNK. By default, CTM will use the closest supply for fulfilling any requirement after 30.08.2008. The supply consumption sequence in backward scheduling will be SNP planned order (40), firmed planned order (10), and stock (10). Using supply categorization with ATP categories, you can categorize these supplies to define a custom search sequence.

3 | CTM Demand and Supply Processing

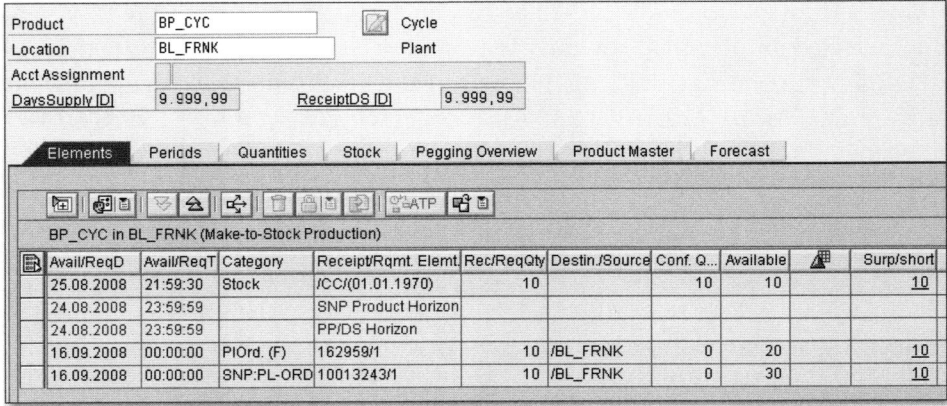

Figure 3.21 Initial Supply Used for Supply Categorization

Figure 3.22 shows how the Categorization Profile CTM is configured to use categorization by ATP categories. The supplies with ATP categories AJ, EE, and CC are assigned custom CTM categories. The CTM categories can now be used to define a custom search sequence to consume stock before consuming unfirmed planned orders. You can also use ATP category groups instead of ATP categories to assign the CTM category. When an ATP category group is used, then all of the corresponding ATP categories will be assigned to the same CTM category.

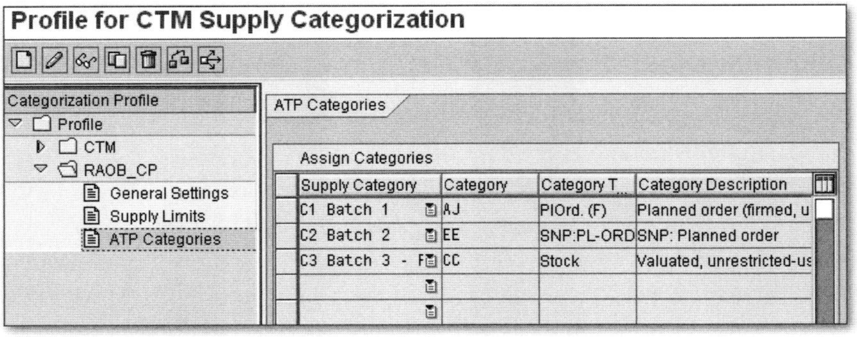

Figure 3.22 CTM Supply Categorization Profile with ATP Categories

The categorization profile can be now used in the CTM planning profile using the Categorization Profile setting under the Supplies tab. All of the CTM supplies selected for planning will be categorized, and the custom categories will be assigned to the supplies instead of the default category 00 (see Figure 3.23).

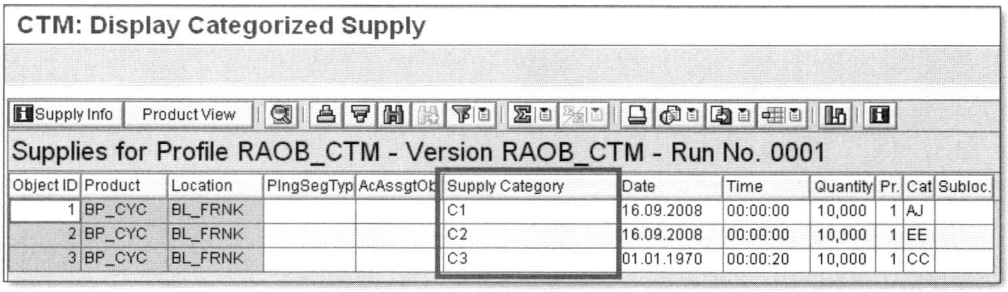

Supply Categorization | 3.5

Figure 3.23 CTM Supply Categorization by ATP categories

These categorized supplies can now be used to define a custom search sequence to consume the supplies with category C1 and C2, before using the C3 category supply that represents the reserved supply. We'll look at the search strategy definition in more detail in the next sections.

3.5.2 Supply Categorization by Supply Limits

Supply limits are used for defining the categorization of a single or a group of supplies using quantity limits. You can use the SAP APO Transaction /SAPAPO/CTM02 to define the quantity limits for a given location product (refer to Figure 3.21). The supply limits defined are used in the CTM categorization profile to assign the CTM categories. Based on the supply limits, a single supply can be split into multiple supplies, or multiple supplies can be aggregated into a single supply to assign the CTM categories. For example, for the product BP_TYR at location BL_FRNK, the supply limits are created as 0-10, 10-50, 50-1000 (see Figure 3.24). 100 units of stock are available for the given product.

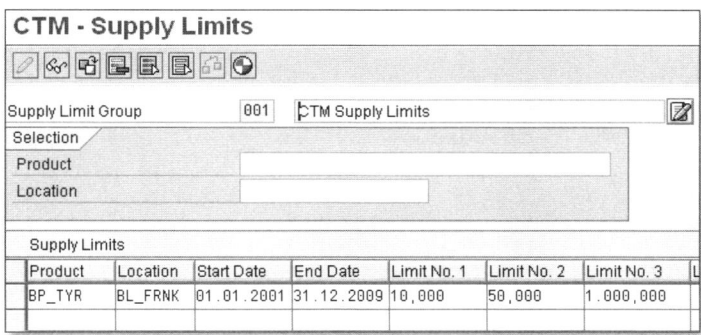

Figure 3.24 CTM Supply Limits Definition

95

As shown in Figure 3.25, the CTM supply categorization profile is used to categorize CTM supplies using supply limits. Supply quantity from 0 – 10 is assigned to the CTM category C3 to represent the reserved stock.

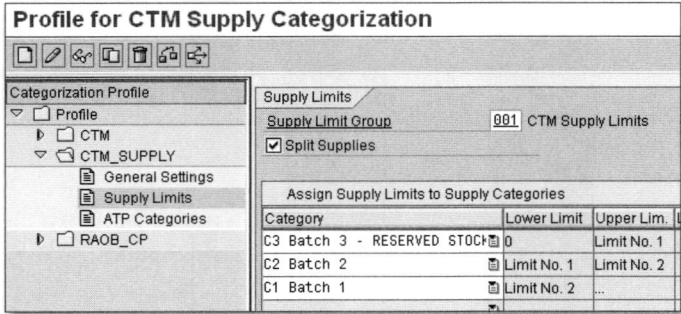

Figure 3.25 CTM Supply Categorization Profile Using Supply Limits

When you use the supply categorization profile in the CTM profile, the existing stock of 100 units for product BP_TYR is split as per the supply categorization definition. For example, 10 units are assigned to category C3, 40 units to category C2, and the rest to category C1 as shown in Figure 3.26.

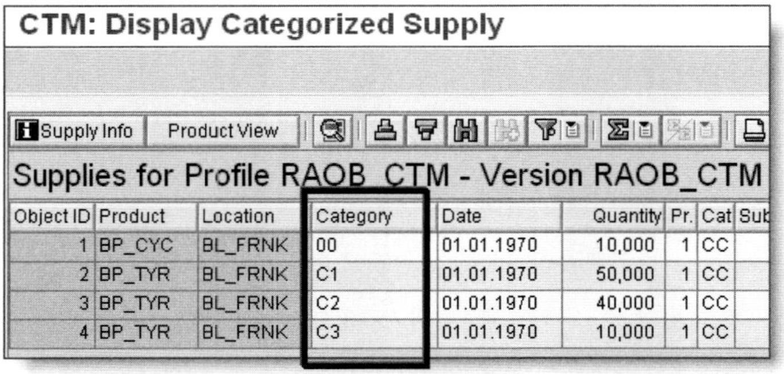

Figure 3.26 CTM Supply Categorization Using Supply Limits

The categorized supplies can be used to define a custom search sequence. It's important to understand that the supply categorization is applied to existing supplies and is applied locally to each location product. Supply categorization must always be used in conjunction with the custom search strategy. Because the CTM supply categories are changed from the default value of 00, if the custom search sequence isn't used, then the supplies won't be used for planning.

3.5.3 CTM Search Strategy for Source Selection

CTM planning uses a predefine search sequence for all of the available sources of supply. A source of supply in CTM is used to fulfill a demand on time. Many possible sources of supplies are used in CTM planning, for example, supply, production sources (PP/DS, PDS), procurement sources (transport lanes), and substitution sources (ATP rules). The selection and sequence of each source depend of the procurement type and the CTM search strategy. The search strategy is defined using the SAP APO Transaction /SAPAPO/CTMSSTRAT or using the SAP Easy Access menu ADVANCED PLANNING AND OPTIMIZATION • MULTILEVEL SUPPLY AND DEMAND MATCHING • ENVIRONMENT • CURRENT SETTING • SEARCH STRATEGIES.

The following search sequence is used by the CTM planning engine:

1. Consume receipts from CTM category 00 of original product.
2. Consume receipts from CTM category 00 of substitute product.
3. Determine source of supply for production/procurement.

The default search sequence can be changed using the custom search sequence. For example, as shown in Figure 3.27, the Search Strategy CTM is defined in such a way that the supply with category C3 is used after the production/procurement defined by the ** category. Category ** represents the CTM internal category and can't be added or deleted by the users in the search strategy definition.

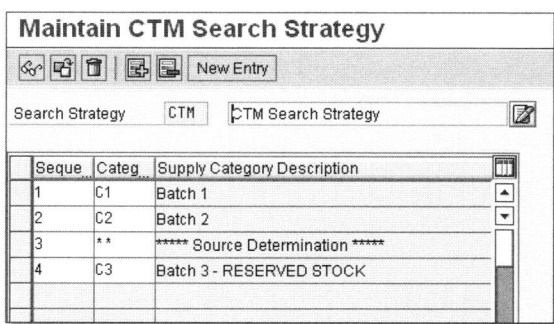

Figure 3.27 CTM Search Strategy Definition

Using the search strategy sequence CTM, the new sequence used by the CTM planning is shown here (if product substitution is used):

1. Consume receipts from CTM category 00 of original product.
2. Consume receipts from CTM category C1 of original product.

3 | CTM Demand and Supply Processing

3. Consume receipts from CTM category C2 of original product.
4. Consume receipts from CTM category 00 of substitute product.
5. Consume receipts from CTM category C1 of substitute product.
6. Consume receipts from CTM category C2 of substitute product.
7. Determine source of supply for production/procurement.
8. Consume receipts from CTM category C3 of original product.
9. Consume receipts from CTM category C3 of substitute product.

Keep in mind that the search sequence is applied locally at each location or planning level. For example, Figure 3.28 shows the current supply and demand situation. The Demand 50 at the DC location can be fulfilled by Plant1 and Plant2 locations with Plant1 having higher priority than Plant2. There are in total four supply elements in both the plants that have categories C1 and C3. CTM will apply the search strategy in each location locally; that is, the supply with category C3 in Plant1 is used before the supply with category C1 in Plant2. It isn't possible to define a search sequence in such a way that CTM will consume C1 category supplies in the complete network before using C3 supplies. You should understand that the search sequence will be applied as long as the demand can be fulfilled on time. If the demand can't be satisfied on time, then the search sequence can be violated by the CTM planning run to fulfill the demand on time.

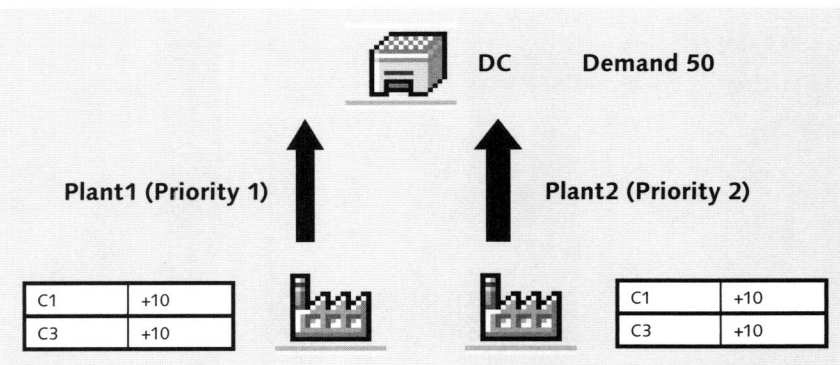

Figure 3.28 CTM Local Supply Search Strategy

In the preceding example, the following search sequence is used by CTM planning to fulfill the demand quantity of 50 units:

1. Consume receipts from CTM category C1 in Plant1.
2. Determine source of supply for production in Plant1.
3. Consume receipts from CTM category C3 in Plant1.
4. Consume receipts from CTM category C1 in Plant2.
5. Determine source of supply for production in Plant2.
6. Consume receipts from CTM category C3 in Plant2.

3.6 Summary

In this chapter, you learned that CTM planning matches the demands and supplies while considering the capacity and material constraints. CTM demands and supplies have predefined attributes relevant for planning. Each of the attributes can be influenced using standard and custom functions. CTM demands and supplies can be aggregated using time buckets to create a weekly or monthly supply plan instead of the daily plan. Demand prioritization represents the most important function in CTM where the demands can be prioritized to allocate constraint materials and resource capacities to the most important customer requirements or products. Several attributes can be used for demand prioritization for sales orders and forecast orders. Demand prioritization and aggregation is applied only for the independent demands and supplies. Supply categorization can be used to define special categories for CTM supplies, which can be used to define custom search sequence.

The next chapter explains the CTM planning algorithm and the standard and custom rules used by the CTM planning engine to generate the constrained supply plan for a given demand.

The CTM planning engine is the core of the CTM planning process. In this chapter, you'll learn the planning algorithm used for creating the multilevel supply plan. The source of supply (SOS) selection rules and scheduling rules are explained in detail in this chapter, and you'll learn the usage of the CTM explanation tools so that you can understand the CTM planning results. We'll also review the common scheduling issues you may encounter with the CTM planning process.

4 CTM Planning Algorithm

The CTM solver is the central component of the CTM planning process. CTM solver (also referred to as the CTM engine) offers a very flexible, scalable, and robust planning algorithm to solve large constraint satisfaction problems in a reasonable amount of time. The CTM engine uses heuristics-based, depth first, finite constraint planning logic. Due to the heuristics-based planning logic, very large and complex models can be evaluated quickly to support several what-if planning scenarios. CTM uses multilevel planning algorithms with depth-first strategy to detect and propagate constraints at all of the levels of the Supply Chain Model (SC Model). You can model several constraints that can be used for finding a feasible solution considering the constraints. The goal of the CTM engine is to find an in-time solution for a demand with the required date and quantity, considering all of the available sourcing alternatives. CTM will create a late solution for the remaining quantity when no or partial in-time solution can be calculated.

CTM planning is based on constraints, which is generally defined as a condition that must be satisfied for the selected solution and represented by a constraint variable. Each constraint variable is defined with domain values or value ranges. The CTM engine tries to generate a feasible in-time solution by satisfying all of the constraints and the allowed domain values. Constraint variables are linked with each other, and as a result, the corresponding domain values are also linked. Any changes or reduction of the domain values for one constraint variable is propagated across all linked constraints.

The following example is provided to illustrate the basic principles of the CTM engine algorithm using constraints.

4 CTM Planning Algorithm

Example		
Constraints	x ∈ [0, ∞)	y ∈ [0, 20]
Constraint Relationship	y = 2x	
Domain Reduction	x ← 10	x ∈ [0, 10]
Constraint Propagation	x ← 10	y = 2x
		→ y ∈ [0, 5]

X and Y represent the constraint variables that are linked using relationship Y = 2X. Due to this relationship, the domain values for Y are reduced with respect to X. This can be further explained in terms of the SC Model. The constraint X represents the resource capacity, whereas Y represents the demand quantity. The relationship indicates the resource capacity requirements for fulfilling 1 unit of demand quantity; that is, to fulfill each unit of demand quantity, 2 units of resource capacity are required. The available resource capacity is limited to 10 units, so the resource capacity constraint is propagated to the demand variable, and the maximum allowed demand quantity is limited to 5 units. You can see a more detailed example in Figure 4.1.

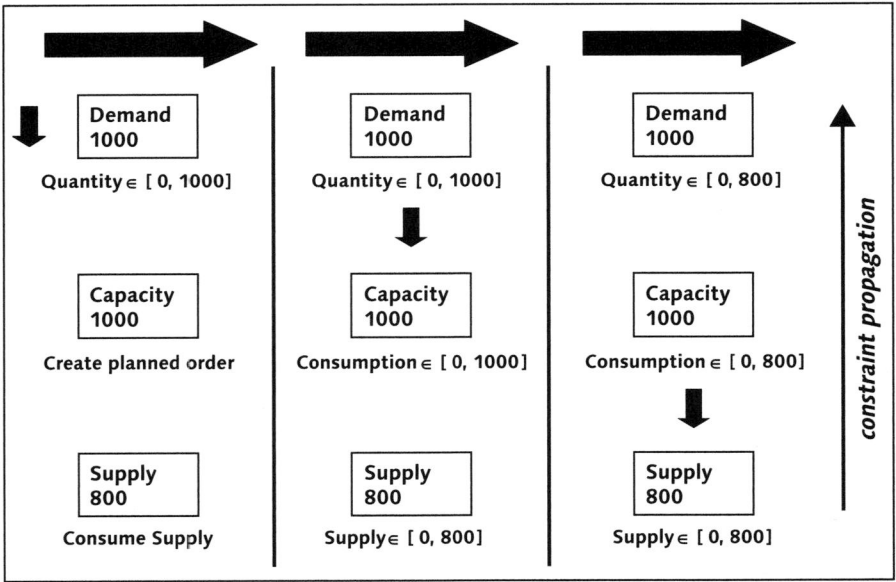

Figure 4.1 Constraint Propagation in CTM Multilevel Planning

The CTM planning algorithm and the underlying scheduling logic is developed in C++, so it requires an additional optimizer server connected to the SAP SCM system. The planning data is exchanged between the SAP SCM system and CTM optimizer server using RFC communication through the SAP gateway.

> **Note**
>
> Before the SAP SCM 5.0 release, the CTM engine was only available for Microsoft Windows 32-bit and 64-platforms.

4.1 CTM Planning Algorithm

The CTM planning engine is started after the data preparation phase of the CTM planning run. Your master data and transaction data are then evaluated based on the CTM profile settings. Next, the selected planning data is uploaded into the CTM engine for generating the supply plan, and the CTM engine creates the solution proposal for each individual demand according to the demand prioritization sequence. CTM uses all procurement alternatives to generate the in-time supply plan for the given demand. You can select to fulfill the demand late, just in case the complete demand quantity can't be fulfilled in time. You can define the allowed time frame for late demand fulfillment. After you process the demand, the generated supply (complete or partial) is saved, and the engine continues to plan the next demand in the demand list. Remember that during the CTM engine demand processing, the supply plan created for demand shouldn't be changed after the demand is planned. As a result, the demand prioritization sequence determines the sequence of supply and resource allocation.

The next section explains the sequence of supply plan creation for a given demand. As CTM plans the complete supply chain network starting with the finished product through to raw materials, the complete network is evaluated as a tree structure. During the search tree generation by CTM, you can use several standard and user-defined decision criteria to influence the supply plan generated by CTM.

4.2 CTM Search Tree Generation

CTM engine uses a *depth first* strategy for creating the supply plan for a given demand. A depth first strategy generates the supply plan based on the complete supply chain network from the finished product demand to the raw material. The

4 | CTM Planning Algorithm

CTM engine's goal when planning in backward scheduling mode is to fulfill the demand quantity as much as possible and as close as possible to the demand date. With CTM, you can evaluate the complete supply chain network for every component in sequence. Then the finished product demand is satisfied by generating the search tree of the components. Each level of the search tree is known as a *node*. You can apply CTM standard search logic and rules at each node locally, which represents the key *decision points* of the search tree. The key *decision criteria* applied at each of the decision points are the following:

- Supply selection
- Substitution rules selection
- Source of supply (SOS) selection

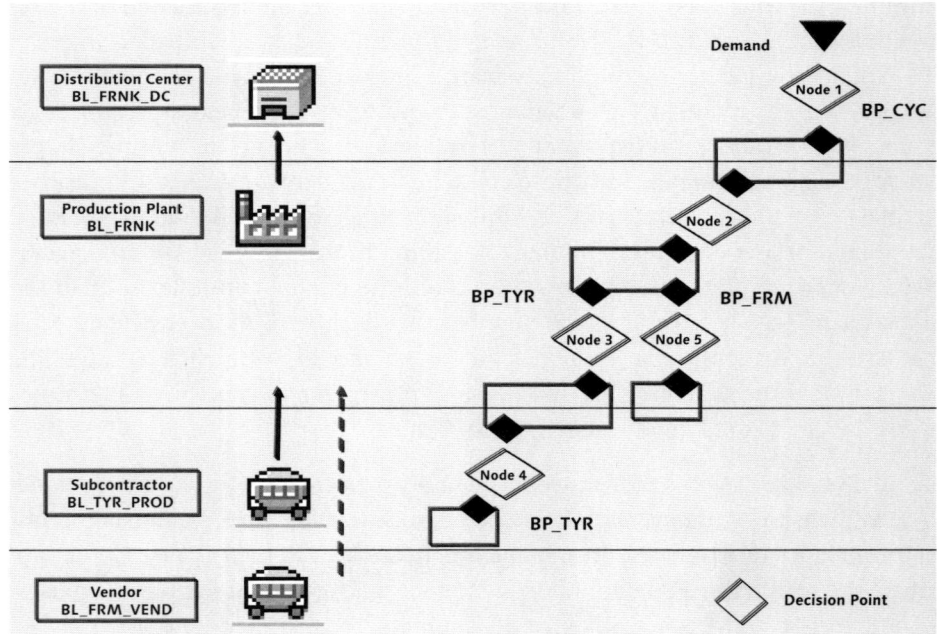

Figure 4.2 CTM Search Tree Generation and Decision Points

Figure 4.2 illustrates the search tree and the nodes for which the CTM model is used. The supply chain network for the finished product BP_CYC consists of four locations. The forecast is released at location BL_FRNK_DC, which is a distribution center. At the demand location, the first node, Node 1, of the supply plan is created. The standard CTM decision criteria are applied at this node. Then CTM searches for existing supplies with the material availability date before the requirement date and then searches for possible sources of supply to create a new order. In this example, because no supply is found at Node 1, CTM creates the stock transfer order using the transport lane from the location BL_FRNK to BL_FRNK_DC. For the dependent requirement at location BL_FRNK, Node 2 is created, which results in the creation of the planned order for BP_CYC.

The planned order generates two dependent requirements for the components BP_TYR and BP_FRM. CTM chooses one of the dependent requirements (BP_TYR) and applies the source selection on Node 3 to generate the stock transfer order from the subcontracting location BL_TYR_PROD. The transfer order requirement represented by Node 4 is fulfilled by the planned order for BP_TYR. If there are any capacity constraints at Node 4, the CTM engine uses backtracking to adjust the solution for BP_CYC created at Node 2.

The solution tree generated so far isn't saved in SAP liveCache yet, however. After Node 3 is satisfied completely, CTM selects Node 5 for the dependent requirement for product BP_FRM and creates the purchase requisition for the vendor location BL_FRM_VEND. The search tree for a given input component is generated by the last node of the supply chain network before generating the search tree for other input components. Because the supply tree is completely generated with respect to the required demand quantity, the solution is saved and the next demand will be selected for CTM planning. After all of the demands are planned by the CTM engine the generated supply tree is saved in SAP liveCache.

For planned orders with multiple input components, the sequence of supply tree generation is governed by the internal sequence and can't be influenced by the user. In any case, this doesn't cause any limitation because CTM will always ensure that all dependent requirements are fully satisfied in time. It's important to understand that the decision criterion is applied locally at each node of the search tree. After the complete in-time supply plan is generated for a given demand, the search tree is saved. For any open demand quantity, a late search is applied to generate the late supply plan. After the in-time and late supply plan creation, the solution is saved, and the next demand is planned. Due to the heuristics-based planning approach, after you create the supply plan and save it for a given demand, the succeeding demands don't influence the supply plan already created for the previous demand.

In the next section, the key decision criteria used by the engine at each level or node is explained in detail.

4.3 CTM Decision Criteria for Source Selection

The CTM engine uses predefined search criteria to generate the supply plan. The default search sequence starts with existing supplies that can be used for a given demand to create an in-time solution. After all available in-time supplies are used, CTM selects other possible sources of supplies (SOS). The selection of SOS by the CTM engine is based on predefined rules that can be influenced by the user.

4.3.1 CTM Supply Selection

As described in Chapter 3, the CTM supply contains the attributes supply quantity, date, and category. At each of the decision points, CTM searches for existing supplies and consumes the supplies at the demand date. By default, all CTM supplies are created with CTM category 00. The CTM engine implicitly searches for a supply with category 00 for both the primary and secondary demands. If no supplies are found for the product before the requirement date, CTM searches for the supplies of the substitute product, provided a rules-based substitution is used in CTM planning. By default, only the supplies with category 00 are used for the substitute product. We'll explain planning with substitution rules in more detail in later chapters.

Because multiple supplies exists that can be used to satisfy the demand, CTM uses the closest supply when planning in *backward scheduling* mode. As shown in Figure 4.3, backward scheduling consumes Supply 2 to satisfy the demand of 10 units, but with *forward scheduling*, the earliest available supply is used. In this example, Supply 1 is used for planning the demand of 10 units. The supply selection rules are applied as long as the demand quantity can be satisfied in time. If the use of the supply will create a late supply plan, then the supply is ignored, and CTM uses alternative SOS to generate a new order to create an in-time supply plan. The supply selection is always applied locally at each node of the search tree.

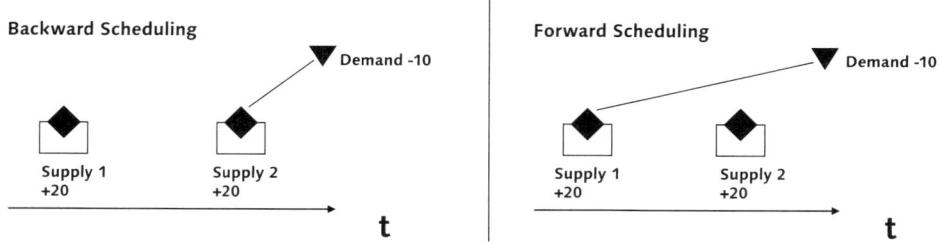

Figure 4.3 CTM Supply Selection in Forward and Backward Scheduling

4.3.2 CTM Source of Supply Selection

Source of supply (SOS) is used in CTM planning to generate the supply plan for the selected demands. In the case of a multiple SOS, selection of the SOS in CTM depends on predefined rules. The sequence of source selection is used as long as the required schedule for the demand can be met. If the source with higher priority leads to creation of late supply, CTM selects the source with the lower priority to meet the demand in time. This is because the primary goal of the CTM engine is to create an in-time supply plan considering all possible SOS alternatives in the complete supply chain.

You can execute CTM planning with three types of supply sources:

- **In-house production**
  CTM planning uses in-house production SOS to create the planned orders using production process models (PPM) and production data structures (PDS). SNP and PP/DS PPM/PDS can be used in CTM based on the planning mode. PPM describes when a plan can be used to manufacture a product. A location and a lot-size interval are defined in the PPM as validity criteria. The temporal validity is adopted from the output product. The production version from SAP R/3 corresponds to the PPM in SAP APO. On the other hand, PDS contains the master data for planning in SAP APO. Production data structures are generated from R/3 data (classic master data such as BOM, routing, and recipe).

- **External procurement**
  CTM planning uses external procurement SOS to create the purchase requisitions or stock transfer orders using transportation lanes and purchasing information records. The transportation lane in SAP APO defines the transportation route between two locations in an SC Model. The use of scheduling agreements and contracts isn't supported in CTM planning.

4 | CTM Planning Algorithm

- **Product substitution**
  Substitution rules can be used to select the supplies of the alternate products. Product interchangeability groups and FFF classes can be used not only to select supplies for alternate products but also to create procurement or production for the alternative products. Substitution orders are created using the substitution rules.

SOS (in-house production, external procurement) selection in CTM uses predefined rules to select the appropriate SOS when multiple SOS exists for a given demand. As shown in Figure 4.4, CTM source selection uses the procurement type as the first selection criteria to determine the SOS that can meet the demand due date. Similar to the supply selection strategy, the SOS selection is also applied locally at each individual node of the supply search tree. The source determination is applied by the CTM engine to select the SOS while considering several planning parameters, product parameters, and the SOS parameters to generate an in-time supply plan for the demand.

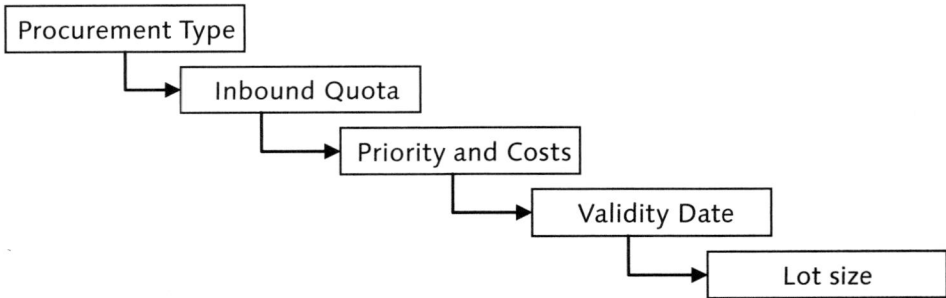

Figure 4.4 CTM Source Determination Sequence

4.3.3 Source Selection with Procurement Type

The procurement type defines how a product is procured and is a classification that indicates whether a material is produced internally, procured externally, or both. The procurement type can be defined for each product location. The SAP SCM system offers four possible procurement types that can be assigned to the individual product location. Source selection in CTM depends on the procurement type of the products selected for planning.

- **External procurement (F)**
  With procurement type F, CTM planning can use transport lanes to create a purchase requisition with a source. If no transport lanes are available, then CTM creates the purchase requisition without a source location.

- **In-house production (E)**
  With procurement type E, CTM planning can use PPM and PDS to create planned orders. If no PPM/PDS is selected in the CTM planning, then CTM can't create any planned order without a source, unlike SNP Heuristics. The selection of the PPM or PDS for planning can be influenced by the Plan Explosion parameter in the product master or by using the global setting in CTM customization as shown in Figure 4.5.

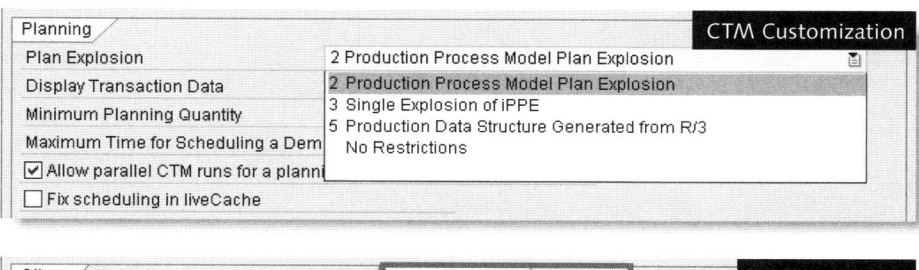

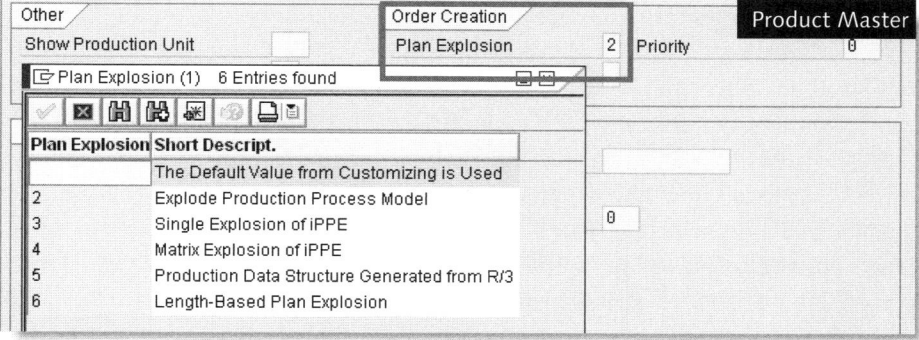

Figure 4.5 Plan Explosion for PPM/PDS Selection

- **External procurement or in-house production (X)**
  With procurement type X, CTM planning can use PPM/PDS and transport lanes to create planned orders and purchase requisitions with a source location. If no PPM/PDS or transport lane is selected in CTM planning, then CTM can create purchase requisitions without any source location.

- **External procurement planning (P)**
  With procurement type P, CTM planning doesn't create any new orders or consume any supplies for the demand. The requirement for the product with procurement type P isn't planned in CTM.

Substitution orders in CTM can be created for procurement type E, X, and F. The selection of a particular SOS in CTM planning can be ignored using the Exclude Procurement Alternatives parameter in the CTM profile. For PPM/PDS, using the Transport Lanes and External Procurement setting available in the CTM profile under Technical Settings, you can exclude the usage of the procurement alternative for CTM planning. It's also possible to temporarily reassign the procurement type for the product used in CTM planning using the Replace Procurement Type setting, which is also available under the Settings tab of the CTM profile.

4.3.4 Source Selection with Inbound Quota

After the SOS selection using the procurement type, further source selection is determined by quota values. The quota arrangement defines which part of a product quantity should be assigned to a given SOS. Quota arrangements represent dimensionless proportions that are used as a basis for splitting a quantity. Quota arrangements are either inbound or outbound. With inbound quota arrangements, the source location of a shipment is defined. For each product, a quota arrangement specifies which part of the quantity should be sourced from which of the possible sources. Possible sources include locations, PPMs, and procurement relationships listed as sources for a specific destination location by transportation lane. For outbound quota arrangements, the destination location of a shipment is defined. For each product, a quota arrangement specifies which part of the quantity should be transported to which of the possible destination locations. Possible destination locations are all the destinations of transportation lanes starting at the defined source location. CTM supply planning considers only inbound quota values, whereas CTM supply distribution considers outbound quota values.

You can use CTM planning with inbound quota to define the percentage of your quantity that must be sourced from a given SOS. If multiple SOS exist for a given product location, the SOS selection function uses inbound quota to select the SOS that can fulfill the quota requirement. Inbound quota can be maintained for a given location and maintained for a given product and planning version. Inbound quota can be maintained and used in CTM planning for locations, in-house production, and means of transports assigned to the transport lanes. For products with procurement type X, the inbound quota can be maintained across transport lanes and PPM/PDS. Inbound quotas (see Figure 4.6) can be maintained using the SAP APO Transaction /SAPAPO/SCC_TQ1 or using the SAP Easy Access menu ADVANCED PLANNING AND OPTIMIZATION • MASTER DATA • QUOTA ARRANGEMENT.

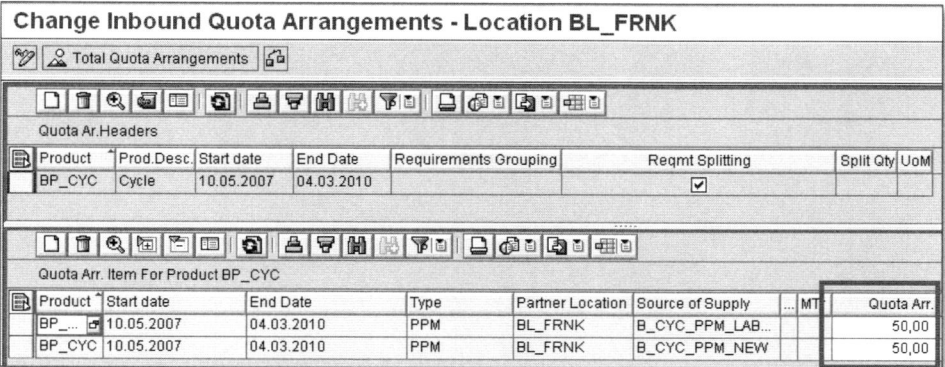

Figure 4.6 Inbound Quota Arrangements Used for CTM Planning

Source selection in CTM using inbound quota is applied either for the total demand quantity of the complete planning run or for each individual demand using the Requirement Split setting of the inbound quota.

▶ **Inbound quota without requirement split**
Source selection with quota is applied as a soft constraint, meaning quota values will be used for CTM planning only if the demand quantity can be fulfilled in time. With inbound quota, CTM uses the SOS to reach the quota levels as much as possible. For each demand (primary and secondary), all possible sources are evaluated to generate the new supply plan that is as close as possible to the required quota values. If you have maintained quota for one of the SOS, then alternatives without any quota values are ignored completely from planning. Similarly, sources with zero quota values are also ignored completely. Quota values are evaluated for each CTM run, and the history of the quota requirement from previous planning runs isn't considered for CTM source selection. For example, if there are purchase orders for a vendor where quota is maintained, then CTM doesn't consider quota from purchase orders for SOS selection during the creation of new purchase requisitions.

4 | CTM Planning Algorithm

To understand the source selection with reference to quota, consider the following example.

> **Example**
> A DC can source from two locations L1 and L2. The required quota of 80/20 is maintained across location L1 and L2.
>
> | Demand | Initial Quota (L1/L2) | Source L1 | Delta L1 (80) | Source L2 | Delta L2 (20) |
> |---|---|---|---|---|---|
> | 100 | 80/20 | 100/0 | 20 √ | 0/100 | 80 |
> | 200 | 100/0 | 100/0 | 20 √ | 33/67 | 47 |
> | 350 | 100/0 | 100/0 | 20 √ | 36/64 | 44 |
> | 200 | 100/0 | 100/0 | 20 | 77/23 | 3 √ |
> | 200 | 77/23 | 80/20 | 0 √ | 61/38 | 18 |

For each demand, both the sources L1 and L2 are evaluated. The new quota value with each source is compared to the required quota values. SOS with minimum deviation (Delta) is finally selected for the given demand. You can apply the same logic for each demand you select for planning in a given CTM run. Because inbound quota values are considered soft constraints, based on the demand situation and the capacity constraints, the net quota values proposed by the CTM run can be different from the required quota values. CTM will apply the quota values only if the demand can be satisfied in-time.

▶ **Inbound quota with requirement split**
With the SAP SCM 5.0 release, CTM planning considers the inbound quota with requirement split. Requirement split can be enabled for the inbound quota values in the master data maintenance of the inbound quota values. The inbound quota values are used in CTM planning to split the original demand quantity in the proportion of the quota requirements. Each proportional demand quantity is planned in CTM using the corresponding SOS. If you use time-phased inbound quota values for CTM planning, then you'll use the demand date (for primary and secondary demand) to select the inbound quota interval.

In unconstrained planning situations without any lot size requirements, the supply plan is generated based on the required quota requirements as shown in the following example.

Example

A DC can source from two locations, L1 and L2. The required quota of 80/20 is maintained across location L1 and L2.

Demand	Source L1	Source L2
100	80	20
200	160	40
350	280	70
200	80	20
200	160	40

Note that the lot size specifications or the resource constraints aren't considered when calculating the proportional demands quantities using the inbound quota values. In constrained planning situations, if the proportional demand quantity can't be fulfilled in time, then CTM uses the procurement priority to select the alternate SOS.

4.3.5 Source Selection with Procurement Priorities and Costs

Because you don't use a quota for planning, you use the procurement priority and costs to select the source for planning. For products with procurement type E, you use the priority assigned to the PPM/PDS. The PPM/PDS with the highest priority is selected that can generate an in-time supply plan. Similarly, the transport lane priority is used to select the transport lanes for products with procurement type F. For products with procurement type X where production and procurement is possible, the priority across PPM/PDS and transport lanes is used to select the source.

Fixed multilevel cost assigned to the PPM is used for SOS selection if priority isn't maintained or if the SOS has the same priority. For transport lanes, the cost assigned to the means of transport (MOT) is used to select the lowest cost MOT.

As shown in Figure 4.7, the priority and costs are applied locally at each node of the search tree. For the demand at the distribution location, the transport lane from Plant 1 and Plant 2 are checked for highest priority. After the lane is selected, the MOT with the lowest cost is selected. For the dependent requirement at the plant, the priority assigned to the PPM/PDS is used in such a way that the high-

4 | CTM Planning Algorithm

est priority PPM/PDS is selected for creating the in-time supply plan. The source selection is applied locally at each location and not across locations. For example, it isn't possible for CTM to check for highest priority PPM from Plant 1 and Plant 2 before using the low priority PPM in Plant 1 and Plant 2. Source selection in CTM is a soft constraint, meaning that if the source with higher priority results in a late supply plan, then the source is ignored, and the low priority source is selected.

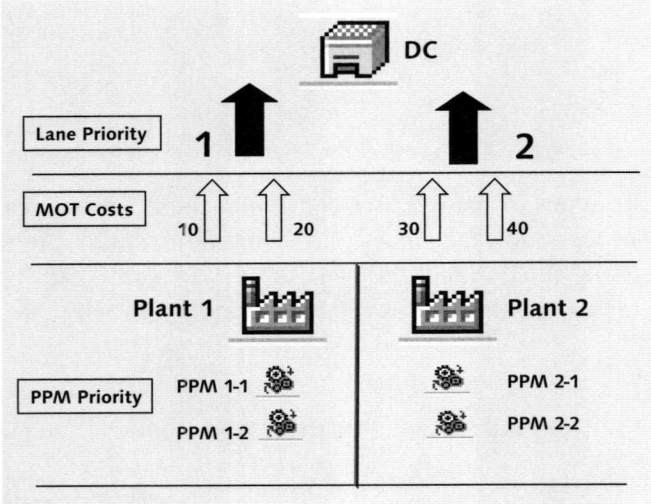

Figure 4.7 CTM Source Selection with Priority and Costs

4.3.6 Source Selection with Validity Date

When source selection using inbound quota and procurement priority doesn't result in a unique source, then CTM selects the SOS using the validity date of the PPM/PDS and transport lanes. The source with the largest end date has the highest priority, provided the source selection results in the in-time solution. SOS with the validity start date after the demand date won't be selected for CTM planning unless late demand fulfillment is allowed for the selected demand.

4.3.7 Source Selection with PPM/PDS Lot Size

If multiple sources have the same priority and validity date, then the source selection is based on the maximum lot size value assigned to the PPM/PDS. The PPM/PDS with the largest maximum lot size has the highest priority. PPM/PDS with the minimum lot size larger than the demand quantity is completely ignored by CTM to avoid creation of excess supply because of the PPM/PDS minimum lot size. Excess supply in CTM can only be created due to the product lot size. The PPM/PDS lot size is only used for source selection. Minimum and maximum lot sizes for the transport lanes aren't used for source selection. Lot size values for the transport lanes maintained using the lot size profile are used mainly by the CTM engine for the new order creation.

PPM/PDS selection with lot size can lead to partial quantity fulfillment.

> **Example**
>
> **Original Demand** = 100 Units
> **PPM Lot Size Requirements [Min, Max]** = [30, 40]
> **CTM Proposed Quantity**
> - Order 1 = 40
> - Order 2 = 40
> - Order 3 = 20 (Fails due to the minimum lot size restriction of the PPM)
>
> Due to the minimum lot size restriction of the PPM of 30 units, the partial demand of 20 units can't be fulfilled. As a result, the demand of 100 units is fulfilled by a supply of only 80 units.
>
> In this example, the complete quantity of 100 units can be fulfilled with three orders of 40, 30, and 30 units. Such lot size optimization isn't supported in CTM planning.

Source selection with CTM is followed by scheduling and creating the order using the selected source. Initial source selection doesn't ensure that the selected source can create a feasible plan. When the selected source fails to create a feasible plan, CTM rejects the source, and the new source determination is carried out using the same rules again.

4.4 CTM Order Scheduling

Order scheduling in CTM follows the same basic principles as SNP and PP/DS. CTM can create planned order, stock transfer order, purchase requisitions, and substitution order in both the bucket planning mode and the time-continuous planning mode. After the source determination, CTM uses the source to schedule the order using the parameter assigned to the source. You can display all of the parameters relevant for scheduling the selected source using the CTM master data check function. CTM planning can be used to create the supply plan using both backward and forward scheduling mode. Scheduling direction is maintained for the CTM profile, so all of the demands planned in CTM with the profile will use the same scheduling mode. It isn't possible to define a product-specific or demand-specific scheduling mode in CTM. You can use backward scheduling in CTM to create the supply plan so that the supply is created as close to the demand as possible, whereas in the forward scheduling mode, you can create the supply plan as early as possible. In both scheduling modes, you can use source selection to determine the source with highest priority that can lead to an in-time supply plan.

In the following section, CTM scheduling logic for each of the order types is explained in detail.

4.4.1 Scheduling Planned Order

Scheduling the planned order in CTM considers several parameters available in PPM/PDS. The parameters available with the activity, input/output component, and mode of the PPM/PDS are used by CTM. Figure 4.8 shows the basic structure of the planned order created by CTM. The PP/DS and PDS parameters assigned to the activity, mode, and components used by CTM scheduling are described in detail in Chapter 2.

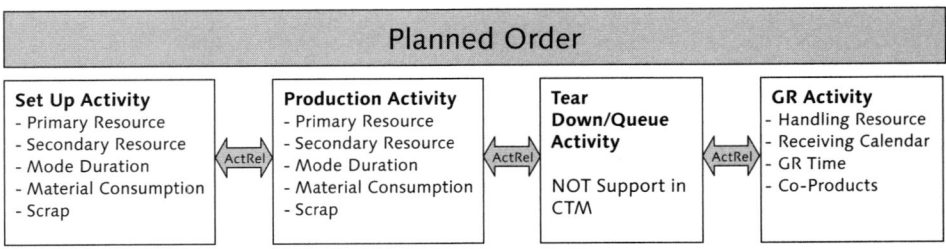

Figure 4.8 Scheduling Parameters for a CTM Planned Order

For CTM scheduling in the SNP and PP/DS planning mode, the earliest start date you can have for planned order creation and deletion is limited by the SNP production horizon for the main output product. The SNP production horizon is maintained in the product master under the SNP 2 tab. If you maintain the extended SNP production horizon, then CTM will use the total production horizon, which is the sum of both the horizons. The PP/DS Horizon in Days parameter maintained for the planning version is used in the case where no product-specific SNP production horizon is maintained. The production horizon in CTM is always calculated from the current date. If you've used the CTM planning in the past, the SNP horizon can be calculated from the planning start date using the Relate Horizons to Planning Start parameter in the CTM profile under the Master Data Settings tab. The planned order is always created with both the start and end dates outside the production horizon. Similarly, the deletion of a planned order in CTM is only possible if both the start and end dates are outside the production horizon.

Planned order scheduling with *co-products* is also supported in CTM planning. For PPM/PDS with multiple output products, the product with the requirement is considered the main product, and any additional output products are planned as co-products. The planned order is scheduled to create the supply for the co-product. You can use the co-product supply for all of the demands planned for the co-products. It's important to understand that the scheduling parameters such as lot size, SNP production horizon, and goods receipt processing time is only considered for the main output product and not for the co-product.

Material consumption is maintained for the output and input components of PPM/PDS. It's possible to maintain both the fixed and variable material consumption values in PPM/PDS. The total output quantity of the planned order is related to the net quantity and the material consumption of the output material that follows.

Quantity_Output

= *Mat Cons<Var> * Quantity_Net + Mat Cons<Fix>*

With Assembly scrap

Quantity_Net

= *Quantity_Net * 100% / (100% - Assembly Scrap %)*

The total output quantity is further influence by the *assembly scrap* maintained for the product.

The net quantity for the output material is used to generate the material consumption for the input components using the conversion factor for the input materials.

Quantity_Input = conv_fact * Quantity_Net + Mat Cons<Fix>

where

conv_fact = Input Mat Cons<Var> / Output Mat Cons<Var>

> **Note**
>
> The material consumption for the input material must always be greater than 0.001 units. If the material consumption of any of the input components is less than 0.001, then CTM will ignore PPM/PDS and won't create a planned order.
>
> For example, output material quantity in the PPM is 100 units, and input material quantity in the PPM is 0.02 units.
>
> For the demand quantity of 1 unit:
>
> The input material consumption is 0.02 / 100 * 1 = 0.0002 (~ 0.000)
>
> CTM won't create any planned order because the input material consumption is less than 0.001 units.

The input material consumption is further influence by the *activity scrap* maintained in the activity of the PPM/PDS. CTM planning doesn't use the Material Flow attribute of PPM, and because of this, the activity scrap isn't propagated across multiple activities. The activity scrap is only applied for the material and resource consumption of the given activity.

The time interval for the scheduling of the planned order is limited by the validity of PPM/PDS. By default, the planned order is scheduled so that the available date of the output product lies within the PPM/PDS validity as shown in the Figure 4.9. As a result, when planning in backward scheduling mode, the end date of the last activity of the planned order always ends inside the PPM/PDS validity.

Using the CTM EffectivityMode planning parameter, you can select different options to schedule the planned order scheduling based on the PPM/PDS validity as shown in the following note.

> **Note**
>
> CTM Planning Parameter = EffectivityMode
>
> Value1 = 0 → Start and end dates inside the PPM/PDS validity
>
> Value1 = 1 → Only end date inside the PPM/PDS validity (default)
>
> Value1 = 2 → Start date inside the PPM/PDS validity
>
> Refer to SAP Note 781974 for more details.

4.4 CTM Order Scheduling

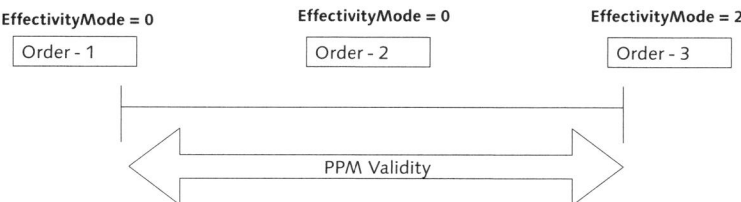

Figure 4.9 Planned Order Scheduling with PPM/PDS Validity Date

The EffectivityMode parameter is also used for scheduling the transport activities.

The validity dates of the input materials are also considered during the CTM scheduling. If the dependent requirement date lies outside the input component validity, then no dependent requirements are created for the planned order. Using the Prevent Product Explosion option of the input components of the PPM/PDS, you can prevent the creation of any new planned orders for the dependent requirements created for the input product. CTM will only use stock and purchase requisitions for fulfilling dependent requirements of these input components.

Resource consumption assigned to the mode of the activity in PPM/PDS is also calculated by the CTM engine, similar to the input material consumption.

*Resource_Cons = conv_fact * Quantity_Net + Resource Cons<Fix>*

where

conv_fact = Resource Cons<Var> / Output Mat Cons<Var>

With finite planning in CTM, scheduling the planned order is limited by the availability of the resource capacity. When planning in the time-continuous mode with mixed resources, the finite capacity constraint is restricted by the time-continuous capacity of the resource. After the planned order is scheduled, the bucket consumption of the mixed resource is calculated for the planned order. The resource capacity consumption is also affected by the activity scrap.

> **Note**
>
> The resource consumption must always be greater than 0.001 units. If it's less than 0.001 units, CTM will ignore PPM/PDS and won't create a planned order.
>
> For example, output material quantity in PPM is 100 units. Resource consumption in PPM is 0.02 seconds.

4 | CTM Planning Algorithm

> For the demand quantity of 1 unit:
> The resource consumption is: 0.02 / 100 * 1 = 0.0002 seconds (~ 0.000)
> CTM won't create any planned order because the resource consumption is less than 0.001 units.

Planned order scheduling for bucket planning with SNP PPM/PDS is limited by the maximum available capacity for each day of order duration. As shown in Figure 4.10, SNP PPM/PDS has a fixed duration of 5 days. In week 1, CTM can schedule the order for 5 days with 50 units because the daily capacity of 10 units is available. On the other hand, CTM can only create a planned order of 25 units because Day 3 of week 2 has a maximum available capacity of 5 units only. CTM will calculate the total capacity requirement for the order with 5 days duration. For finite scheduling of the planned order, the capacity requirement for each day must be satisfied considering the resource is maintained with daily capacity profile.

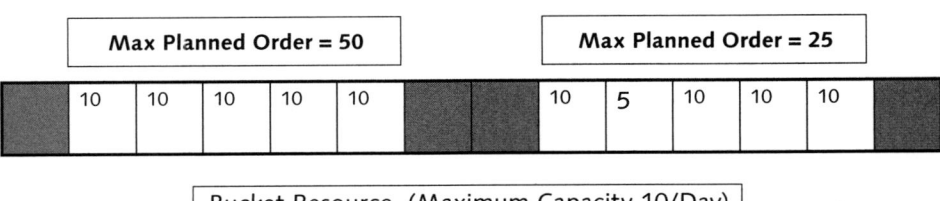

Figure 4.10 Bucket Resource Consumption for the SNP Planned Order

Mode definition in PPM/PDS defines the allowed resources and the duration of the activity. For multiple modes, you can define the priority of the modes for both the SNP and PP/DS planning in CTM. The order duration for SNP PPM/PDS is fixed, and you can only maintain the order duration in a multiple of days with minimum duration of 1 day. On the other hand, the order duration for PP/DS PPM can be maintained as a variable duration with a minimum duration of 1 sec. For scheduling a time-continuous order, the total order duration is calculated as follows:

> **PP/DS Order**
>
> *Order Duration = conv_fact * Quantity_Net + Order Duration<Fix>*
> *where*
> *conv_fact = Order Duration <Var> / Output Mat Cons<Var>*

Scheduling a planned order in CTM is slightly different compared to SNP Heuristics and SNP Optimizer when in bucket planning mode. CTM orders are created so that the order always ends at the end of the daily bucket, which is defined as [24:00:00]. SNP Heuristics and SNP Optimizer, on the other hand, consider the end of bucket as [23:59:59]. As a result, the planned orders scheduled by CTM are displayed in the SNP interactive planning with an offset of one day. This causes the SNP capacity view and order view also to be offset by one day. To avoid this, you can use the BAdI /sapapo/ctm_orders. The sample code delivered with the BAdI using the CTM 1_SECOND_PULL planning parameter can be used to align the CTM scheduled planned orders in the SNP Interactive planning book.

Both the SNP order and PP/DS order in CTM can be scheduled over the break, as long as the Break Not Allowed parameter setting isn't used in the mode of PPM/PDS. If break is allowed, you can use the Maximum Break Duration setting to limit the allowed break for scheduling an activity. The order can be scheduled to start and end in a break.

PPM/PDS with multiple activities are defined with *activity relationships*. CTM will schedule the activities with only the end-start relationship, irrespective of the setting in PPM/PDS. It's possible to define the minimum and maximum allowed duration between the end and start of two activities for the PP/DS PPM/PDS. For SNP PPM/PDS, the minimum and maximum constraint can't be defined in PPM/PDS. By default, the minimum and maximum interval between two SNP activities is considered as zero seconds. As a result, CTM scheduling can generate an early or late supply plan. To avoid this, you can use the Maximum Interval Between Activities (SNP) setting in the CTM profile. This setting defines the maximum allowed duration between the activities in the SNP PPM/PDS.

Activity relationships can also be used to define *mode linkage* to link the modes using the same resource name (Type 2) as shown in Figure 4.11.

Mode linkage in activity relationship is useful if you use setup and production activities with multiple modes and resources. Using mode linkage, CTM scheduling will ensure that you use the same resource for scheduling the setup and production activities.

CTM scheduling can also be used to finitely plan for secondary resources assigned to the mode. The secondary resource can be used to model labor resources or any other additional resources required for the activity. During scheduling an activity where a secondary resource is used, CTM evaluates the capacity requirements for both the primary and secondary resource simultaneously. As shown in Figure 4.12, the net capacity available for CTM scheduling is limited by the minimum available capacity of both primary and secondary resources.

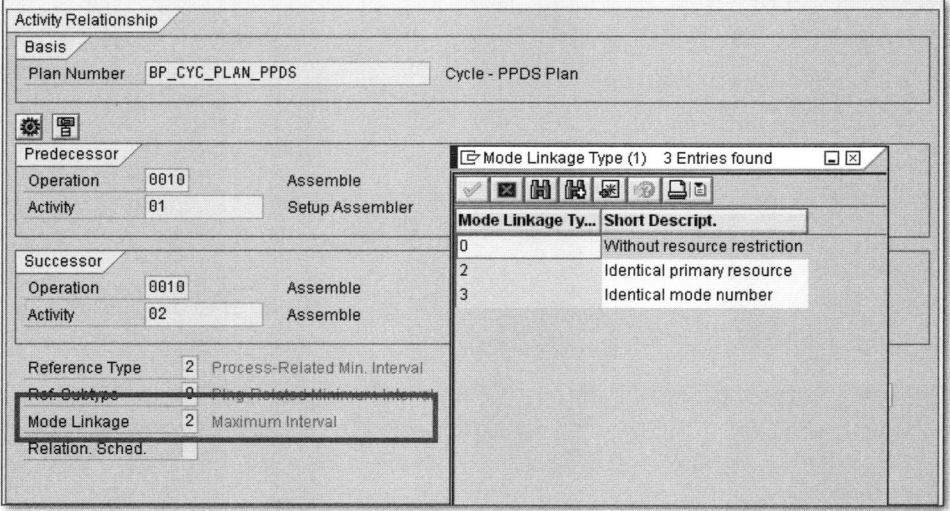

Figure 4.11 Mode Linkage for Activity Relationships

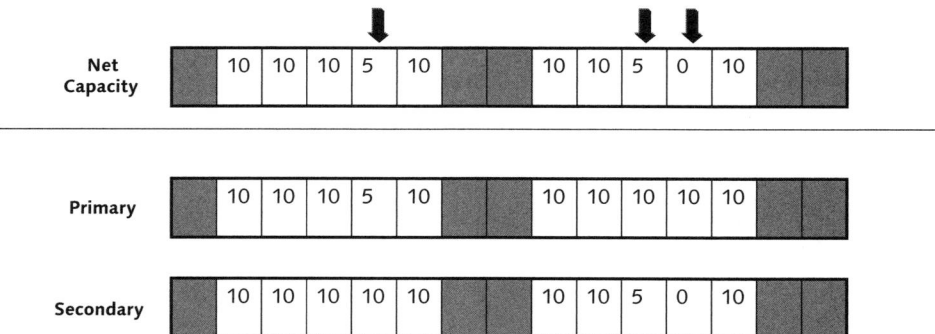

Figure 4.12 CTM Scheduling with Secondary Resource

For scheduling the time continuous planned order with secondary resource using PP/DS and PPM, CTM will ensure that the net duration of the activity on both the primary and secondary resource is identical.

CTM supports scheduling both setup and production activities. The setup matrix isn't used for scheduling planned orders. PI (Process Industry) operation and PI phase are also not supported in CTM scheduling.

Time dependent planning parameters (TDPP) assigned to the material consumption, activity scrap, mode duration, and resource consumption of PPM/PDS are used for scheduling planned orders in CTM. It's possible to define the version-specific time-phased values to execute what-if analyses. TDPP planning parameters are useful to model the production process improvement. The increase of production efficiency can be modeled with TDPP where input material and resource consumption is reduced over time. TDPP are maintained for a given time interval. By default, when planning in backward scheduling mode, the activity end date is used to determine the interval of the TDPP. For forward scheduling mode, the activity start date is used for the selection of the TDPP interval. Using the Swap Selection Time of Time-Dependent Parameters setting in the CTM profile, you can select the activity start date for TDPP interval selection in backward scheduling mode.

Planning and scheduling planned orders with *phantom assemblies* is supported in CTM planning. A phantom assembly defines a logical grouping of materials. A phantom assembly is created in engineering to describe a number of components and manage them as a whole. The components in a phantom assembly are immediately placed in the superior assembly. Components in an assembly are first assembled to produce the header material. Then the header material is placed in the superior assembly. Phantom assembly is used to define a group of products to manage the individual products as a group and is defined in SAP ERP using the BOM definition. The BOM created for the phantom assembly is also transferred to SAP SCM as an independent PDS. During planned order scheduling with CTM, the phantom assembly is evaluated so that the requirement and supply elements are created for the individual products, as shown in Figure 4.13.

The phantom assembly itself isn't included in the planned order created by CTM. This is different for the planned orders created by PP/DS where the phantom assembly and the actual components are included in the planned order, but only the actual components are relevant for creating a reservation during the planned order to production order conversion.

4 | CTM Planning Algorithm

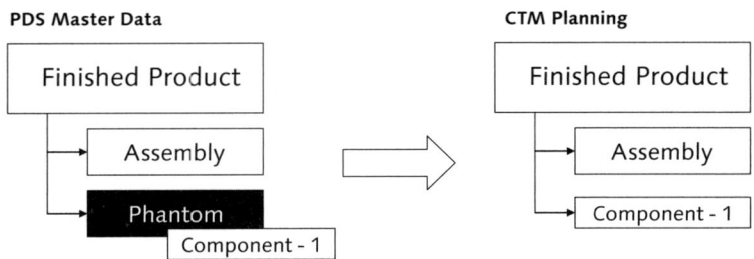

Figure 4.13 CTM Scheduling with Phantom Assembly

Goods receipt (GR) time maintained for the product is used by CTM for scheduling the GR time for the planned order. GR time is maintained in the product master. Based on the GR time for the product PPM/PDS used in CTM, planning is extended with an additional activity referring to the GR time. As shown in Figure 4.14, additional activity is added to PPM/PDS with the fixed mode duration representing the GR time.

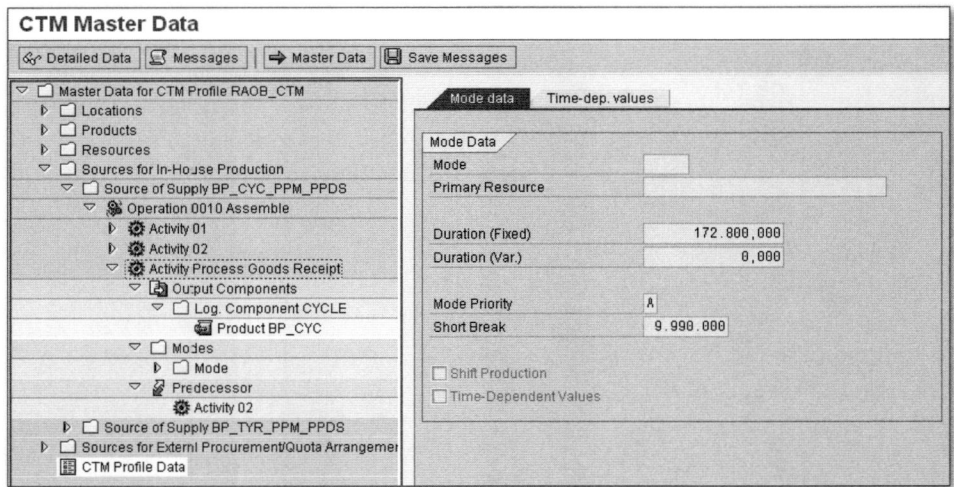

Figure 4.14 Scheduling GR Processing Time for a Planned Order

The planned order created with GR processing time will have the material availability at the end of the GR activity instead of the end of the production activity. The handling resource or the receiving calendar assigned to the location will be used for scheduling the GR activity. The handling resource will be used if the handling resource consumption is maintained for the product. By default, the minimum and maximum interval between the production and GR activity is set as 0 to ensure that the GR activity can start as soon as the production activity is completed.

GR activity and mode properties are derived from Table 4.1.

Duration	Main Product GR Time from Product Master
Handling Resource	Location Master
Receiving Calendar	Location Master

Table 4.1 GR Activity and Mode Property Derivations

Because the GR times are scheduled in CTM by adding an additional activity in PPM/PDS, it's mandatory to maintain identical GR times for the main product and the co-products. Similarly, if the plan contains multiple PPM/PDS for different planning locations, then it's also mandatory to define the same GR processing times for the product in all of the planning locations.

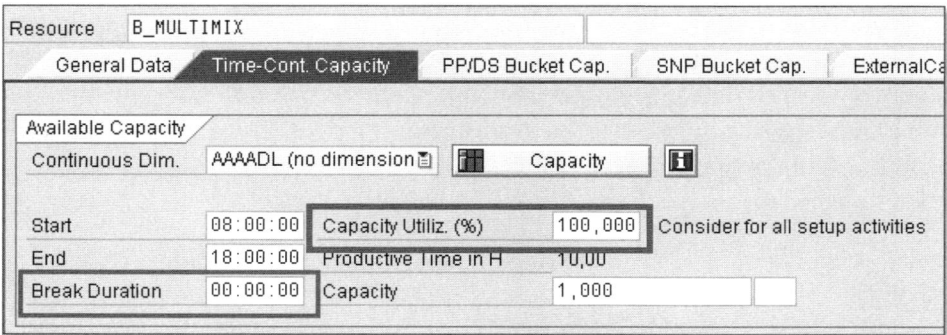

Figure 4.15 Resource Parameter for Utilization and Unscheduled Break

Resource utilization and unscheduled breaks in CTM aren't supported in the CTM planning run with the PP/DS planning mode. These parameters are shown in Figure 4.15. When planning in the SNP bucket mode, the available resource capacity is automatically adjusted according to the resource utilization factor. The capacity of SNP bucket resource is also adjusted to consider any unscheduled break duration. As a result, the CTM scheduling in bucket mode in not influenced with these parameters assigned to the bucket resource. In the CTM time-continuous planning mode, CTM uses 100% utilization factor for all time-continuous resources. If the resource has a utilization factor that isn't equal to 100%, then SAP liveCache will reschedule the activity created by CTM. This can cause scheduling differences between CTM and liveCache scheduling. The dependent requirements will also be offset, which causes date alerts.

To identify and log the scheduling errors, you can use the Check liveCache Scheduling. If Errors Exist Create Error Log in the CTM Global Customization setting. Using this setting, CTM will log all of the scheduling differences between CTM and liveCache.

4.4.2 Scheduling Stock Transfer Order

Stock transfer order or purchase requisitions with source location are scheduled in CTM with reference to the transport lane. The transport lane is selected for CTM planning if the product is maintained in the source and destination location. The creation and the deletion of the transfer order are limited by the *SNP stock transfer horizon* in both the SNP and PP/DS planning mode. By default, the stock transfer horizon of the destination location is considered for order scheduling. Using the Consider Stock Transfer Horizon of Source Location option in the planning version, you can use the stock transfer horizon of the source location for order scheduling. As shown in Figure 4.16, the transfer order is scheduled with goods issue (GI), transport and goods receipt (GR) activities.

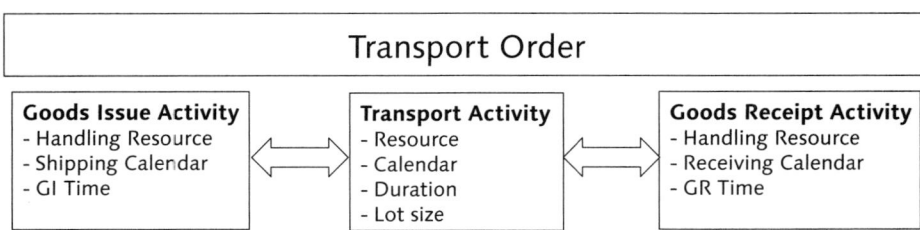

Figure 4.16 Scheduling Parameters for CTM Transport Order

The duration of the GR and GI times are maintained in the product master, and you can define fixed GR/GI times for scheduling. As a result, the GR/GI times are independent of the output quantity. Similarly, the transport duration is also independent of the transport quantity and is maintained in the transport lane.

Scheduling the GR/GI handling resource is similar to scheduling the production resources. However, scheduling and capacity consumption for transport resources is different from the production resource. As shown in Figure 4.17, the production activity is scheduled with the daily capacity requirement for the total order quantity. On the other hand, because the transport resource is fully occupied for the duration of the transport activity, the same daily capacity consumption is used for the complete activity duration.

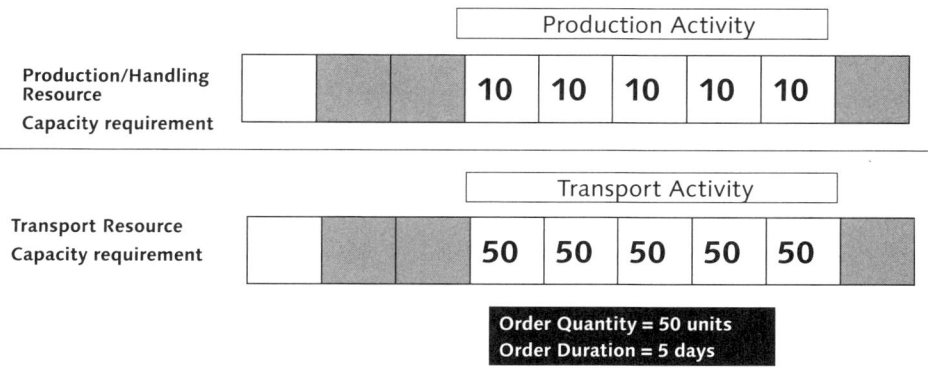

Figure 4.17 Resource Capacity Consumption — Transport and Production

Scheduling GR/GI and transport activity can use the receiving, shipping, and transport calendars. If the GR/GI times and transport duration are set to zero, then the GR/GI and transport activity isn't created, and the calendars are ignored. Similar to the production activities, the transport activities can't be scheduled to start or end in a calendar break. The activities can, however, be scheduled over the calendar or resource breaks.

The transport order is created with GR/GI activities, and, by default, the activity relationship between GI – Transport – GR activities is created with no maximum time constraint for activity scheduling. So, due to capacity constraints, the GR activity could start much later than the transport activity has ended. Similarly, the transport activity could start after the GI activity has ended, as shown in Figure 4.18. In many cases, such a large time lag between the activities of the transport order isn't feasible. By default, CTM would schedule the activities to reduce the time lag among all three activities. Using the CTM bMaxConstraintTrans planning parameter with Value1 = true, it's possible to schedule the transport order with GR/GI activities without any time lag. Because the activity relationship definition is a hard constraint for CTM scheduling, the complete transport order can be created much earlier or later than the required date.

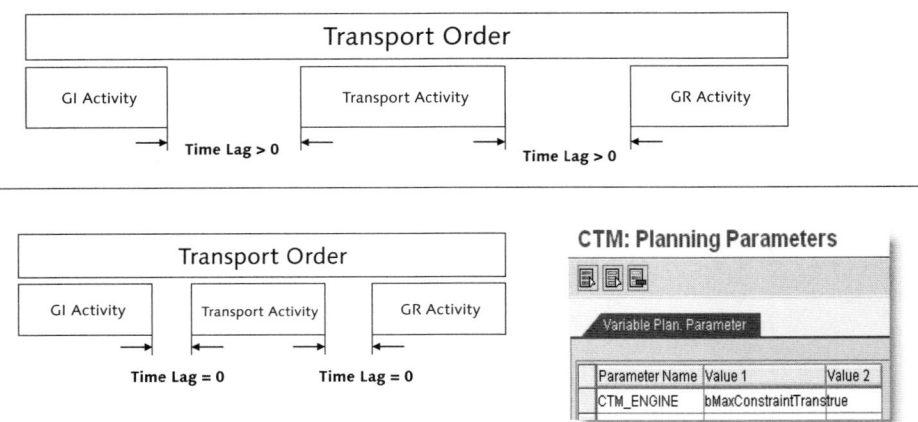

Figure 4.18 CTM Transport Order Scheduling with Constraint Capacity

CTM assigns the start and end times for each of the activities of the transport order. These times are required to ensure that the CTM created transport orders can be successfully published to the R/3 system without causing any scheduling differences. The key times assigned to the transport orders (see Figure 4.19) are the following:

- Requirement time
- GI end time
- Staging time
- Delivery time
- GR start time
- Available time

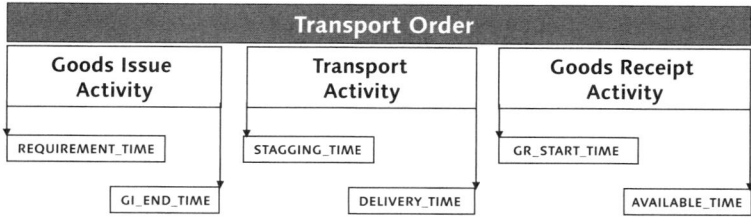

Figure 4.19 Transport Order – Key Scheduling Times for Each Activity

4.4.3 Scheduling Purchase Requisitions

Scheduling the purchase requisition is similar to scheduling the stock transfer order. The purchase requisitions are created without any reference to transport lane and would therefore only create the supply at the destination location. The purchase requisition doesn't contain any source information. Scheduling a purchase requisition using purchasing info records is supported in CTM where the purchasing info records attributes such as planned delivery time is considered for scheduling purchase requisitions. Only GR activity is relevant for scheduling purchase requisitions. CTM can create and delete purchase requisitions after the planned delivery time (PDT) maintained for the product in the product master. PDT can also be maintained in the purchasing info records, which is used for scheduling and deleting purchase requisitions. The GR activity can also be scheduled for purchase requisitions with handling resources and a receiving calendar.

4.4.4 Scheduling Substitution Order

Substitution orders are used in CTM for planning with substitution rules. Scheduling substitution orders is fairly simple because no constraints are used during substitution order creation. The substitution order doesn't contain activity and hence it isn't possible to use any duration for the substitution process. Similarly, no resources are used for scheduling the substitution order. Creation and deletion of the substitution orders is limited by the production horizon of the main product. As a result, no substitution orders can be created and deleted inside the production horizon of the main product.

Figure 4.18 (shown earlier) shows the complete scheduling results of the CTM planning engine for the model shown in Figure 4.20. The figure shows the planned

4 | CTM Planning Algorithm

order, transport order, and purchase requisition created for the finished product demand.

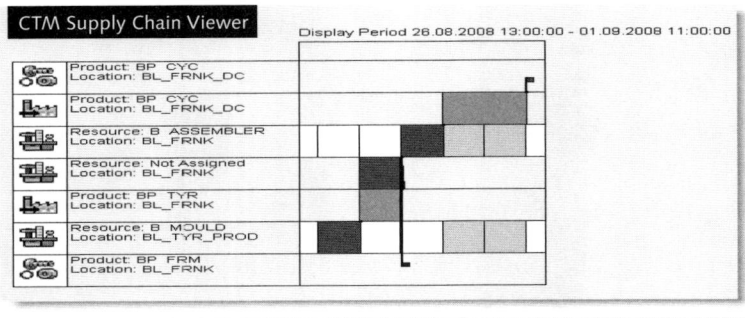

Figure 4.20 CTM Scheduling Results Display

In the next section, you'll learn the various late demand strategies that are available for CTM planning.

4.5 Scheduling Techniques for Late Demands

The primary goal of CTM scheduling is to create full or partial supplies= as to meet the demand in time. Due to capacity or material constraints, it's possible that in-time supply plan creation isn't feasible. In such scenarios, you can allow CTM to schedule late orders. There are two main options that are available to select the late demand strategies. You can define the late demand processing strategy in the CTM global customization. The two options for late demand strategy are the following:

- **Domino strategy**
  Using the domino strategy, CTM will try to find an in-time and late solution for a given demand before planning for the next demand. Late fulfillment of a

demand can lead to late fulfillment of subsequent demands during demand prioritization. This may be the case if the capacity has already been exceeded.

- **Airline strategy**
  Using the airline strategy, CTM will first try only in-time solutions for a given demand. If a demand can't be fulfilled by the demand date, the subsequent demands are fulfilled first during demand prioritization. CTM doesn't attempt to fulfill the late demand until the end of the demand list. The advantage of using this strategy is that late demand fulfillment doesn't delay the fulfillment of subsequent demands.

  If all demand elements have moved to the end of the demand prioritization list, CTM switches automatically to the domino strategy for the late demands.

The CTM demand attribute late demand frame (LDF) defines the allowed lateness of a demand. CTM will limit the creation of the orders per the LDF. CTM offers several options to define LDF as shown in Figure 4.21. The following options are available for defining LDF for each of the demand selected for planning:

- **Global LDF**
  CTM global customization can be used to define a constant LDF for all product locations across all CTM profiles.

- **CTM profile-specific LDF**
  If there are several CTM profiles used for planning different subsets of a model, then you can use the profile-specific LDF value using the CTM planning parameter nLateShipGlobal with Value2 = <Number of Days of LDF>.

- **Demand-specific LDF**
  Using the calculation profile assigned to the ATP rules, it's possible to define a different LDF for each product location. This is mainly useful when working with products with different LDF requirements. In some scenarios, it's required to have demand-dependent LDF. For example, when planning with sales orders and forecast orders, you want to have different LDFs for sales order and forecast orders.

Using the user exit APOBO020, it's also possible to define a demand-specific LDF, which is calculated with reference to the demand date considering only the calendar days. If you use demand aggregation, then LDF is applied with respect to the new aggregated demand date instead of the original demand date.

4 | CTM Planning Algorithm

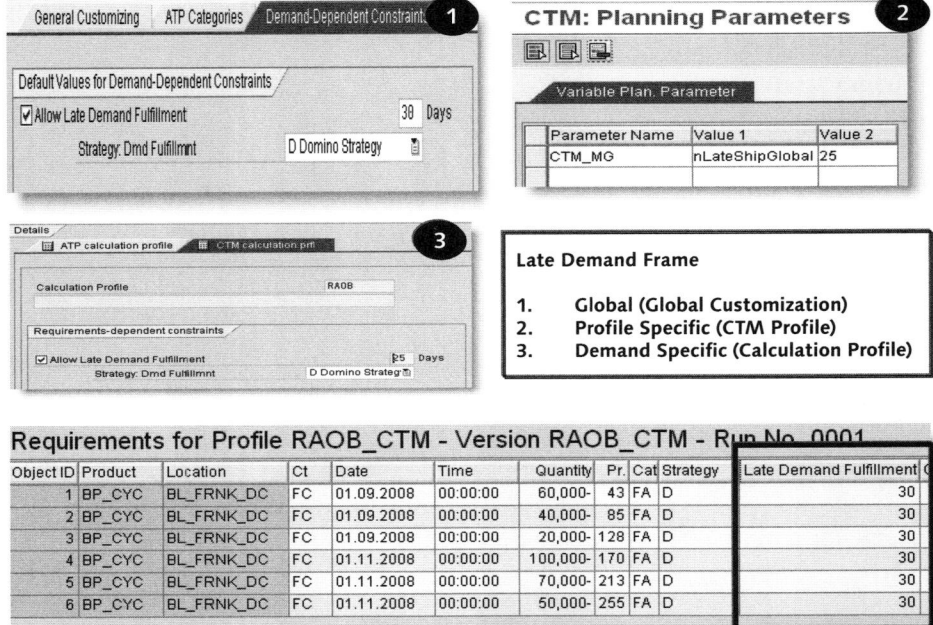

Figure 4.21 Late Demand Frame Maintenance Options

LDF can be displayed in the CTM demand simulation list and is used only for normal demands. For safety stock demands, CTM calculates the allowed LDF for each of the virtual safety stock (SS) demands. You can also select a user-specific LDF for SS demands using the setting in the CTM profile. This is described in more detail in the next chapter.

4.5.1 Late Demand Scheduling Modes

Late demand scheduling in CTM is executed when the in-time solution with all possible sources of supplies doesn't fulfill the required demand quantity. Scheduling for the remaining quantity is executed in LDF. There are three main scheduling options that are available for late demand planning in CTM (see Figure 4.22). You can select the late demand scheduling modes in the CTM profile using the settings available in the CTM profile.

4.5 Scheduling Techniques for Late Demands

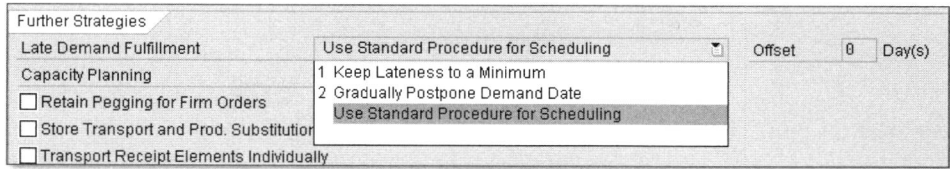

Figure 4.22 CTM Late Demand Handling Modes

The scheduling logic for all three scheduling modes is shown in Figure 4.23. The figure shows two sources of supplies (PPM/PDS), each with a maximum capacity of 10 units/day. The demand of 75 units can't be fulfilled in time. The scheduling logic for all three different scheduling modes is described in detail in the following sections.

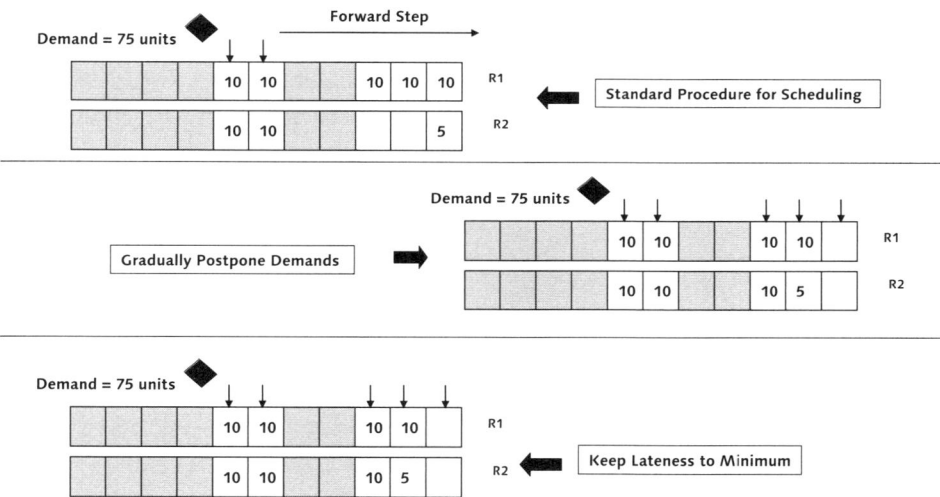

Figure 4.23 CTM Late Demand Scheduling Modes

Option 1: Standard Procedure for Scheduling

With this method for scheduling late demands, CTM gradually postpones the demand date by each day until a partial solution is found. At each day, CTM will check for all possible sourcing alternatives to fulfill the demand. Any partial supply that can be created is saved. The daily search sequence is stopped as long as no new supply can be created. CTM will use the remaining quantity to determine the new possible date within LDF. Using the new date, CTM will apply the backward scheduling mode to fulfill the remaining quantity. As shown in Figure 4.23, after Day 2, CTM doesn't find any new supply due to a resource break. As a result, the remaining quantity of 35 units is used to determine the new date using the forward scheduling logic. CTM will select the highest priority SOS and find a possible date on Day 7. Using this new date, the remaining quantity is scheduled, causing suboptimal late supply using the second priority SOS.

Option 2: Gradually Postpone Demands

Using this option, you can search for the late solution with predefined intervals. The intervals are defined using the Offset parameter in the CTM profile under the Special Strategies tab. As shown in Figure 4.23, the Offset value of 1 is used. The demand is fulfilled at each day until the complete solution is found within the LDF. In this option, the forward scheduling mode to determine the new possible date isn't used, resulting in better use of all possible sources of supplies to create the late supplies as close to the demand date as possible. Using the offset of 1 day isn't optimal for performance. It's possible to define an offset of larger granularity to avoid performance issues. This won't generate an optimal solution for products planned with short lead times and would cause much later supply creation. You have to select the late demand offset parameter while considering the lead times of the products and the allowed lateness for the demands.

Option 3: Keep Lateness to Minimum

With this option, CTM will schedule the orders to reduce the lateness as much as possible by using all of the possible sourcing alternatives. This method is similar to Option 2 but without any serious performance limitation.

Note that late demand scheduling is only applied for the primary demands selected for CTM planning. The dependent demands or secondary demands are always fulfilled in time.

4.6 Additional Parameters Influencing CTM Scheduling

Scheduling the orders in CTM depends on the individual attributes of the source of supplies (PPM/PDS, transport lanes). Additional parameters that can influence the scheduling of orders in CTM can be maintained in the CTM profile or global customization. Some parameters are defined with reference to the planning start date, whereas the other parameters are defined with reference to the demand date. Figure 4.24 shows the key parameters that can influence the scheduling of orders in CTM.

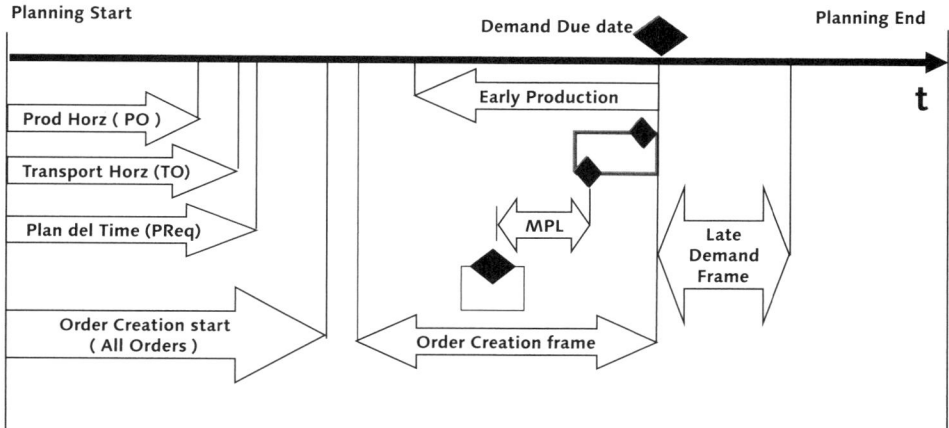

Figure 4.24 Time-Based Constraints for CTM Order Scheduling

4.6.1 Scheduling Horizons

Production horizon, *transport horizon*, and *planned delivery time* influence the creation and deletion of the planned order, stock transfer order, and purchase requisition. You can define the horizons in the product master for each product location.

By default, the horizons refer to the current date. You can use the Refer Horizons to Planning Start Date setting to consider the scheduling horizons with respect to the planning start date. This setting is available under the Technical Settings tab of the CTM profile.

4.6.2 Order Creation and Deletion Start

The *Order Creation Start (OCS)* parameter is used in CTM scheduling to limit the earliest start date of any order created in CTM. The OCS parameter is applied in addition to the respective horizons during order creation. Similarly the *Order Deletion Start (ODS)* parameter is used for order deletion and limits the earliest start for selecting the orders for deletion. The OCS and ODS parameters are maintained in the CTM profile under the Planning Strategies tab. By default, the OCS and ODS parameters refer to the current date.

4.6.3 Demand Selection Horizon

The *demand selection horizon* parameter defines the time frame for demand selection inside the planning time fence. You can maintain the demand selection horizon in the product master under the SNP 2 tab.

To better influence the CTM scheduling results and avoid early build of the supplies, you can define demand dependent scheduling parameters. These parameters are applied for each demand planned in CTM. They can be maintained globally at the CTM profile level or at the detailed level for each demand. These parameters are used in general in backward scheduling mode, where due to capacity constraint, the supply plan is created much earlier than the demand requirement date. Due to storage cost and material expiry issues, the generated plan is neither desirable nor optimal. To avoid early builds in backward scheduling mode and to maximize the use of all possible sources of supplies, the following parameters can be used to influence CTM scheduling of orders.

4.6.4 Order Creation Frame

Order Creation Frame (OCF) is calculated with respect to the demand date. OCF defines the allowed time interval for scheduling all of the orders required for fulfilling the demand quantity. All of the orders created for the dependent requirements must start inside OCF. OCF value is calculated without any reference to the calendar and therefore represents only the calendar days and not the working days. OCF constraint is applied for the CTM demands in both the backward and forward scheduling mode. OCF constraint can be enabled using the global parameter in CTM global customization or by defining a product-specific OCF in the product master. Demand-specific OCF can be set using the user exit APOBO020. The selected value for OCF can be displayed in the CTM demand simulation list as shown in Figure 4.25.

4.6 Additional Parameters Influencing CTM Scheduling

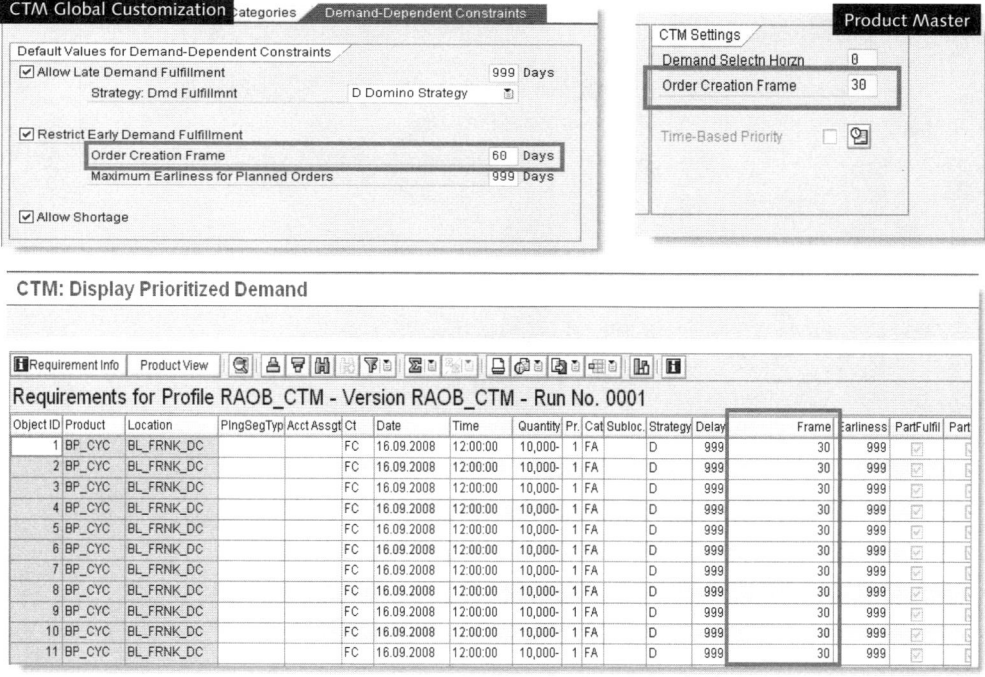

Figure 4.25 Order Creation Frame for CTM Demand

By default, the OCF parameter is applied for all newly created orders in a given CTM planning run. If you have existing stock or supply elements, then the supplies aren't constrained by the OCF parameter. As a result, CTM can use the supplies outside OCF. The OCF constraint can be applied to the existing supplies using the CTM OrderCreationFrame planning parameter with Value1 = S as shown in Figure 4.26.

CTM ensures that all of the orders are scheduled inside OCF and reduces and prevents early supply situations. If the dependent requirements are generated for products that have a very short shelf life, then OCF won't ensure that the supplies are consumed in time. Early supply for dependent requirements can be controlled using the Maximum Earliness for Planned Orders parameters as described in the next sections.

4 | CTM Planning Algorithm

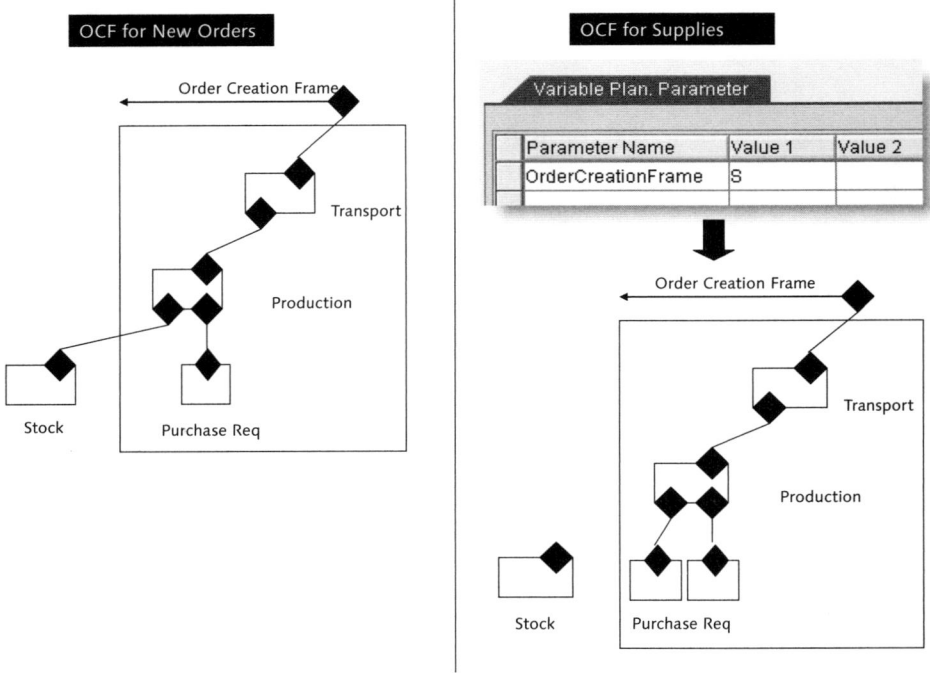

Figure 4.26 CTM Scheduling with Order Creation Frame for Supplies

4.6.5 Maximum Earliness for Planned Orders

The Maximum Earliness for Planned Orders parameter defines the earliest end time of the first planned order created to satisfy the demand. This parameter is useful in situations where the demand exists at the distribution center, and the production happens at the production plant. This parameter can be used to control the early build of the planned orders in the production plant.

As shown in Figure 4.27, the Maximum Earliness for Planned Orders parameter is maintained globally in the CTM global customization. This value is assigned to all of the demands planned in the CTM profile and can be displayed in the demand simulation list.

The Maximum Earliness for Planned Orders parameter is applied with respect to the demand date and is applied for the first planned order created for the demand. The rest of the supplies created for the demand aren't influenced by this parameter. The Maximum Earliness for Planned Order parameter is also calculated without any calendar breaks. If the transport duration is used, you must take it into account when maintaining the Maximum Earliness for Planned Orders parameter. Profile-specific Maximum Earliness for Planned Order parameters can be maintained using the calculation profile of the ATP rules. Similar to other demand attributes, the parameter value can also be influenced using the user exit APOBO020 to maintain a demand-specific value.

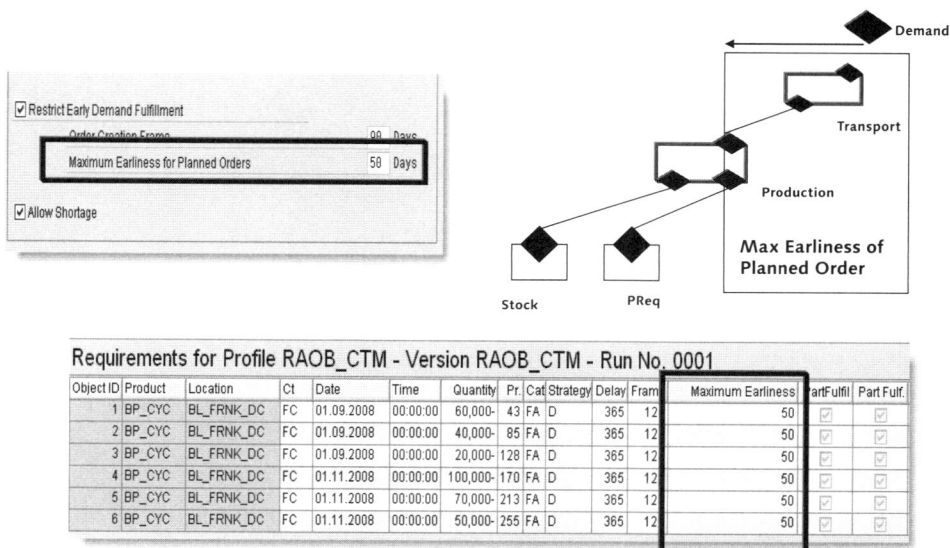

Figure 4.27 CTM Scheduling with Maximum Earliness for Planned Order

4.6.6 Maximum Earliness for Dependent Demands (MPL)

The maximum earliness parameter is also referred to as the maximum pegging length (MPL), which defines the maximum time between any demand and supply element created by CTM. MPL offers the maximum flexibility to control the scheduling of CTM supply to avoid any early build of supplies. The MPL parameter limits the maximum time between any demand and supply element planned in CTM. Using the MPL constraint, you can define the maximum storage time for supplies created for any given product at all of the levels of the supply chain. As shown in Figure 4.28, the Maximum Earliness setting in the CTM profile under the Supplies tab is used to enable CTM scheduling using the MPL parameter.

4 | CTM Planning Algorithm

The MPL value itself can be maintained as a time-independent value in the product master. MPL value is defined at the product location level using the Maximum Earliness of a Receipt field in the Pegging tab of the product master. It's important to remember that this field is also used by SAP liveCache as a parameter for creating dynamic pegging. CTM only uses the value of this field for scheduling the demands and supplies irrespective of the pegging type selected in the CTM profile. If you're required to maintain a time-phased MPL parameter, then you can use the SNP time series key figure to maintain the MPL value using the function 13. The MPL value is converted to the number of seconds in CTM planning and can be displayed in the CTM master data check results.

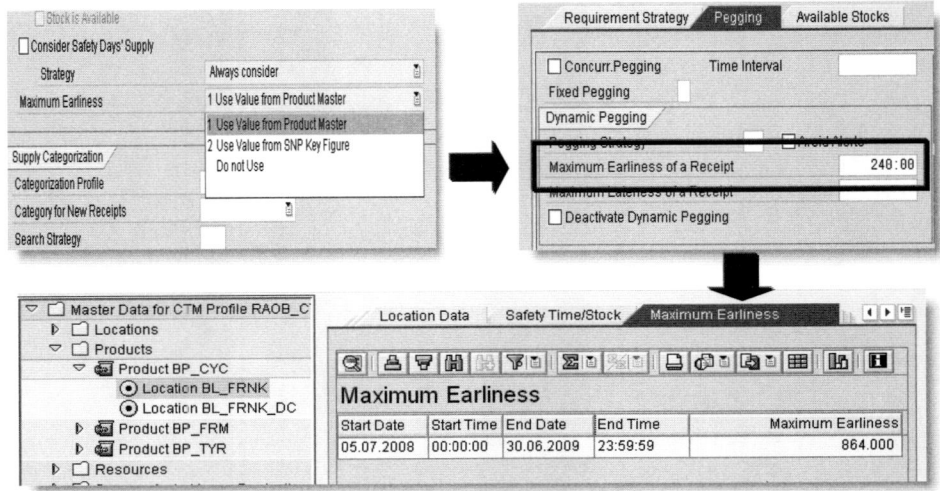

Figure 4.28 Maximum Pegging Length for CTM Demand and Supply

Scheduling with MPL in CTM is shown in Figure 4.29. The MPL constraint is applied only on the order end date or the material availability date, but the order can start before the MPL constraint. MPL is mainly useful in the backward scheduling mode because the orders are created close to the demand date. In resource-constrained situations at the production plant, the planned order can be created much earlier than the requirement date of the transport order. This can result in high storage costs at the plant. Using MPL constraint for the product at the production plant, you can define the maximum allowed storage time after the production is completed. CTM creates the planned order and transports the supply within the MPL time frame.

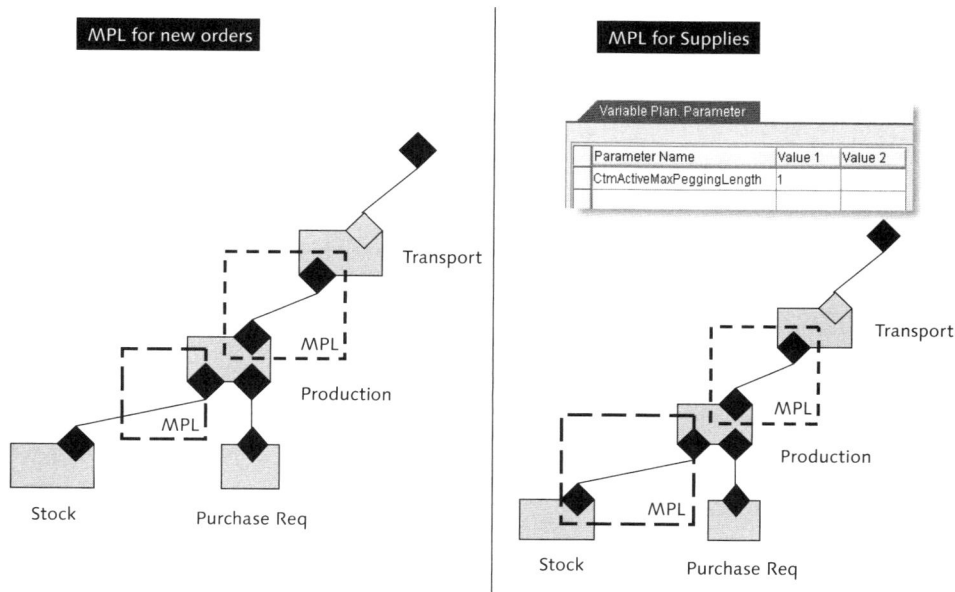

Figure 4.29 CTM Scheduling with Maximum Pegging Length (MPL)

An MPL value of 0 indicates that no MPL constraint is applied, whereas an MPL value of -1 indicates that MPL of 0 is applied for all demands and supplies planned in CTM. An MPL value of -1 can only be maintained in the SNP time series key figure. By default, the MPL constraint isn't applied to the existing supplies, similar to the OCF constraint. The existing supplies outside the MPL constraint can be used by the CTM engine to fulfill the given demand. This function can be influenced by using the CTM CtmActiveMaxPeggingLength planning parameter with Value1 = 1. Using this planning parameter, you apply the MPL constraint for the existing supplies as well. You need to pay special attention to the stock elements when working with MPL for supplies. Stock elements in SAP SCM are created with the available date of 01.01.1970. As a result, when MPL is applied for supplies, then the stock elements with date 01.01.1970 are always ignored because they would violate the MPL value. This can be avoided using the BAdI /SAPAPO/CTM_SUPPLY to adjust the date for CTM stock elements to the planning start date.

The MPL constraint is applied as a hard constraint, so the complete demand quantity can be unfilled due to the MPL constraint. The MPL parameter value for a specific demand can't be maintained because MPL isn't a demand attribute. MPL is applied to all of the demands of a given location product planned in a single CTM run.

> **Note**
> See SAP Note 1073004 for more details about the Maximum Earliness parameter for the supply elements.

4.7 CTM Planning Results Analysis

CTM planning is used for multilevel simultaneous capacity and material constraint planning. Each demand is planned by considering the capacity and material constraint for the entire supply chain. In addition to the material and capacity constraints, CTM planning considers other planning relevant constraints, such as safety days of supply, order creation frame (OCF), inbound quota, lot sizes, and so on. Each of the planning constraints can have a very significant impact on the overall planning results. For example, a demand can be totally unfilled, partially fulfilled, fulfilled too early, or fulfilled too late. The complexity of the planning results grows significantly when several demands are planned together in a single CTM planning run. It can be very challenging to understand the CTM planning results generated due to incorrect master data. In addition to the planning constraints, incorrect master data can also create unexplainable planning results. To better understand the CTM planning results, you can use the CTM explanation tool available in SAP SCM 5.0.

4.8 Explanation of CTM Planning Results

After a CTM planning run has been performed, you can have the system explain the possible reasons why CTM only partially fulfilled demands or didn't fulfill them at all. Here you use the explanation tool that saves the relevant information in the CTM application log. You can use the reasons listed to check whether you can solve a problem by increasing capacities or extending horizons, for example.

4.8 Explanation of CTM Planning Results

The explanation tool provides explanations as standard for all demands for each location product in the master data selection that you're using in the current CTM profile. You can, however, restrict the scope of the explanations and thereby make the information clearer. To do this, you can use an explanation profile (see Figure 4.30) in which you can make the following settings:

- Specify an alternative master data selection to have the system explain demands for critical location products only.
- Reduce the number of demands that need to be explained for each location product.
- Reduce the explanations of the search steps in the CTM planning run to the last search step only.
- Hide the demand search if CTM checks other procurement options too.

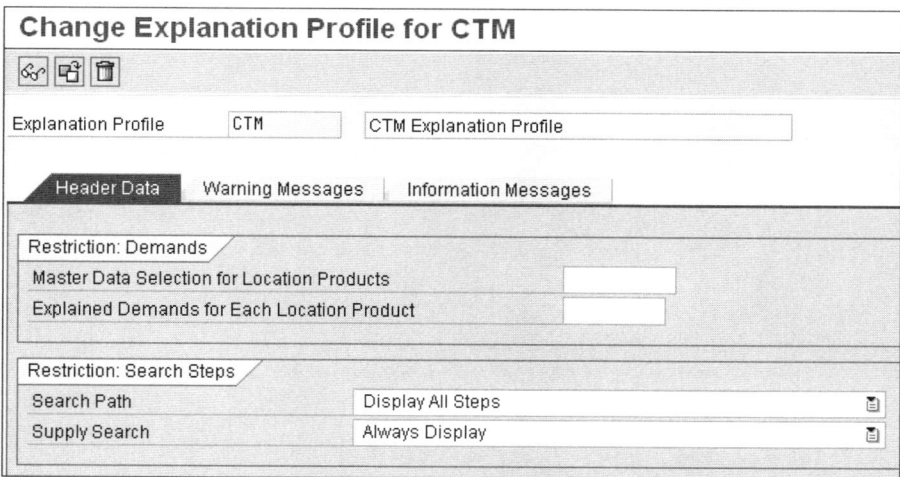

Figure 4.30 CTM Explanation Profile

The explanation tool can be maintained in SAP SCM system using the SAP APO Transaction /SAPAPO/CTMEXPL or using the SAP Easy Access menu path ADVANCED PLANNING AND OPTIMIZATION • MULTILEVEL SUPPLY AND DEMAND MATCHING • ENVIRONMENT • EXPLANATION PROFILE.

In the explanation profile, you can define a subset of location products for which explanation information must be generated. This is very useful when a large num-

4 CTM Planning Algorithm

ber of demands are planned in the CTM profile. Generating the explanation for all of the demands can have a negative impact on the overall performance. Using the Explained Demands for Each Location Product option, you can select the number of demands for a given product location that will be selected for explanation.

The Search Path option can be used either to generate the complete supply tree for the demand or to display only the last step of the supply tree that caused the demand to be unfilled. Existing supplies are used for demand fulfillment as the first search sequence for both the independent and dependent demand. Using the Supply Search option, you can select whether the supply search is displayed for all of the search nodes. Due to performance reasons, it's recommended to select Only Display as Single Procurement Option.

You can also reduce the possible information messages and warning messages in the explanation profile. The warning messages (see Figure 4.31) are used for explaining the planning results when the demand fulfillment is either late or not fulfilled at all.

Display	Message Text
☑	Resource &3: No dispatching possible with duration &1 / capacity reqmt &2
☑	Activity &2 / Mode &1 cannot be scheduled
☑	Resource &3: Dispatch not possible from &1 to &2
☑	No stock found
☑	Procurement alternative excluded: &1
☑	Source of supply validity starts after demand date &1
☑	Demand quantity &1 falls below minimum lot size &2 of source of supply
☑	Fell short of minimum consumption: Activity &1 / mode &2 / resource &3
☑	Fell short of minimum consumption: Activity &1 / product &2 / location &3
☑	Fell short of minimum duration: Activity &1 / mode &2
☑	No source of supply found in subcontractor
☑	Product explosion for component requirements is not allowed
☑	Source of supply cannot be used in forecast segment
☑	Source of supply generates cyclical product explosion
☑	Empty scheduling interval: No scheduling after &1 or before &2

Figure 4.31 CTM Messages Used for Demand Explanation Log Generation

To enable CTM demand explanation, you have to assign the explanation profile to the CTM profile using the Explanation Profile field available under the Technical Settings of the CTM profile. After the planning run, the explanation data can be displayed from the CTM application log as shown in Figure 4.32.

4.8 Explanation of CTM Planning Results

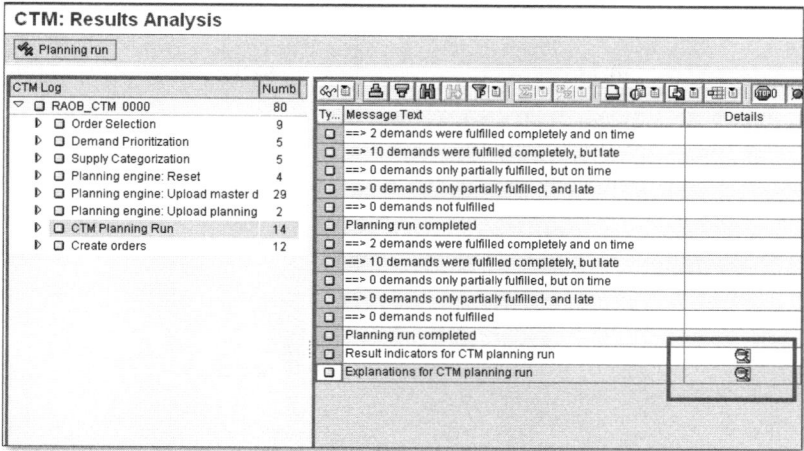

Figure 4.32 Starting Explanation Results from the CTM Application Log

The SC Model shown in Figure 4.33, is the basis for the next section. CTM will generate the explanation for the complete supply chain network and logs any constraints that can't be satisfied causing the demand to be unfilled or delayed.

The explanation results are displayed with the demand list that was selected for explanation. Each demand contains the following attributes:

- Original demand quantity
- On-time supply quantity
- Delayed supply quantity
- Number of delay days

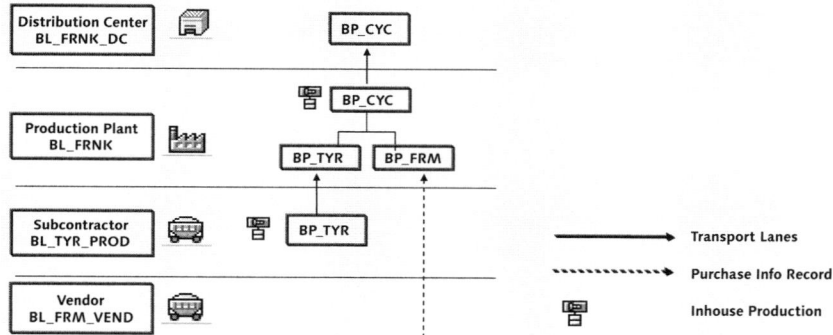

Figure 4.33 CTM Model for Explanation Tool

4 | CTM Planning Algorithm

Figure 4.34 shows the explanation results for the planning scenario where the CTM engine fails to find an in-time solution due to the production horizon for one of the components required for the finished product. The last node of the explanation tree indicates that the order can't be scheduled in time due to the production horizon using the yellow triangle. The rest of the supply chain displays green squares where no constraints are detected.

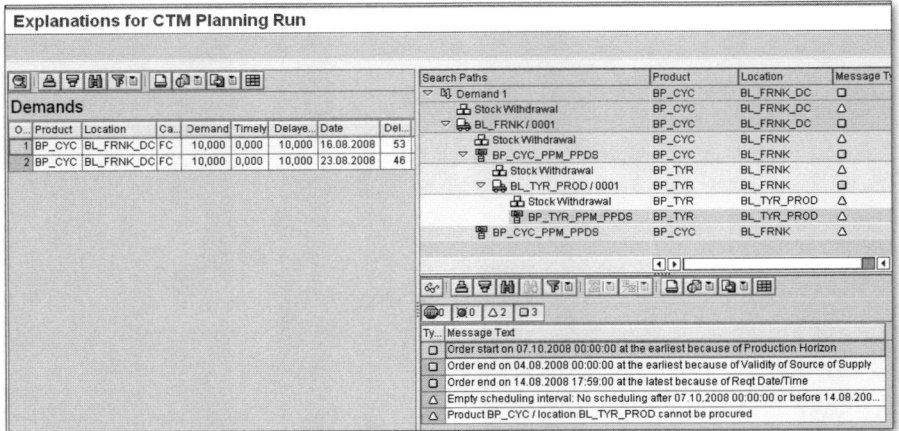

Figure 4.34 CTM Explanation for the Demand Fail Due to Production Horizon

Figure 4.35 shows the explanation results for the planning scenario where the CTM engine fails to find an in-time solution due to the capacity constraint for the production resource. The message displays the activity, mode, and the bottleneck resource that resulted in the finished product demand to be fulfilled late or not be fulfilled at all.

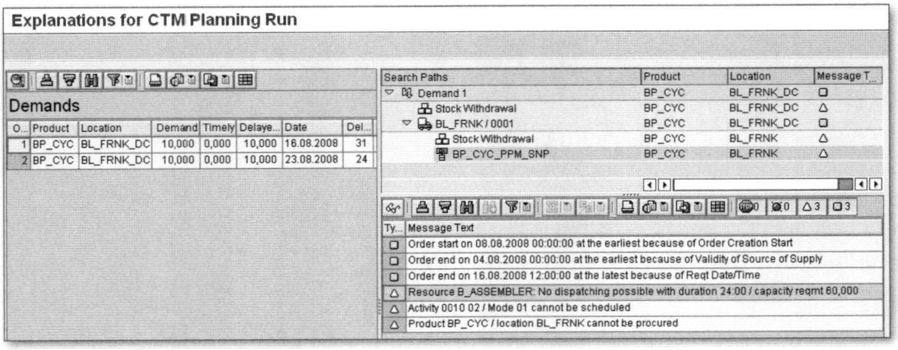

Figure 4.35 CTM Explanation for the Demand Fail Due to Resource Capacity

4.9 CTM Planning Result Indicators

Result indicators in CTM are aggregated measured values that provide meaningful information about the result of a CTM planning run. You can display the following result indicators in the CTM application log:

- Demand fulfillment per location product and demand type. The system displays the quantity per demand that was on time, the quantity that was delayed, and the shortage.
- Sources of supply used per location product.
- Resource utilization.

The result indicators in the CTM application log can be enabled using the CTM profile parameters as shown in Figure 4.36.

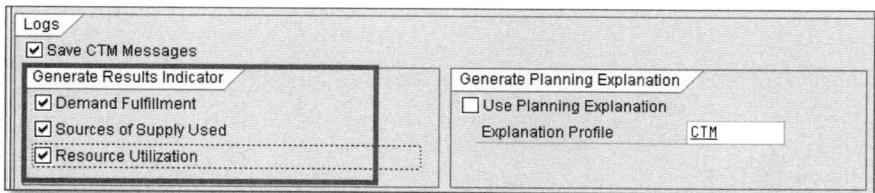

Figure 4.36 CTM Profile Settings for Result Indicators

Figure 4.37 shows the solution indicators for the SOS used in the CTM planning run. The solution indicators provide the aggregate view of the total quantity that was fulfilled using the particular SOS. You can have in-house production, transport lane, external procurement, and supplies as possible SOS.

Result Indicators	Product	Location	CTM Source Category	Source Description	Loc. Type	Unit	Receipt	Consumptn	Reqmts
Demand Coverage									
Sources of Supply Used	BP_CYC	BL_FRNK	Production	BP_CYC_PPM_SNP	1001	DE	120,000	120,000	12
Resource Utilization	BP_CYC	BL_FRNK_DC	Stock Transfer	BL_FRNK / 0001	1002	DE	120,000	120,000	12
B_ASSEMBLER	BP_FRM	BL_FRNK	External Procurement	BL_FRM_VEND / 0001	1001	DE	120,000	120,000	12
B_MOULD	BP_TYR	BL_TYR_PROD	Production	BP_TYR_PPM_SNP	1001	DE	240,000	240,000	12
	BP_TYR	BL_FRNK	Stock Transfer	BL_TYR_PROD / 0001	1001	DE	240,000	240,000	12

Figure 4.37 CTM Result Indicator for SOS Used for Planning

The solution results of the CTM planning run for total demand fulfillment can be used in user-defined reports using SAP NetWeaver Business Intelligence (SAP NetWeaver BI) using the DataSource APO_SDM_INDC_DEMSAT (see Figure 4.38).

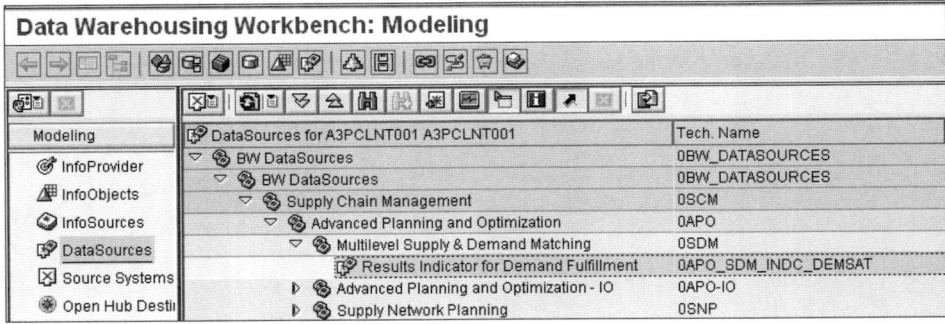

Figure 4.38 DataSource of Results Indicator for CTM Demand Fulfillment

4.10 Common Scheduling Issues with CTM Planning

As described in detail in the earlier chapters, CTM planning is a heuristics-based, multilevel, finite-capacity planning algorithm. CTM uses a top-down planning approach for each demand selected for planning and uses a local search strategy for SOS selection. Due to the inherent nature of the planning algorithm, CTM planning can generate infeasible and undesired plans for certain SC Models. These limitations must be carefully evaluated because they can severely impact the success of any CTM project. Some of these limitations in CTM scheduling logic can be addressed using special modeling techniques.

4.10.1 CTM Planning with Multilevel Fixed Lot Sizes

CTM planning with fixed lot sizes can generate highly infeasible supply plans when a fixed lot size is used at multiple levels of the supply chain network and BOM. This issue commonly occurs in the backward scheduling mode. As shown in Figure 4.39, the finished product has a net demand of 300 units. A fixed lot size of 100 is used for the finished product and a fixed lot size of 500 is used for the assembly or components used for the finished product. In the backward scheduling mode, CTM will create the first planned order for the finished product in the closest bucket to the demand date. Because CTM uses multilevel planning logic, the dependent requirements generated for the finished products are also planned.

The dependent requirement of -100 units is fulfilled using the planned order of 500 units (due to fixed lot size) for the assembly, which creates an excess supply of 400 units. This partial solution is saved internally by the CTM engine, and the remaining quantity (for the finished product) of 200 units is planned again. CTM will again create the planned order of 100 units for the finished product.

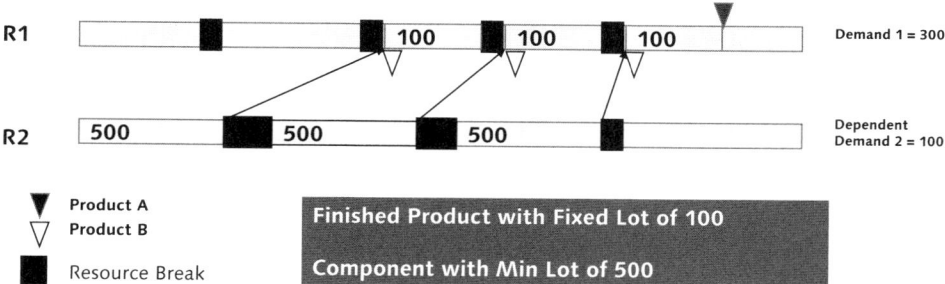

Figure 4.39 CTM Fixed Lot Size Planning Issue

The dependent requirement of -100 units can't use the excess supply because the supply is available much later than the dependent requirement time. To fulfill the dependent requirement for the assembly, CTM will create a new planned order of 500 units for the assembly. The same phenomenon occurs for the third lot of planned orders created for the finished product. As a result, 1,200 units of excess supply for the assembly are created. Even though the excess supply is used for the successive demands, due to the storage capacity limitation, the plan is highly undesirable. Additionally, if the planned order for assembly is scheduled on a resource that is also used for other assemblies, then this can result in unfulfilled demands for all successive demands. Consequently, the use of fixed lot sizes in CTM planning must be carefully evaluated.

In infinite planning mode, you can address this limitation using individual CTM planning steps at each of the planning levels (low-level code). You can create a new CTM profile to select and plan for the product with the fixed lot size. This CTM profile can be executed after the normal planning run where all of the dependent requirements are generated. The dependent requirements are planned with a material requirement date to sort the demands according to the demand date. The excess orders are deleted and planned again for each level of the supply chain network. Using this method, you can correct the material and resource consumption, but any constraints at the component level aren't propagated to the finished product demands.

149

4.10.2 CTM Planning with Local Search Strategy

CTM planning uses a search strategy to select the SOS using predefined rules. The search strategy is applied locally at each level of the supply chain network. As a result, it isn't possible to define global source selection rules in CTM planning. This can generate the supply plan that isn't cost optimal and can lead to early build of the supply plan. As shown in Figure 4.40, there are two production alternatives with priority 1 and 2. With CTM backward scheduling mode, CTM will use the production alternative with the highest priority and schedule the order between the planning start and the demand date. The production alternative with lower priority is only selected after the higher priority alternative can no longer be used due to capacity constraints. This would generate the supply plan that starts much earlier than desired. The CTM planning won't use the lower priority alternative if an in-time solution can be generated using a higher priority alternative.

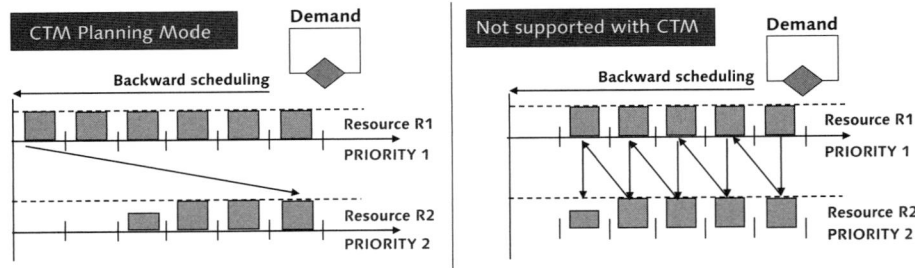

Figure 4.40 CTM Planning with Alternative Sources Across Locations

Additionally, if there are two production locations, and each location has a higher priority PPM/PDS, then CTM won't apply the SOS search across the locations. As described earlier, the CTM search strategy is applied locally at each node of the supply chain. As a result, CTM will use the lower priority PPM at a location when a higher priority PPM is available in alternative locations.

4.10.3 Bucket Planning with Fixed Lot Size and Resource Underutilization

SNP bucket resources are defined with a daily capacity profile. Available capacities for the bucket resources are always stored in the SAP liveCache using a daily grid definition that starts at 00:00:00 and ends at 24:00:00. During CTM planning, SNP activities must be scheduled so that the start of the activity is always at the start of the resource grid or capacity bucket. For CTM finite planning in SNP bucket mode, the net capacity requirement for each day (or bucket) must not exceed the required capacity requirement for the activity. SNP activities in CTM are scheduled with fixed duration, and cross-period activities aren't supported in CTM planning. As a result, when planning in the SNP mode using fixed lot sizes, bucket resources can be underutilized. For example, as shown in Figure 4.41, the demand of 480 units must be planned on a resource with a maximum available capacity of 100/Day or 500/Week. The product also has a fixed lot size of 60 units. CTM planning will schedule the first planned order of 60 units consuming a capacity of 60 units. The remaining 40 units of resource capacity can't be used for scheduling another order with a fixed lot size of 60 units. CTM schedules the order in the second or earlier bucket. Due to this scheduling logic, CTM can only create five planned orders of 60 units each for a given week resulting in only 60% of resource utilization. When planning with lot-for-lot specification for the products, CTM can schedule the orders considering all of the available capacities.

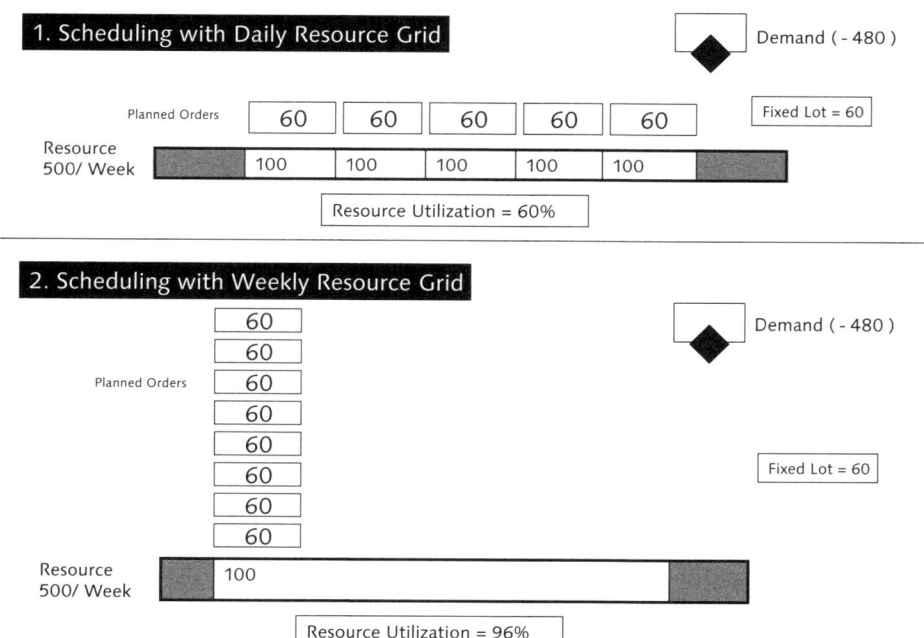

Figure 4.41 CTM Scheduling with Weekly and Daily Resource Capacity Profiles for SNP Bucket Resources

4 | CTM Planning Algorithm

To avoid resource underutilization, you can plan for the resources in larger buckets instead of daily bucket sizes. In the resource master using the Capacity Profile definition, you can define the resource capacity using weekly, quarterly, or monthly buckets (see Figure 4.42).

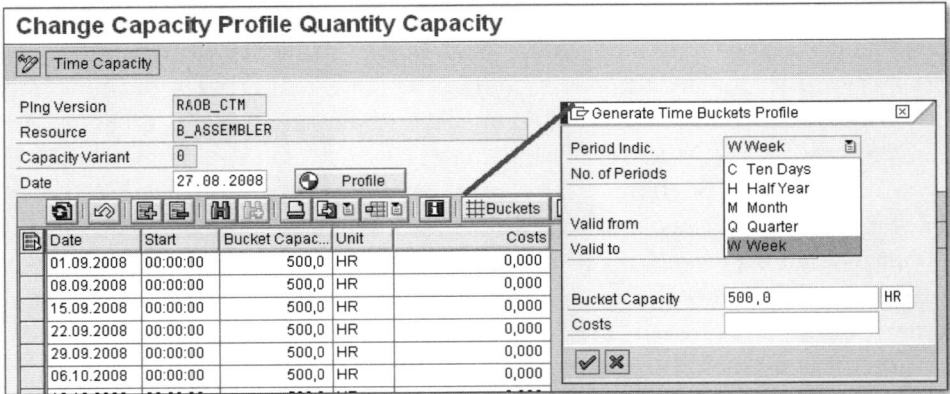

Figure 4.42 Define Weekly Bucket Resource Profile

Weekly capacity profile is used for CTM order scheduling. The SNP activities must always be scheduled at the start of the resource capacity definition. All of the SNP orders are created as shown in Figure 4.43. Each order is aligned with the start time of the weekly bucket definition. CTM planning will now consider the total weekly capacity instead of the daily capacity for order scheduling. The overall resource utilization is considerably improved when a weekly capacity profile is used for CTM planning. On the other hand, when using CTM for multilevel planning, the material requirement dates can be impacted due to a weekly or monthly resource capacity profile. The overall production lead time for the finished product will be significantly higher due to the weekly resource capacity profile. As shown in Figure 4.43, the order can only be scheduled at the start of the bucket using the weekly capacity profile. As a result, for two levels of the BOM, the overall production times increased from two days to two weeks.

To avoid the long production times due to the weekly resource capacities, you define an additional SNP dummy activity to the SNP PPM/PDS without any resource. All of the input and output components are assigned to the dummy activity. As a result, all of the SNP activities are now scheduled in the same weekly bucket as long as the first level of production has the longest production time.

Common Scheduling Issues with CTM Planning | **4.10**

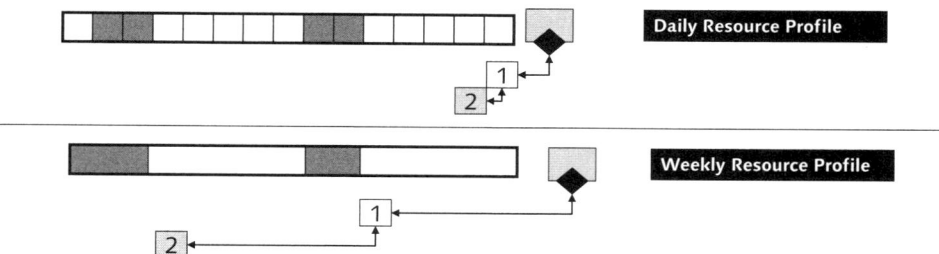

Figure 4.43 Multilevel Planning Issues with Weekly Resource Capacities

4.10.4 Fair Share Planning with CTM

CTM planning is based on prioritized demands. Each demand selected for CTM planning gets a unique sequence number after demand prioritization. All of the demands selected for CTM planning are planned in a predefined sequence. The available supplies and resource capacity is allocated to the demands in the sequence of demand priority. The first demand in the demand list can consume all of the constrained resource capacity and supply. For example, if two products have the same material priority, then the demand prioritization doesn't assign a unique priority to the demands. As a result, the first demand that is selected for planning can consume all of the available resource capacity and supply. CTM planning doesn't ensure fair share distribution of resource capacity and supply to the demands for products with the same priority, as illustrated in Figure 4.44. The three demands for products A, B, and C are planned in sequence even though the material priority is identical. The constrained resource capacity of 200 units is only allocated to the first two demands for A and B products. The third demand for product C can't be satisfied because all of the available capacities are already allocated.

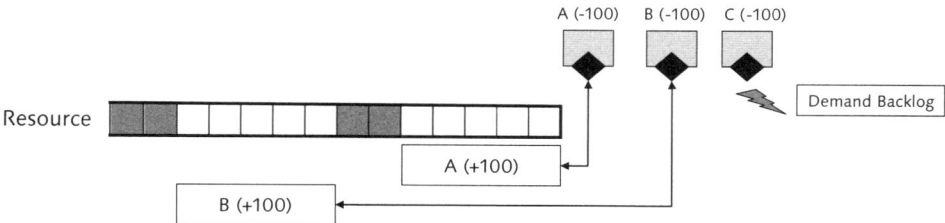

Figure 4.44 Demand Backlog Created Due to Sequential Demand Planning in CTM

4 | CTM Planning Algorithm

To achieve fair share distribution in CTM planning, you can release the forecast from DP into separate demand streams. Each demand stream represents a smaller proportion of the original demand quantity and is assigned a different ATP category (see Figure 4.45).

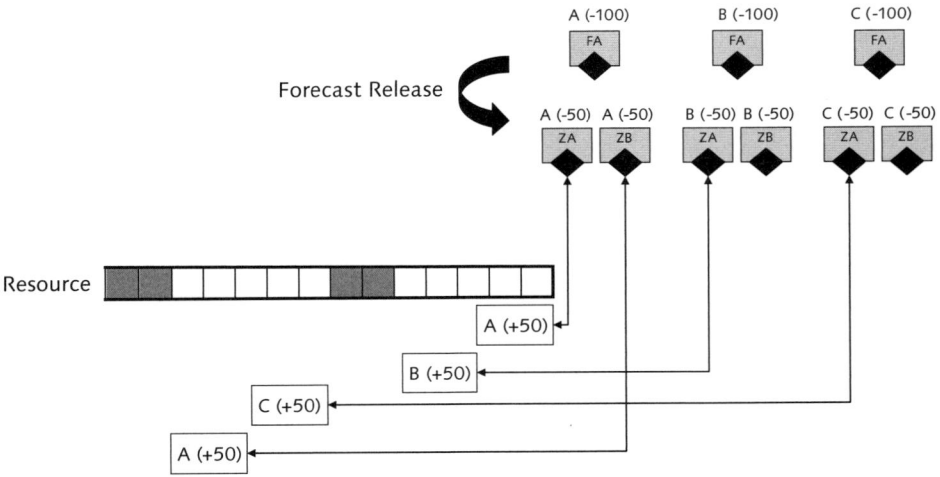

Figure 4.45 Fair Share Supply and Resource Allocation with CTM

Because each forecast demand is now identified using a different ATP category, you can use ATP category (ATPCAT) as the demand prioritization sequence in the CTM profile. As a result, the demands are prioritized and planned in such a way that the resources and supplies are allocated to the partial demand quantities. In Figure 4.45, all of the demands with ATP category ZA are planned before demands with category ZB. This modeling approach can be used to achieve fair share planning in CTM. On the other hand, you must understand the following limitations to use this modeling approach:

- The demand split model uses static calculation of the fair share quantities without considering any capacity or material constraints.
- Demand split can only be achieved for forecast orders. When planning with the make to order (MTO) scenario, the sales orders can't be split into smaller quantities using custom ATP categories.
- When planning with smaller demand quantities, the fair share rule can be violated due to minimum or fixed lot sizes.

- SOS selected using minimum lot size can result in demand backlog. For example, if PPM/PDS has a minimum lot size restriction, then the smaller demand quantity can't be fulfilled using PPM/PDS.
- Safety stock requirements planned in CTM using virtual demands can't be planned using this fair share model. The virtual demands are generated by CTM during planning and hence can't be split using the fair share requirements.

4.11 Summary

This chapter explained the rules used by the CTM planning engine to select the appropriate SOS to generate the supply plan for a given demand. The CTM planning algorithm uses a finite heuristics-based planning method to generate a constrained and feasible supply plan. The goal of CTM planning is to create an in-time supply plan that considers all of the procurement alternatives before switching to the late demand fulfillment. You now understand how to use the CTM explanation tool to see why the demand can't be satisfied or is satisfied late. Finally, you also learned about common scheduling issues that are encountered with CTM planning, and you can identify the different modeling techniques that you can use to avoid or correct those issues.

In the next chapters, you'll learn about the various supply control functions that are available in CTM. Safety stock planning and safety days of supply are explained in detailed.

Safety stock planning in constrained resource scenarios is a complex process. You'll learn different safety stock scenarios that can be planned using different CTM planning modes. This chapter will also introduce you to new CTM functions available in SAP SCM 5.1 release.

5   Supply Control with CTM Planning

Supply control or safety stock planning is required to manage the uncertainties in the supply chain. Safety stock planning is an integral part of the supply planning process, which is used to determine the optimal safety stock quantity and safety stock location. The optimal deployment of the stock is crucial for any business.

As the supply chain becomes complex, so do the factors that can influence the safety stock planning in the supply chain. When managing hundreds of products distributed across several locations in the enterprise, you should have an optimal safety stock to avoid excess stock at each level of the supply chain. Although it's required to maximize the service level requirements by planning for sufficient safety stock at all levels of the supply chain, having such a strategy isn't feasible from the cost perspective. The goal of multilevel safety stock planning is to meet the end user customer service levels with optimal stock in various locations of the supply chain. By using the safety stock planning methods available in SAP SCM, you can create optimal safety stock.

Standard and extended safety stock planning methods are available in SAP SCM. Using standard methods, it's possible to define the safety stock quantity and location based on the planner's experience or using third-party inventory optimization tools. Extended safety stock planning methods in SAP SCM are available to calculate the optimal safety stock for a given service level using alpha and beta service level methods.

Safety stock planning in CTM is available for the standard safety stock methods. CTM generates the constrained supply plan using the safety stock requirements maintained for the products. The extended safety stock methods aren't supported in CTM planning. Safety stock planning in CTM can be used to create the supply plan based on the required safety stock (SS) or using the safety days of supply

5 | Supply Control with CTM Planning

(SDS) to create the supply plan for future requirements. Additionally, using the supply distribution (SD) function in CTM, it's possible to deploy excess stock in the next level of the supply chain using the outbound quota values. Supply control for the dependent requirements can be achieved using the Maximum Earliness parameter in CTM planning. In the SC Model where the storage of products isn't desired at the production plant, CTM planning offers functionality to store the products at the distribution location instead. With SAP SCM 5.1, you can build a supply for a given product location based on the minimum build (MB) requirements. This is useful in scenarios where special contractual agreements exist for the subcontractors.

The standard SS planning methods that are available in SAP SCM are defined individually for each product location in the product master as shown in Figure 5.1.

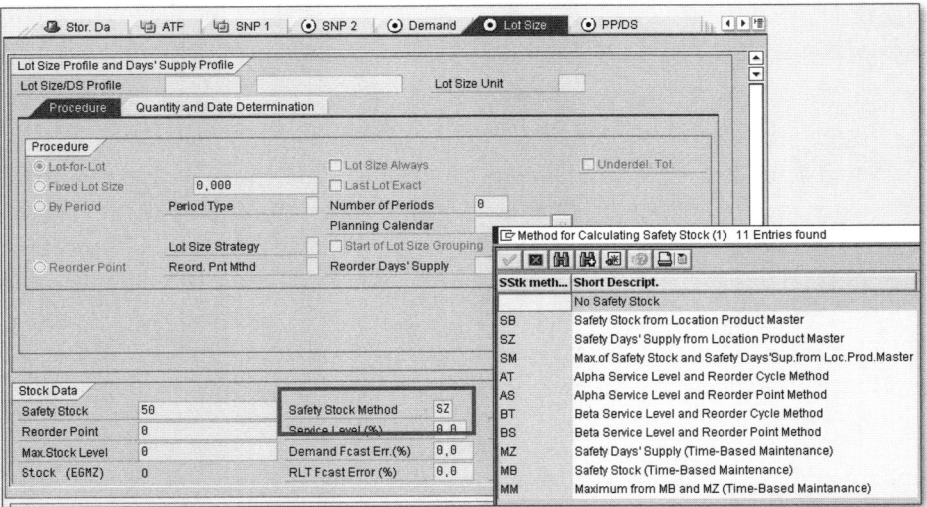

Figure 5.1 Safety Stock Planning Methods

The following SS methods are available in SAP SCM:

▶ **SB**
Safety Stock from Location Product Master

▶ **MB**
Safety Stock (Time-Based Maintenance)

▶ **SZ**
Safety Days' Supply from Location Product Master

Supply Control with CTM Planning | **5**

▶ **MZ**
Safety Days' Supply (Time-Based Maintenance)
▶ **SM**
Max. of Safety Stock and Safety Days' Supply from Location Product Master
▶ **MM**
Maximum from MB and MZ (Time-Based Maintenance)

It's important for you to understand the key difference between CTM planning and other planning tools in SAP APO for the SS methods SM and MM. For CTM planning using the SM and MM methods, both the SS and SDS values are used instead of the maximum of the SS and SDS.

For the constant safety stock (SS) and Safety Days of Supply(SDS) methods (SB, SZ, SM), the SS values are maintained in the product master using the Safety Stock and the Safety Days Supply fields under the Lot Size tab of the product master. The SS value is maintained in the base unit of measure (UOM) of the product. SDS is maintained as the number of days and must be maintained in multiples of days.

The SS methods that are available in CTM planning are shown in Table 5.1.

Safety Stock Methods	Constant	Time-Phased
Safety Stock	SB	MB
Safety Days of Supply	SZ	MZ
Both SS and SDS	SM	MM

Table 5.1 Safety Stock Methods Available in CTM Planning

When planning with SS methods MB, MZ, and MM, time-phased SS and SDS values can be maintained for CTM planning using the time series key figure of the SNP planning area (see Figure 5.2).

SNP PLAN	Unit	21.07.2008	28.07.2008	04.08.2008	11.08.2008	18.08.2008
Total Demand	DE		100	100	100	100
Total Receipts	DE		200	50	75	75
Stock on Hand	DE		100	50	25	
Supply Shortage	DE					
Safety Stock (Planned)	DE		100	50	25	
Safety Days' Supply	D					
Safety Stock	DE		100	50	25	

Figure 5.2 Time-Phased Safety Stock and Safety Days of Supply

5 | Supply Control with CTM Planning

The SNP key figure used for maintaining the time-phased values must be made available for CTM planning using the customization Make SNP Key Figure Available as shown in Figure 5.3. The customization setting can be accessed using IMG • ADVANCED PLANNING AND OPTIMIZATION • SUPPLY CHAIN PLANNING • MULTILEVEL SUPPLY AND DEMAND MATCHING • CAPABLE TO MATCH • MAKE SNP KEY FIGURE AVAILABLE.

The key figure functions 11 and 12 are available to define the key figure used for SS and SDS. The planning object 9AMALO must be used for the SNP planning area that you want to use for CTM planning. If you maintain multiple key figures for the same function, then CTM will use the first key figure for time-phased data selection. The planning area that can be used for CTM planning can be defined in the CTM global customization under the ATP Categories tab. It's also possible to define a CTM profile-specific planning area under the Technical Settings tab of the CTM profile. In this case, CTM the profile-specific planning area is used for key figure selection before using the planning area maintained in the CTM global customization.

9ASNP02	9AMALO	9APSUBZU	24 Product substitution: Rece
9ASNP02	9AMALO	SAFTY	13 Maximum earliness
9ASNP05	9AMALO	9ASAFETY	12 Safety stock
9ASNP05	9AMALO	9ASVTTY	11 Safety days' supply
			11 Safety days' supply
			12 Safety stock
			13 Maximum earliness

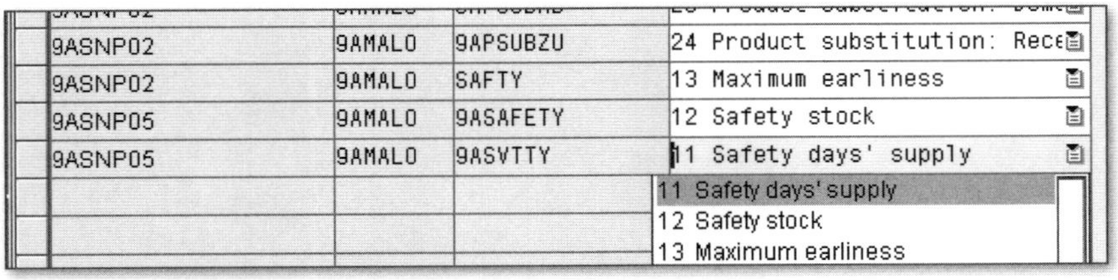

Figure 5.3 Make SNP Key Figure Available for CTM

When using the SNP time series key figure, the key figure values are selected based on the storage bucket profile of the planning area. The time bucket profile used in the planning view isn't used for data selection. If you plan to use time buckets that are different from the storage buckets, you must use the No Disaggregation function for the key figure to ensure that the SS and SDS values are selected for CTM planning with the appropriate time buckets.

Using the CTM master data check function, you can validate the time-phased key figure values used for CTM planning as shown in Figure 5.4. This is a very useful function where you can check whether all of the appropriate customization is made to make the SNP key figure values available for CTM planning.

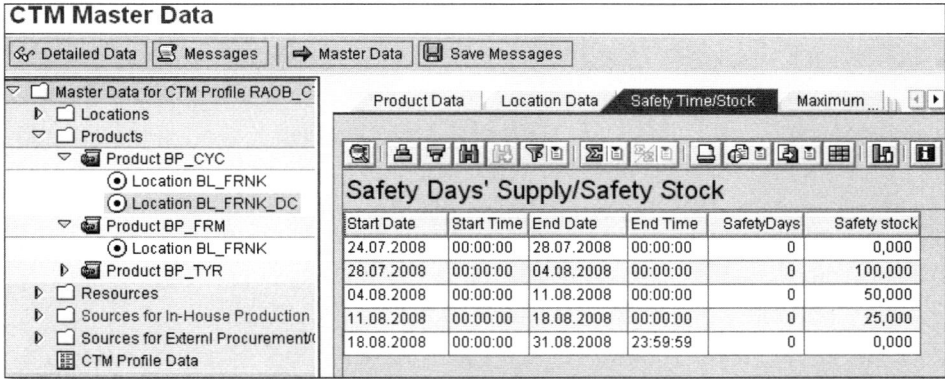

Figure 5.4 CTM Master Data Check for Time-Phased Safety Stock Values

After you've made the appropriate selection of the SS planning methods and the relevant SS and SDS values, the CTM planning run will generate the supply plan to fulfill SS and SDS. In the next sections, we'll take a detailed look at planning for SS and SDS in CTM.

5.1 CTM Planning for Safety Stock Quantity

CTM planning with SS quantity is performed for the SS methods SB, MB, SM, and MM. SS planning with SS quantity is enabled in CTM by using the Build Up Safety Stock setting, which is available under the Supply tab of the CTM profile.

SS planning in CTM can be executed with the following methods:

- Constant SS planning with SAP liveCache demands
- Constant SS planning with CTM virtual demands
- Time-phased SS planning with CTM virtual demands

For planning with the constant SS requirement, it's possible to create SS requirements persistency in the SAP liveCache. These demands can be planned along with the normal demands (forecast, sales orders, etc.) in CTM planning.

Alternatively, SS requirements can be planned in CTM using virtual demands. CTM planning for SS quantity uses a unique method to determine the SS requirements. With finite planning in CTM, the supply plan is created while considering the resource capacity constraints. Due to capacity constraints, the supplies are created per the available capacity rather than the requirement date.

After the normal demands are planned in CTM, the net SS requirement for each product location is calculated based on the available inventory. The net SS requirement for each product is translated into SS virtual demands that have the same attributes as other CTM demands. The virtual demands are planned by the CTM engine as regular demands using the same search sequence and SOS selection rules as normal demands. The SS virtual demands are only generated during the CTM planning run and aren't persistently saved in SAP liveCache.

Because the SS requirement using virtual demands doesn't exist in SAP liveCache, it isn't possible to create fixed pegging for the SS requirements. The virtual demands for SS requirements represent only the required SS quantity and the date. The supply plan generated for the SS virtual demands is created considering the capacity and material constraint. When planning in infinite capacity mode, the supply plan is created according to the SS requirements. For finite planning, the supply plan for the SS virtual demands can be created earlier or later than the requirement date.

Using the virtual demand attributes and other planning parameters in the CTM profile, it's possible to control the allowed earliness and lateness for the supply plan of virtual demands. To plan for reducing time-phased SS values, the CTM interval planning method is used. The interval planning method can be used to control fluctuations in the SS requirements more accurately. In this method, the complete planning horizon is planned with smaller intervals, thus providing more accuracy and control of the SS variations.

Depending on the accuracy and the granularity of the SS builds, the intervals can be defined as daily, weekly, monthly, quarterly, or yearly using the CTM time stream. Using the SAP APO time stream, you have the option to define the intervals with more flexible start and end times. The main disadvantage with interval planning is the performance of the CTM planning run. Because the CTM planning is executed multiple times for each planning interval, the overall runtime can be very poor based on the number of intervals selected for planning. You have to carefully select and compare the accuracy of the SS planning result with respect to the overall runtime requirements for the CTM planning run.

5.1.1 Safety Stock Requirement in SAP liveCache

To create constant SS requirements in liveCache, the planning version must be set with the Consider Safety Stock Requirements in SAP liveCache parameter as shown in Figure 5.5.

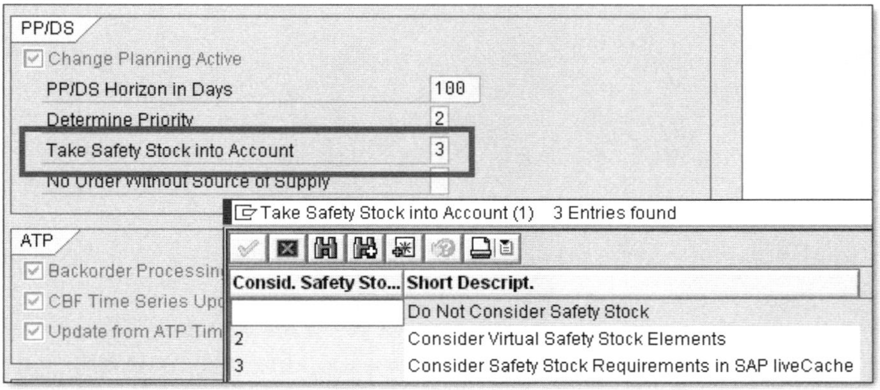

Figure 5.5 Create SS Requirement in SAP liveCache

The SS requirement can be created using the PP-Heuristics algorithm /SAPAPO/ HEU_PLAN_SAFETY_STOCK, which is part of the standard SAP SCM system. Using this heuristics algorithm, the SS requirement is created in SAP liveCache with ATP category SR. This SS demand can be planned with CTM normal demands and can be used for demand prioritization along with the normal demands. The planning method doesn't consider the open inventory and always creates the SS demand on the current day. The time-phased SS values can be used to create the SS demands in SAP liveCache. Consequently, the SS method MB isn't supported for this method.

5.1.2 Safety Stock Requirements as Virtual Demands in CTM

The CTM SS calculation algorithm uses the open supplies and SS requirements to generate the virtual demands. CTM checks the complete planning horizon for any SS backlogs and creates a virtual demand to fulfill the SS backlog. The SS backlogs are checked for a minimum duration of one day. The virtual demands have the same attributes as normal demands. By default, CTM calculates the early production and late demand frame (LDF) attributes of the virtual demand to avoid any early or late build of the SS supplies.

As shown in Figure 5.6, you can use the Early Fulfillment and Late Fulfillment parameters in the CTM profile to define the user-specific early and late demand frame. This is useful in constraint planning scenarios to allow a larger time frame for SS supply creation without causing SS backlogs. All of the remaining attributes are selected from the global customization or the product master, similar to the normal demands.

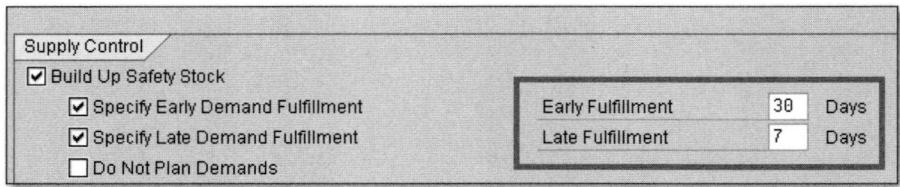

Figure 5.6 CTM Safety Stock Demand Attributes

Unlike the normal demands that exist in SAP liveCache, the SS virtual demands in CTM are calculated during the CTM run. As a result, it isn't possible to use the demand simulation function to check the SS virtual demands before the CTM planning run. After the CTM planning run, the SS virtual demands calculated by CTM for planning can be checked in the demand simulation list, as you can see in Figure 5.7.

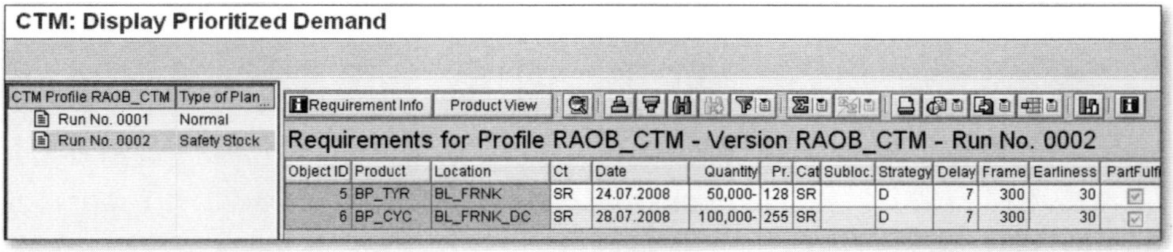

Figure 5.7 CTM Safety Stock Virtual Demand Attributes

- *Demand aggregation* of SS virtual demand aggregation isn't enabled by default even if you use the aggregation function in the CTM profile. The SS virtual demand in CTM is created by considering the daily net inventory levels. If you want to aggregate the SS virtual demand to the buckets larger than one day, you can use the planning parameter SRCAT_AGGREGATION with Value1 = X. The SS virtual demand is created in CTM with the ATP category SR. In the demand aggregation setting, you can include the SR category. As a result, CTM aggregates the SS virtual demands per the required time buckets.

CTM Planning for Safety Stock Quantity | 5.1

> **Note**
>
> See SAP Note 1007721 for more details about the usage of the planning parameter SRCAT_AGGREGATION.

- *Demand prioritization* of SS virtual demand is possible with CTM planning. The SS demands are prioritized using the prioritization sequence maintained in the Demand tab of the CTM profile. The user exit APOBO020 available for the normal demands is also called for the SS demands.
- *Fixed pegging* for the SS virtual demand can't be created in CTM planning because the demand isn't persistently created in SAP liveCache. This is valid only for the finished product demand or the planning level where SS is planned. The dependent requirements and the receipts created for the dependent requirements can be fixed pegged in CTM planning.

5.1.3 Safety Stock Virtual Demand Generation in CTM

SS virtual demand is generated for the SS method with constant SS (SB) and time-phased SS (MB). The planning sequence and generation of the virtual demand for SS requirements can use either the *two-phase* or *single-phase* SS method, as shown in Figure 5.8.

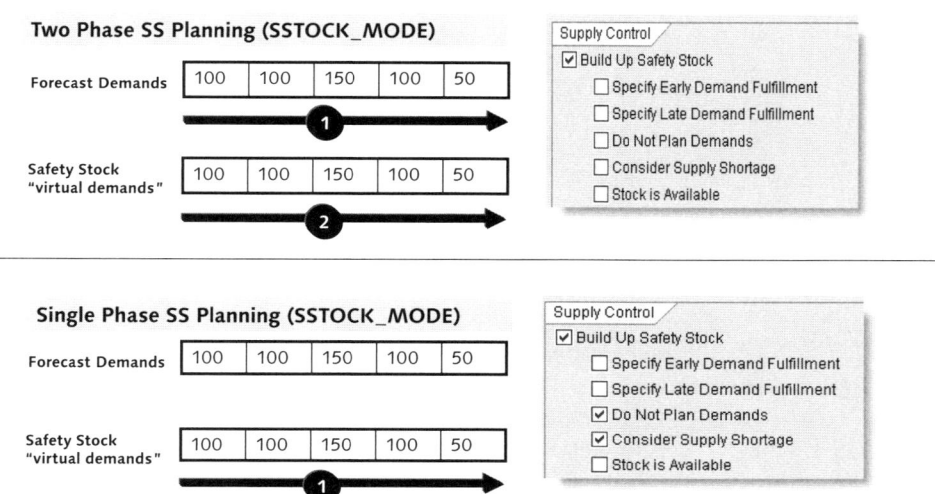

Figure 5.8 Two-Phase and Single-Phase CTM Safety Stock Planning Modes

165

Two-phase SS planning in CTM is the default method in which the SS virtual demands are generated and planned after all of the normal demands are planned. The SS virtual demand planning is similar to the normal demand planning in which a completely new CTM planning run is executed with all of the planning steps such as order selection, demand aggregation, demand prioritization, and CTM planning. In this mode, the SS virtual demand is planned after all of the normal demands, and as a result, the SS demands can be backlogged due to material and resource constraints.

To plan the normal demands and SS demands together with the same priority, you can use the single-phase planning mode. Using this mode, CTM combines the normal demands and SS virtual demands in the daily bucket and plan as one virtual demand. The main advantage of this single-phase mode is that the SS demand in the near horizon has much higher priority over the normal demands that are far out in the future.

On the other hand, because the normal demand and SS demand are planned as a combined virtual demand, fixed pegging can't be created even for the normal demands that exist in SAP liveCache. Additionally, the SS demand Early Fulfillment and Late Fulfillment attributes are applied to the combined SS virtual demand. As a result, it isn't possible to define different LDF and early fulfillment parameters for the normal and SS virtual demand.

The single-phase SS planning can be activated in the CTM profile using the Do Not Plan Demands and Consider Supply Shortage settings. Using these two options, CTM doesn't plan the normal demands. CTM executes SS planning while considering the supply shortage due to normal demands. The normal demands are combined with the SS requirements to generate a combined SS virtual demand.

Until SAP SCM 4.1, single-phase SS planning is enabled in the CTM planning run using the planning parameter SSTOCK_MODE with Value1 = X and Value2 = X.

The main advantages and disadvantages for the constant and time-phased SS method using the single-phase and two-phase SS planning mode are discussed in detail in the next section.

Constant Safety Stock Planning (SB)

With the two-phase SS planning method, CTM provides very good results for the constant SS method. In this mode, the normal demands are planned in the first

CTM run. Based on the net demand and supply generated for the normal run, SS virtual demands are generated and planned in the second CTM run. As you can see in Figure 5.9, in the two-phase method, CTM generates the SS virtual demands after planning the normal demands. Run 0001 indicates the CTM run executed for the normal demands, and Run 0002 indicates the CTM run executed for the SS virtual demands. The demand list for the SS virtual demands must be used to check the demand date and demand attributes that were used for planning. For the constant SS, the SS calculation is performed from the planning start date without considering any firmed horizon (production, transport, etc). As a result, the supply plan generation for the SS virtual demands can fail. It's important, therefore, to adjust the SS virtual demand attributes using the Early Fulfillment and Late Fulfillment parameters available under the Supply tab of the CTM profile.

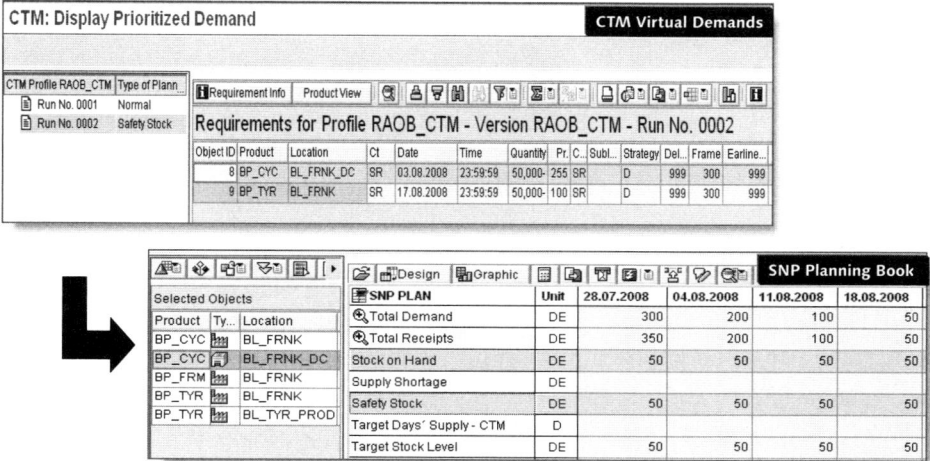

Figure 5.9 Constant SS planning with the Two-Phase Method

It's also possible to use the single-phase method for planning constant SS. For unconstrained or infinite planning with CTM, both the single-phase and two-phase method will generate a similar supply plan. For the single-phase mode, the SS virtual demands in the near horizon are prioritized over the normal demands in the later time buckets. The normal demands and SS demands are combined in the single-phase method, thus allocating resources and supplies to the combined virtual demand.

5 | Supply Control with CTM Planning

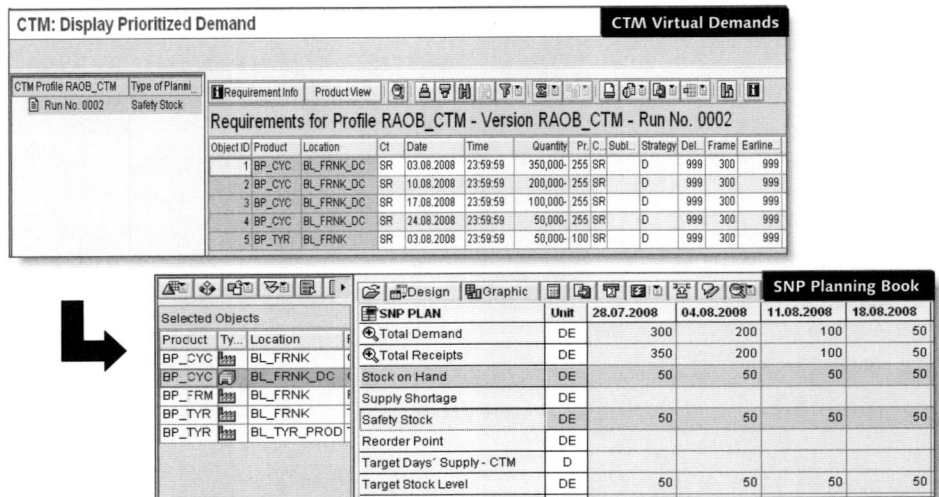

Figure 5.10 Constant SS Planning with the Single-Phase Method

When demand prioritization is based on the demand date (MBDAT), then the SS demands in the current time bucket are prioritized over the normal demands in the later time buckets. As shown in Figure 5.10, with the single-phase method, the CTM run for the normal demands isn't executed. The normal demands are combined with the SS virtual demands in Run 0002. The SS requirement of 50 units is combined with the normal demand of 300 units on 03.08.2008 and planned before the normal demands in the later buckets. This is useful in constrained planning scenarios where SS demands in the near future have higher priority over the normal forecast orders in the later buckets. It's imperative that in the unconstrained planning mode, the demand prioritization sequence is inconsequential.

Time-Phased Safety Stock (MB) Planning

Planning for time-phased SS in CTM can be done with both the two-phase and single-phase modes. When the time phased SS is increasing over time, both the planning methods generate accurate supply plans. Time varying or reducing SS planning in CTM with the two-phase method suffers from serious limitations. These limitations must be clearly understood before using the two-phase method for products with reducing SS requirements.

In the two-phase method, the SS virtual demands are calculated starting from the planning start until the planning end time frame. The calculated SS virtual demands are planned after all of the normal demands are planned and the supply plan is created. The virtual demand for the larger SS in the near horizon generates the supply plan. The SS generated for the initial buckets isn't reduced or consumed in the later buckets because all of the normal demands are already planned, and the supply plan is firmed in SAP liveCache. As a result, the two-phase SS planning method creates excess stock for all of the future buckets when the SS requirement is reducing over time, as shown in Figure 5.11.

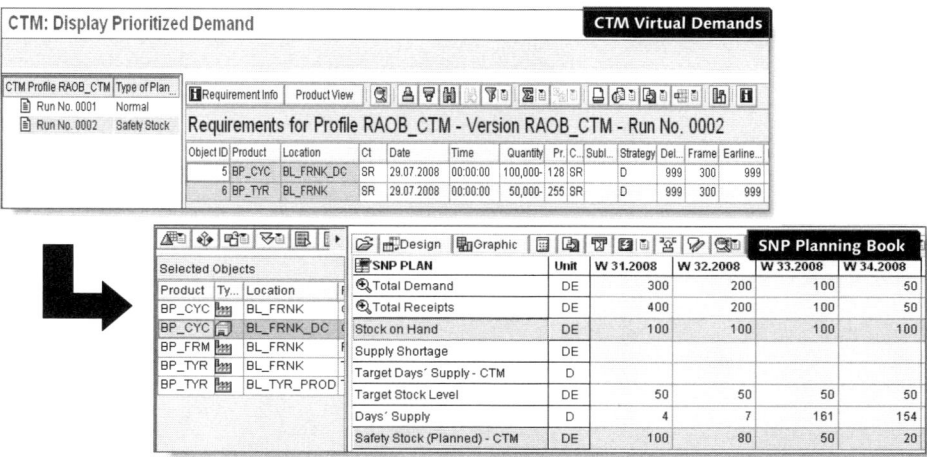

Figure 5.11 Time-Phased Reducing SS Planning with the Two-Phased Method

In the two-phase method, the normal demands are planned in Run 0001, and the supply plan is generated to fulfill the normal demands. In the second run for SS virtual demand planning in Run 0002, the SS virtual demands are generated from the planning start until the planning end. The SS requirements over the planning period are reducing with values 100, 80, 50, and 20. Because the SS requirement creation starts from the planning start, CTM creates the SS virtual demand of 100 at the planning start time. The planning run generates the corresponding supply of 100 units. Because there are no open normal demands, the stock on hand of 100 remains until the planning end, causing an oversupply in all of the later buckets where the SS requirement is less than the initial bucket. This is a very serious limitation of using the two-phase SS method in CTM for planning reducing SS requirements.

Planning with the single-phase method for reducing SS requirements is a better approach. With the single-phase method, the normal demands aren't planned but instead are combined with the SS virtual demands. In this mode, CTM generates the net demand to avoid any excess supply in the future buckets (Figure 5.12). In contrast to the two-phase planning method, during planning with the single-phase method, the net SS virtual demands are calculated from planning end to planning start time frame. This method is used to detect any oversupply situations in the later time buckets. The excess supplies aren't created for the later buckets, however, so undersupply can result for some initial time buckets depending on the SS values and forecast values.

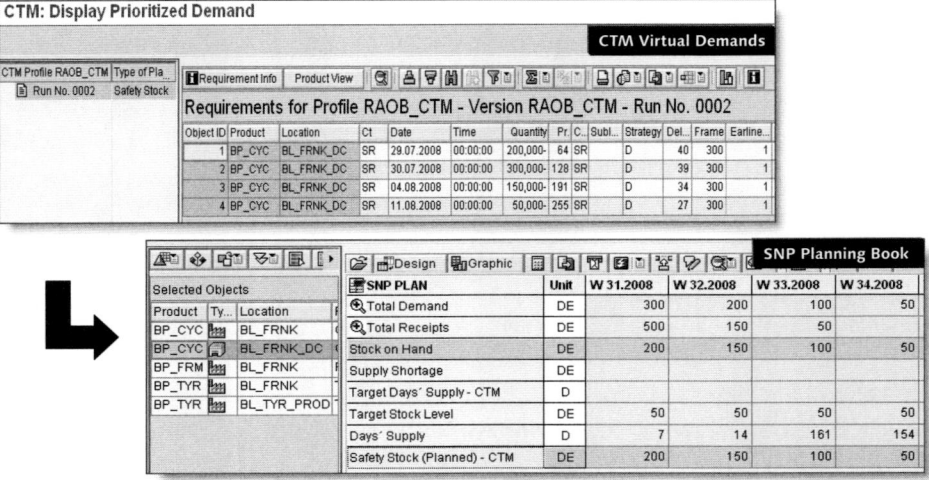

Figure 5.12 Time-Phased Reducing Safety Stock Planning with the Single-Phase Method

Products with some seasonal demand patterns can have time-varying SS requirements. Due to the seasonal demands, some time buckets could have very high SS, whereas the remaining time buckets could have very limited SS requirements. In such scenarios, planning with single-phase SS planning can cause backlogs in some time buckets. This is to ensure that no oversupply is created in the buckets where the SS requirement is very low. This is required for products that have very high production or storage costs. As shown in Figure 5.13, the product BP_CYC has a time-varying SS requirement of 300, 50, 100, and 25. With the single-phase method, the objective is to avoid any oversupply and to fulfill the SS requirement as much as possible. As a result, CTM will generate the virtual demands to avoid oversupply in buckets (CW32 and CW34) with an SS requirement of 50 and 25. This will lead to an undersupply in buckets with an SS requirement of 300 and 100 in buckets (CW31 and CW33).

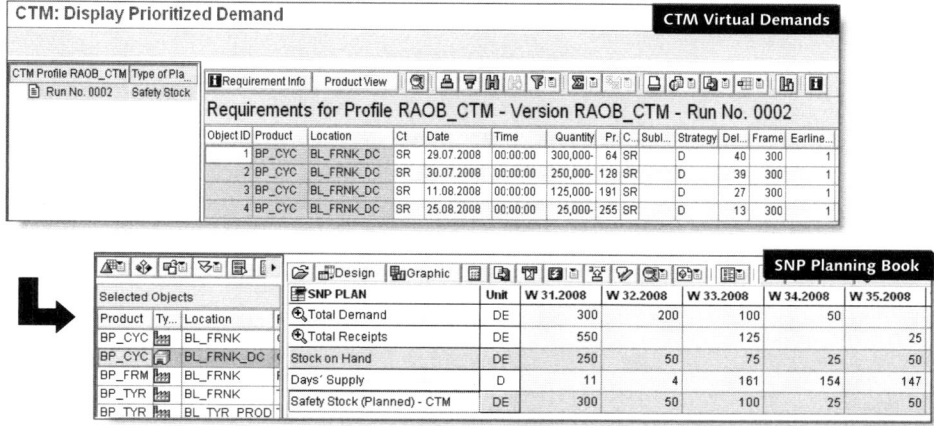

Figure 5.13 Supply Backlogs Created During Time-Varying Safety Stock Planning with the Single-Phase Method

The two-phase SS method is useful in this scenario where the SS build is required even though it causes excess supply in some time buckets. When using the two-phase method as the SS, virtual demand is generated from the planning start until the planning end. CTM will generate the virtual demands to avoid any undersupply. As shown in Figure 5.14, CTM will meet the SS requirement in CW31 but will cause oversupply in the rest of the buckets.

5 | Supply Control with CTM Planning

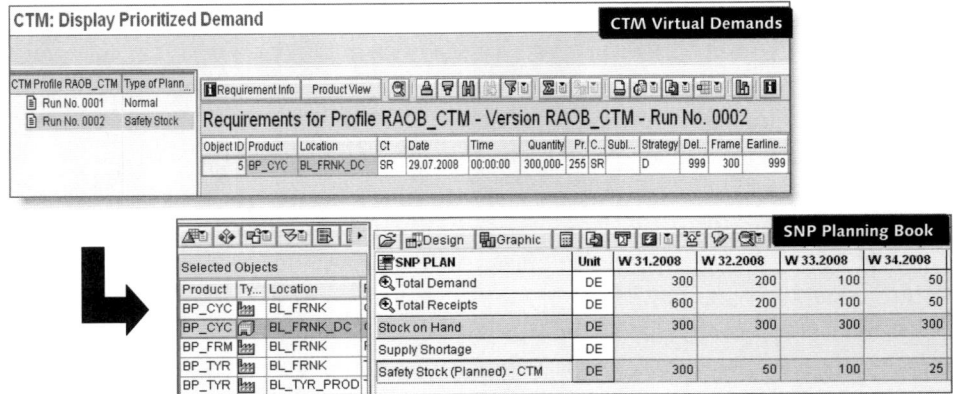

Figure 5.14 Excess Supply Created During Time Varying SS Planning with Two Phase Method

To plan for the time-phased reducing and time-varying SS more accurately, the interval planning method can be used in CTM SS planning.

5.1.4 Interval Planning with CTM for Reducing Time-Phased Safety Stock

Interval planning is the most optimal SS planning method in CTM for reducing time-phased SS. Interval planning in CTM can be enabled by using the Interval Planning option (see Figure 5.15) in the Special Strategies tab of the CTM profile. The interval is defined with the CTM time stream using the SAP Easy Access menu ADVANCED PLANNING AND OPTIMIZATION • MULTILEVEL SUPPLY AND DEMAND MATCHING • ENVIRONMENT • CURRENT SETTINGS • MAINTAIN CTM PLANNING CALENDAR.

In the interval planning method of SS planning for time-phased reducing SS, CTM planning is executed for each interval starting from the planning start time of the planning horizon. By default, the interval planning method is used with two-phase CTM SS planning; that is, CTM the two-phase method is executed for each interval until all of the intervals are planned sequentially. As a result, the SS build for the current interval is used for the normal demands of the succeeding intervals. In other words, the normal demands in the current interval can consume the SS build in the previous intervals.

CTM Planning for Safety Stock Quantity | **5.1**

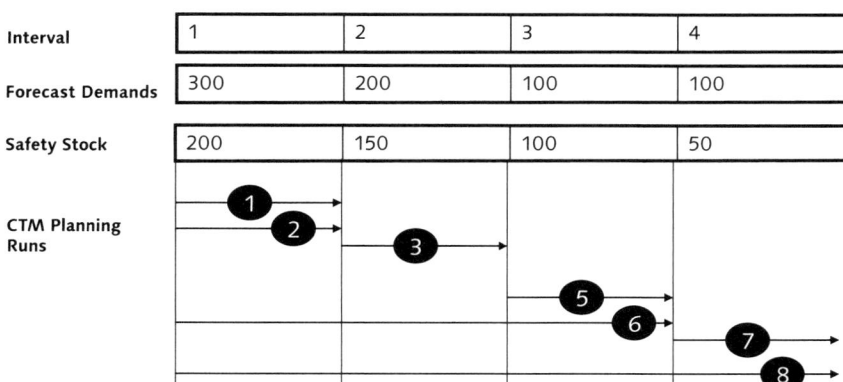

Figure 5.15 CTM Interval Planning Method for Time-Phased SS Planning

As shown in Figure 5.16, the complete CTM planning run is executed for each interval. When using the two-phase method for interval planning, the first run is used for planning the normal demands of the interval. CTM selects all of the demands inside the current interval and all supplies in the complete planning horizon. Although the demand selection is restricted by the interval duration, the supply creation is only limited by the complete planning horizon. Similarly, the supply consumption is also limited by the planning horizon.

Interval	1	2	3	4
Forecast Demands	300	200	100	100
Safety Stock	200	150	100	50
CTM Planning Runs				

Figure 5.16 CTM Interval Planning for Reducing Safety Stock Values

After the normal demands of the current interval are planned, the SS planning of the current interval is started. The SS virtual demands selection is limited by the

173

5 | Supply Control with CTM Planning

planning start and the interval end time. This is required to detect any backlogs that m might have been created by the planning of the normal demands. Runs 1, 3, 5, and 7 are executed for planning the normal demands, whereas Runs 2, 4, 6, and 8 are executed for planning SS virtual demands.

As shown in Figure 5.17, both normal and SS virtual demands that are selected for planning for each interval are displayed in the demand simulation list. Each planning run for a given interval is identified by the Run number. Each Run number signifies a complete new CTM run for the given interval and is characterized by order selection and creation from SAP liveCache, demand prioritization, supply categorization, and planning. Because CTM uses the two-phase SS planning method during interval planning, the first run signifies the planning for normal demands, and the second run for SS virtual demands.

Interval planning provides very good results for reducing SS using the two-phase method but at the cost of longer runtimes. Because each interval is planned as a separate CTM run, the runtimes of the overall CTM planning run for the complete planning horizon can be increased substantially.

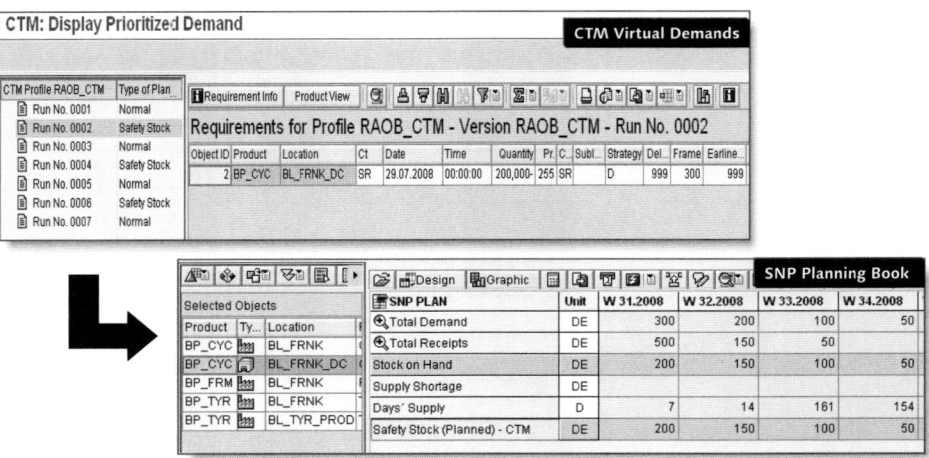

Figure 5.17 CTM Interval Planning Results for Reducing Time-Phased SS

With interval planning, only the normal demands are selected for each interval. Supply consumption and supply creation is restricted by the planning horizon and not by the planning intervals. As a result, SS virtual demands are recalculated from the planning start until the planning end of the current interval. The CTM planning parameter SSTOCK_INTERVAL can be used to limit the SS virtual demands calculation with respect to the intervals. As shown in Figure 5.18, the SS run is executed for the current interval similar to the normal demands planning.

> **Note**
>
> Refer to SAP Note 1153809 for more details about the usage of the planning parameter SSTOCK_INTERVAL.

Careful analysis must be made before using interval planning in CTM. Note that dynamic pegging can't be used when planning in the interval planning mode because CTM uses the pegged quantities to generate the SS virtual demands for each interval. If the supplies created for the SS requirement in the previous interval are dynamically pegged to any future demands, then CTM would calculate incorrect open supply and consequently incorrect SS virtual demands. Dynamic pegging creation can be avoided using the Deactivate Dynamic Pegging setting under the Demand tab for each product location in the product master. Deactivation of dynamic pegging for the products can have a negative impact on other planning tools in SAP SCM, so it must be carefully evaluated. Additionally, the intervals used in the CTM interval planning are created without any reference to the location time zone. The intervals are always created with the UTC time zone. As a result, the supply plan can be created in incorrect time buckets when planning for locations with non-UTC time zones. Although it's possible to use the single-phase planning method with interval planning, it's recommended not to combine these two methods.

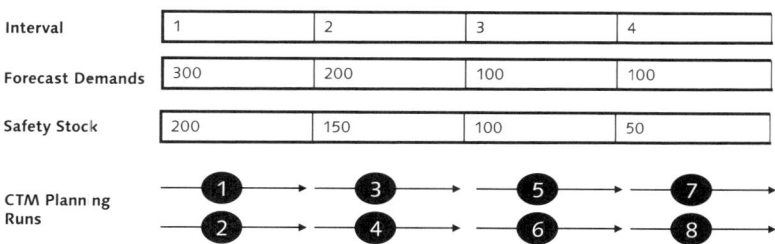

Figure 5.18 CTM Interval Planning Using the SSTOCK_INTERVAL Parameter

Table 5.2 provides a summary of the CTM SS planning methods for different SS requirements.

5 | Supply Control with CTM Planning

SS	Two Phase	Single Phase	Interval Planning
Constant SS	OK	OK	OK
Increasing SS	OK	OK	OK
Reducing SS	Excess Supply	Undersupply	OK

Table 5.2 CTM Safety Stock Planning Methods for Different Safety Stock Requirements

5.1.5 Additional Planning Parameters for CTM SS Planning

By default, CTM SS planning is executed to fulfill the SS requirements for the daily buckets. The SS virtual demands are created considering the net inventory and SS requirements for each day. All of the open demands, supplies, and SS requirements are aggregated on daily buckets to generate the net SS virtual demand at the end of day. This SS planning method provides the accurate results for the time-phased PP/DS planning mode.

When planning in the SNP bucket oriented planning mode with planning buckets greater than one day, this method can generate excess supply. If you use weekly time buckets for SNP planning in CTM and maintain the weekly SS requirements, then CTM will check for the net SS requirements for each of the weeks to fulfill the SS requirements. Any open supplies in the middle or end of the week are ignored for SS requirement calculation.

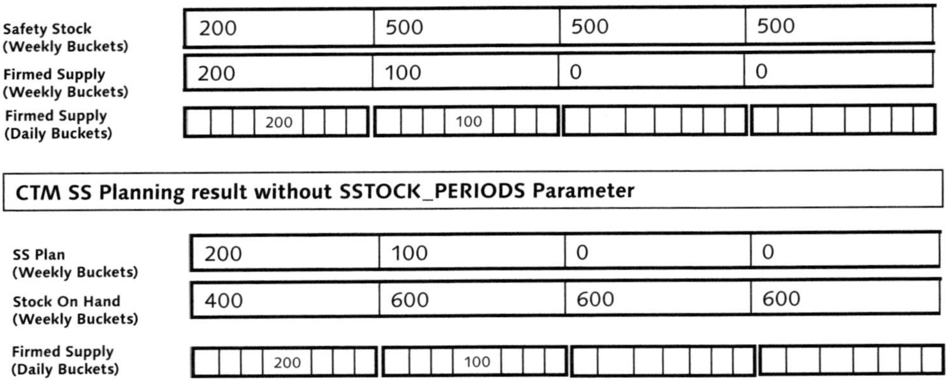

Figure 5.19 CTM Safety Stock Planning Without the SSTOCK_PERIODS Parameter

As shown in Figure 5.19, SS of 200, 500, 500, 500 is required for the weekly time buckets. In buckets 1 and 2, firmed supplies of quantity 200 and 100 exists in the middle of the week. There are no open demands in these 4 weekly buckets. In the default SS planning mode, CTM will generate the SS virtual demands to fulfill the SS requirement for each day, that is, the SS requirement of day 1 of bucket 1 and day 1 of bucket 2, ignoring the firmed supplies that are available on day 4 of each of the weekly buckets. As a result, the net stock on hand for each of the buckets will be higher than the expected SS requirements for each of the weekly buckets.

Using the CTM planning parameter SSTOCK_PERIODS with Value 1 = X, it's possible to define the buckets used for net inventory calculation. The buckets are defined in the CTM planning stream. Depending on the requirement, you can use weekly, monthly, quarterly, or yearly time buckets. As shown in Figure 5.20, when using weekly buckets for SS requirement calculation, CTM will generate the SS virtual demand at the end of the weekly bucket instead of the start of day. As a result, CTM can consider all of the open demands and firmed supplies available in the given time bucket for the calculation of net inventory. The overall stock on hand is generated according to the expected SS requirement for each time bucket.

Note

For more details about the SSTOCK_PERIODS parameter, refer to SAP Note 1001921.

Safety Stock (Weekly Buckets)	200	500	500	500
Firmed Supply (Weekly Buckets)	200	100	0	0
Firmed Supply (Daily Buckets)	200	100		

CTM SS Planning result with SSTOCK_PERIODS Parameter

SS Plan (Weekly Buckets)	0	100	0	0
Stock On Hand (Weekly Buckets)	200	500	500	500
Firmed Supply (Daily Buckets)	200	100		

Figure 5.20 CTM Safety Stock Planning with the SSTOCK_PERIODS Parameter

CTM planning is based on the individual orders in SAP liveCache, unlike SNP Heuristics where the planning can be executed based on time buckets. As a result, during SS planning for time varying SS, the existing supply is reserved for fulfilling the SS requirement of the current bucket. As you can see in Figure 5.21, the initial stock of 200 units is reserved for the SS requirement of the first time bucket. When planning for the normal demands (forecast D1, D2) available in time bucket 3 and 4, the stock (S1) isn't available for planning these demands even though the SS requirement in bucket 3 and 4 is 0. Because the planning time frame for demands D1 and D2 is only restricted by the CTM time frame, reserving supply S1 for the SS requirement ensures that the SS requirement isn't violated in the first bucket. This can cause a backlog for demands D1 and D2 if no other SOS exists. Using the Stock is Available setting, you can make the stock or any other firmed supplies available for planning demands in the future.

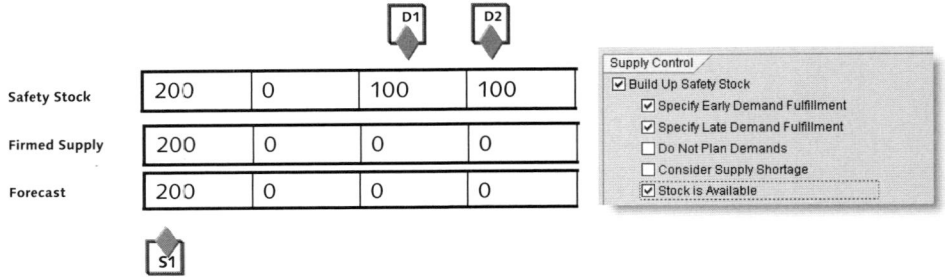

Figure 5.21 Reserving Supply for Safety Stock Requirements

5.2 CTM Planning with Safety Days of Supply

CTM SS planning with the safety days of supply (SDS) is possible using the SS methods SZ (constant SDS) and MZ (time-phased SDS). The methods SM and MM are also supported when planning for SDS. Advanced SS methods (AT, AS, BT, and BS) aren't supported in CTM SS planning. SDS planning is used in CTM to generate an inventory buffer to plan for the demand variations between the forecasted and actual demands. Unlike SS planning with SS quantity where additional stock is planned for managing the demand fluctuations, SDS planning is used to plan for the safety time for the actual demands. The supply plan is generated by CTM while considering the SDS requirement for each product. SDS can be planned for any level of the supply chain.

SDS planning in CTM is enabled using the Consider Safety Days' Supply setting under the Supply tab of the CTM profile, as you can see in Figure 5.22.

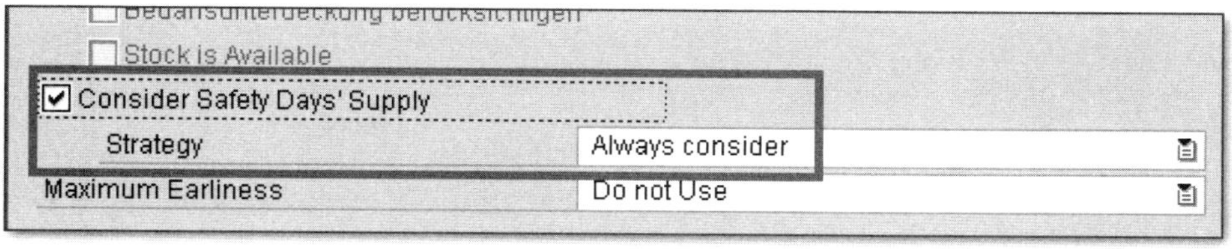

CTM Planning with Safety Days of Supply | 5.2

Figure 5.22 Safety Days of Supply Planning in the CTM Profile

SDS planning in CTM can use both the constant SDS with method SB and time-phased SDS with the MB methods that can be maintained in the product master. The constant SDS values are maintained using the Safety Day's Supply field under the Quantity and Date Determination tab of the product master. The time-phased SDS values are maintained using the time-series key figure as described in the earlier sections and shown in Figure 5.3.

5.2.1 Safety Lead Time Calculation for Constant SDS

SDS planning in CTM uses the safety lead time (SLT) method. The SDS values are converted into the SLT, which is represented in seconds. For SDS planning in CTM, the demand date of the CTM demand is adjusted using SLT.

> **Note**
>
> SDS adjusted demand date = Actual demand date - SLT

SLT is calculated based on the calendar days. The calculated SLT values can be displayed using the CTM master data check function. CTM will create the supply plan, which is SLT days ahead of the actual requirement date. The SDS adjusted demand date is used only for the CTM planning. The original demand date isn't modified in the SAP liveCache. When SLT is applied for the demand date that is near the planning start, it's possible that the SDS adjusted demand date lies before the planning start date. To avoid this situation, SLT is calculated in daily increments from the planning start date as shown in Figure 5.23. The SDS value of 10 days is converted to SLT. From the planning start date, the SLT value increases from 0 to the required value of 10 days. Based on the original demand date, the corresponding SLT interval is selected for adjusting the demand date.

5 | Supply Control with CTM Planning

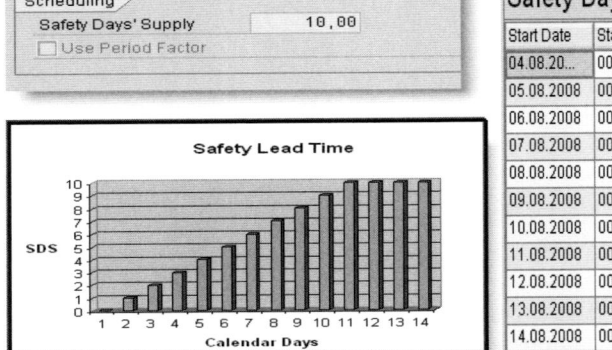

Figure 5.23 Safety Lead Time Calculation Using Constant SDS

If the product is maintained with the planned delivery time horizon, then SLT is calculated from the end of the planned delivery horizon. The incremental SLT calculation can be switched off for CTM planning using the planning parameter SSTOCK_TDS with Value1 = X.

> **Note**
>
> For more details about the SSTOCK_TDS parameter, refer to SAP Note 483694.

5.2.2 Safety Lead Time Calculation for Time-Phased SDS

CTM planning for SDS can use the time-phased SDS method MZ. In this method, the SDS values are maintained in the planning area key figure. The SLT calculation for the time-phased SDS is different from the SLT calculation for the constant SDS. For time-phased SDS, the SLT values are calculated for each day for each of the SDS values. As shown in Figure 5.24, the maximum SLT value is used for the net SLT selection for that given day. The net SLT selected for planning can be displayed using the CTM master data check function.

The CTM planning parameter SSTOCK_TDS is also valid for calculating time-phased SLT values. Using this parameter, SLT is calculated directly using the SDS value of the given bucket.

CTM Planning with Safety Days of Supply | 5.2

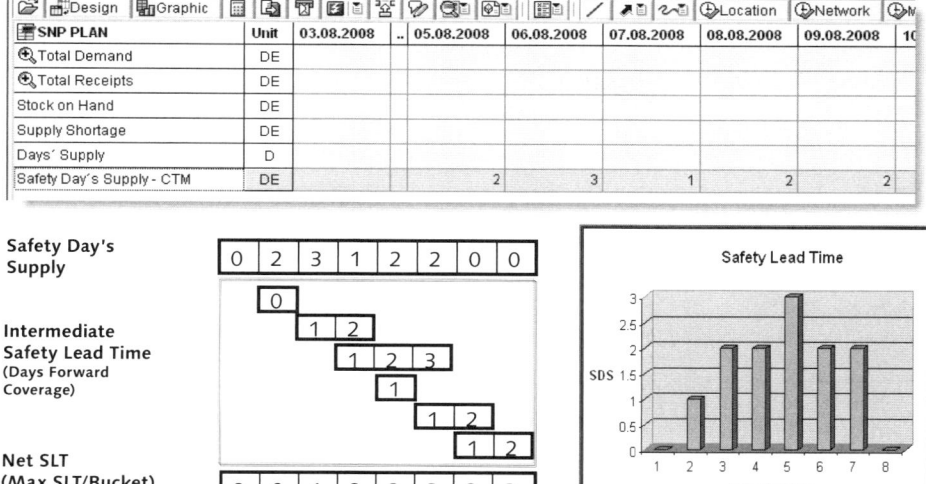

Figure 5.24 Safety Lead Time Calculation Using Time-Phased SDS

5.2.3 CTM Scheduling of Demands Using Safety Lead Time

SDS represents the days of forward coverage of the demands. Because CTM planning is demand driven, the SDS value of the product is converted to SLT, which is used during the scheduling of the demands. Unlike other demand attributes, SLT isn't demand specific and hence can't be maintained for a specific demand planned in CTM. Instead, the SLT value is a product-specific parameter that is applied for all of the demands planned for the given product.

To understand the CTM scheduling for SLT and other available parameters for SDS, it's important to understand the CTM demand tree structure. Any independent or dependent demand that is planned with CTM and is available before the CTM planning run is referred to as the top demand or primary node. All of the dependent demands generated during the CTM planning run to fulfill the primary demand are referred to as secondary demands or secondary nodes of the CTM demand tree. When scheduling with SLT, both the primary demand and the secondary demand date is adjusted according to the SLT. As illustrated in Figure 5.25, using the SLT of 5 days, the primary demand date is adjusted, and the new supply is created according to the adjusted date. For the secondary demand, the SLT of 10 days is used to adjust the demand date. The new supply is created 10 days ahead of the actual required date of the secondary demand.

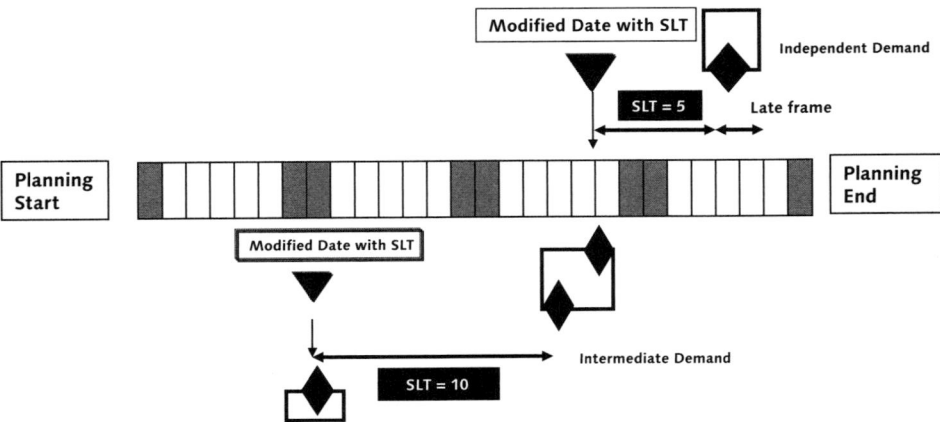

Figure 5.25 CTM Scheduling with Safety Lead Time

The primary demands can be fulfilled late when the SDS or the SLT constraint is applied. As a result, SDS/SLT is applied as a soft constraint for the primary demand; that is, if the demand isn't fulfilled using the adjusted date for the primary demand, then the demand is fulfilled late with respect to the adjusted date. Late demand strategies in the CTM profile are used to fulfill the demand late.

The LDF is calculated with respect to the original demand date of the primary demand and not the adjusted demand date. For the secondary demands, if no supply can be found in time for the adjusted demand date then it isn't possible to fulfill the secondary demand late. As a result, the SDS/SLT constraint is applied as a hard constraint for the secondary demand; that is, CTM will always try to schedule the orders to fulfill SLT for the secondary demand. This is the default CTM scheduling logic used for the SLT planning for the secondary demands. The scheduling logic for the secondary demands can be adjusted using the CTM Strategy setting (see Figure 5.26) available under the Supplies tab of the CTM profile. Note that the Strategy settings are applied only for the secondary demands and not for the primary demands planned in CTM.

CTM Planning with Safety Days of Supply | 5.2

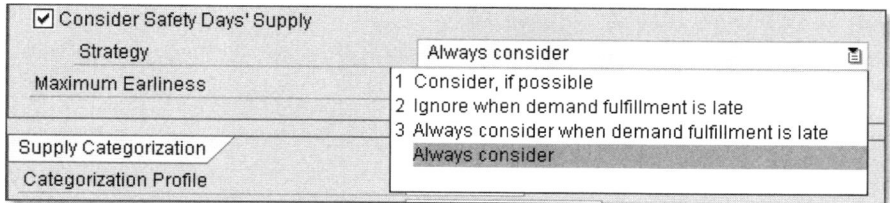

Figure 5.26 Scheduling Strategy for Secondary Demands Using Safety Lead Time

The following options are available for the scheduling strategy of secondary demand using SLT:

- **Always consider**
  In this mode, the primary demand is planned considering the SLT for secondary demands in both the in-time and late planning mode. If the primary demand can't be satisfied using the SLT of the secondary demands, then the primary demand is fulfilled late using the SLT of the secondary demands.

- **Consider, if possible**
  In this mode, the primary demand is planned first by considering the SLT of the secondary demand. If the demand can't be satisfied in-time, then the SLT for the secondary demand is ignored. If the primary demand can't be satisfied even by ignoring the SLT of the secondary demand, then the primary demand is fulfilled late using the SLT of the secondary demand. If any remaining quantity exists for the primary demand, then the primary demand is fulfilled late by ignoring the SLT for the secondary demand.

- **Ignore when demand fulfillment is late**
  In this mode, the primary demand is planned first by considering the SLT of the secondary demand. If the demand can't be satisfied in-time, then the SLT for the secondary demand is ignored. If the primary demand can't be satisfied even by ignoring the SLT of the secondary demand, then the primary demand is fulfilled late ignoring the SLT of the secondary demand. In this mode, when the primary demand is fulfilled late, then the SLT for the secondary demand is completely ignored.

- **Always consider when demand fulfillment is late**
  In this mode, the primary demand is planned first by considering the SLT of the secondary demand. If the demand can't be satisfied in time, then the SLT for the secondary demand is ignored. If the primary demand can't be satisfied even by

183

ignoring the SLT of the secondary demand, then the primary demand is fulfilled late using the SLT of the secondary demand. In this mode, when the primary demand is fulfilled late, then the SLT for the secondary demand is always applied.

To better understand these scheduling strategies used for the secondary demands, consider the following possible cases:

- **Case A:** On-time demand with SDS applied for secondary demands.
- **Case B:** On-time demand without SDS applied for secondary demands.
- **Case C:** Late demand with SDS applied for secondary demands.
- **Case D:** Late demand without SDS applied for secondary demands.

Based on these cases, the sequence shown in Table 5.3 is used for each of the scheduling strategies:

SDS Strategy	Scheduling Sequence
Always consider	Case A , Case C
Consider, if possible	Case A , Case B, Case C , Case D
Ignore when demand fulfillment is late	Case A , Case B, Case D
Always consider when demand fulfillment is late	Case A , Case B, Case C

Table 5.3 Scheduling Strategies

SS planning with SDS is applied in both the forward scheduling mode and the backward scheduling mode. SDS planning can be successfully used for all of the levels of the supply chain. The SDS values are applied to the primary and secondary demands in the CTM engine with a single planning run, unlike the SS planning with quantity where the second CTM planning run is required to plan for the SS quantities. As a result, it's generally recommended to use the SS planning using SDS.

5.3 Additional CTM Supply Control Techniques

CTM planning offers several supplementary supply control techniques in addition to the SS and SDS planning. CTM planning is demand driven, where the supply plan is created with respect to the requirement date. When planning in the backward scheduling mode, CTM will create the supply as close to the demand date as possible. When planning in a multilocation supply chain network with capacity constraints, supply build up at certain locations can be undesirable. To balance the inventory across the supply chain network, the CTM Store Transport and Prod. at Destination Location function and the Execute Supply Distribution after CTM run function can be used. It's important to understand that the CTM techniques offer very limited functions as compared to more advanced functions offered in SAP SCM (deployment, TLB). Additional functions such as minimum build (MB) in CTM can be used to generate the minimum supplies irrespective of the demand situation.

5.3.1 Store Transport at Destination Location

In backward scheduling mode, CTM will create the supply plan in a multilocation supply chain network, as shown in Figure 5.27. The demand of 100 units at the distribution center (DC) is fulfilled by the stock transfer order with the receipt date close to the demand date. The distribution requirement at the production plant can be fulfilled much earlier than the required date due to capacity constraints. In this case, the planned order is scheduled according to the available capacity, and the produced quantity is stored at the plant. The produced quantity is shipped at a much later time to ensure that the product arrives at the DC in time.

This solution meets the just-in-time requirement for the DC but isn't optimal for production plant due to high storage costs. In this scenario, you want to produce and ship the product immediately from the production plant. The produce and ship strategy can be applied in CTM using the Store Transport and Prod. Substitution Receipts at Destination Location setting. Using this technique, CTM will schedule the transport and substitution orders as close as possible with the supplies to minimize the storage costs at all levels of the supply chain. The produce and ship strategy is shown in Figure 5.27. The produce and ship strategy is similar to using the maximum pegging length (MPL) constraint of 0 seconds at the production plant. The main difference is that the MPL constraint is applied as a hard constraint for the demand, whereas the Store Transport and Prod. Substitution Receipts at Destination Location setting is applied as a soft constraint. CTM will try to produce and ship as early as possible.

5 | Supply Control with CTM Planning

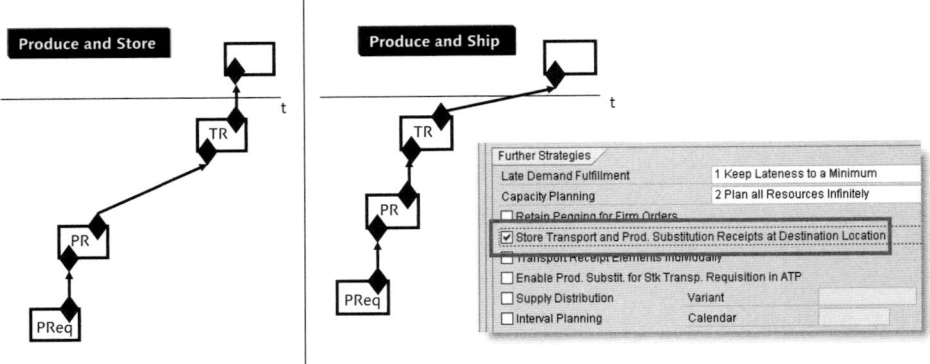

Figure 5.27 Store Transport and Prod. Substitution at Destination Location

If multiple planned orders or firmed supplies are used for fulfilling the distribution requirement, then the latest supply limits the earliest ship date for the transport order. This method is useful for situations where you want to combine the production quantity into one transport order. On the other hand, due to high storage costs, you want to ship the individual planned orders or firmed supplies immediately. In this scenario, CTM will create individual transfer orders for each of the planned orders and supplies. The techniques can be enabled using the Transport Receipts Elements Individually setting available in the Further Strategies tab of the CTM profile. As shown in Figure 5.28, when the Store Transport and Prod. Receipts at Destination Location setting is combined with the Transport Receipts Elements Individually setting, CTM will produce and immediately ship the products individually.

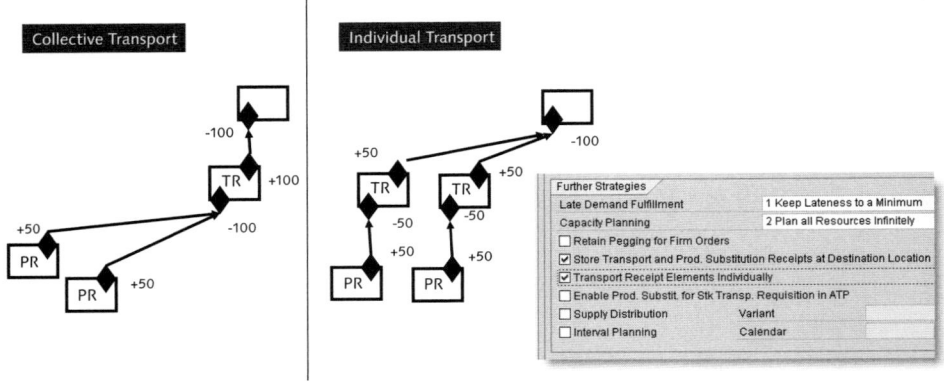

Figure 5.28 Transport Receipt Objects Individually

186

The produce and ship immediately strategy is applied to all levels of the supply chain and for all products planned in the CTM profile. For certain SC Models that include warehouse for the raw materials, it isn't optimal to ship the raw materials immediately to the production plant. Similarly, the produce and ship strategy isn't optimal for all location products planned in the CTM profile.

5.3.2 Supply Distribution

The Supply Distribution function in CTM is used to transfer excess inventory to the succeeding locations of the supply chain. CTM supply distribution (SD) offers very restricted functions as compared to the SNP deployment function. As shown in Figure 5.29, the CTM SD function can be started using the Transaction /SAPAPO/CTM10 or using the SAP Easy Access menu ADVANCED PLANNING AND OPTIMIZATION • MULTILEVEL SUPPLY AND DEMAND MATCHING • PLANNING • SUPPLY DISTRIBUTION.

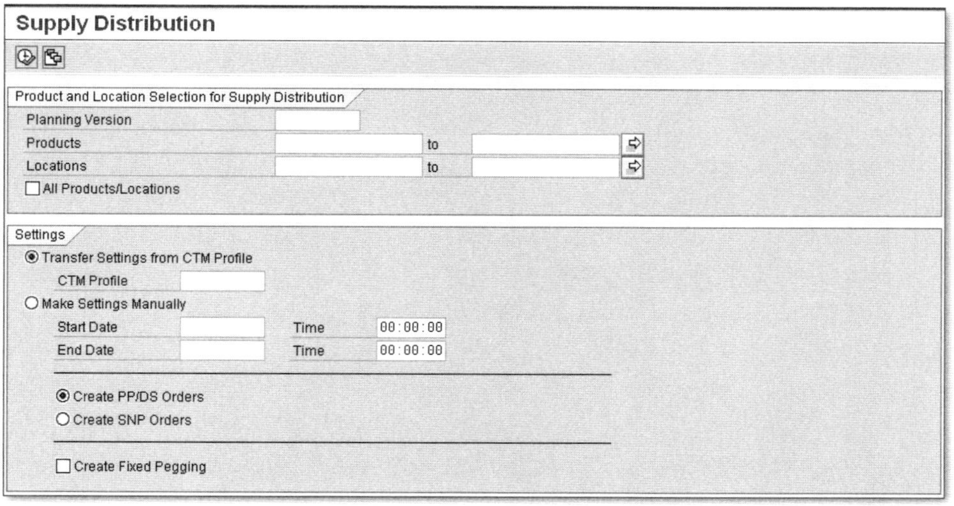

Figure 5.29 CTM Supply Distribution

CTM SD is executed only for a single level; that is, the transfer of unrestricted-use receipts or supplies is created for one location at a time. The stock transfer orders are created using the transport lanes between locations. All of the transport lanes used for SD must have outbound quota values from the source location to the destination location. The available supplies selected for distribution are split according to the outbound quota for the each of the destination locations. All individual supplies are aggregated using the daily buckets before distributing the supplies.

If the time-phased quota is used, then the supply availability date is used for selecting the appropriate interval. The stock transfer order is scheduled using the forward scheduling mode from the supply available date. Until SAP SCM 5.0, CTM SD doesn't consider the transport lot size, GR/GI time, or transport and handling resources. Scheduling of stock transfer orders for SD considers only the shipping, transport, and receiving calendars. SD isn't supported for the subcontracting transportation lanes.

In the SAP SCM 5.1, the CTM SD function is enhanced to consider transport lot size, GR/GI time, and transport and handling resources similar to the scheduling of normal transfer orders. As shown in Figure 5.30, the CTM SD function itself can be started from the CTM profile under the Supply Distribution tab. Using the Execute Supply Distribution after CTM run setting, the SD is started immediately after the CTM run in both the online and batch mode. The Allow Multiple Distribution setting can be used to combine residual supplies when planning with transport lot sizes.

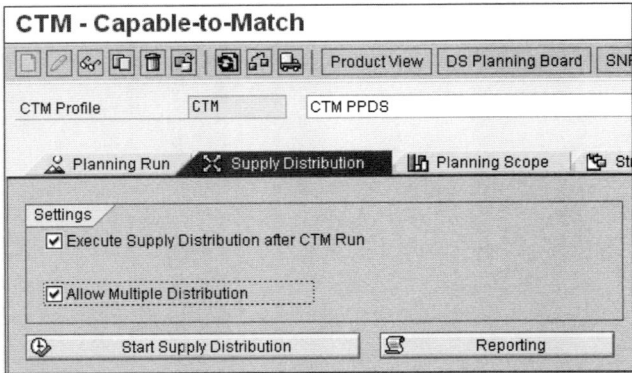

Figure 5.30 CTM Supply Distribution Function in SAP SCM 5.1

5.3.3 Minimum Build of Supply

Another important technique used for supply control in CTM is the minimum build (MB) planning function. The MB planning function is available in CTM starting from SAP SCM 5.1. This function is used mainly in the high-tech industries, where the contract manufacturers expect a constant production irrespective of the demand. To use the production capacities optimally and constantly, the MB quantity is agreed with the manufacturer. CTM will create the planned orders to fulfill the MB requirements even if there are no demands. If the normal demand exists, then the MB supplies can be used for satisfying the normal demands.

The MB function is enabled in the CTM profile using the Plan Min. Receipts Quantity setting available in the Further Strategies tab of the CTM profile. The MB values are maintained using the SNP planning area time-series key figure. The time-series function Minimum Receipt Quantity (see Figure 5.31) is used to select the planning area key figure similar to the selection of time-phased SS and SDS as described in the earlier sections. When planning with production lot sizes or capacity constraint the production quantity may be smaller or larger than the required MB quantity. Using the Balance Surplus and Shortfall Quantity setting, you can transfer the excess or shortfall quantity of the current bucket to the next bucket. Based on the MB bucket size, CTM limits the time frame for order creation for the MB quantity.

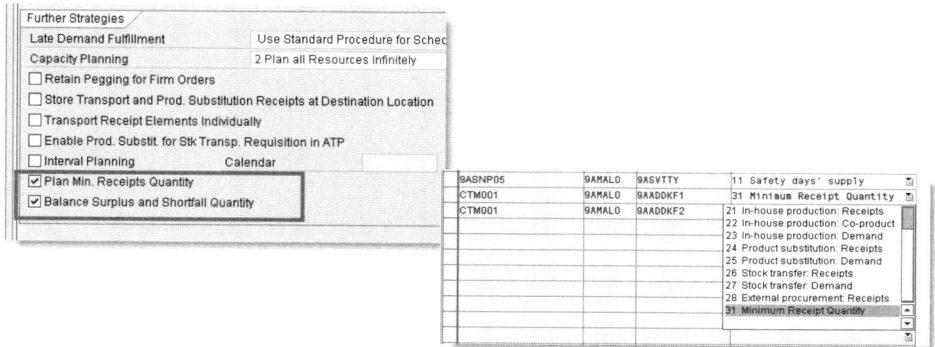

Figure 5.31 CTM Minimum Build for Production Available in SAP SCM 5.1

5.4 Summary

In this chapter, you learned about the various safety stock (SS) planning techniques available in CTM. You now understand the advantages and disadvantages of each of the planning modes. The configuration settings required for SS planning using SS quantity and safety lead time is explained in detail. Planning for time-varying SS is very complex, and you learned different options available in CTM to plan for time-varying SS. You also learned the CTM virtual demand calculation process.

Additional supply control techniques using supply distribution (SD) and minimum build (MB) are introduced in the next chapter. These functions are available in SAP SCM 5.1.

In the next chapter, you'll learn about the advanced planning techniques that are available in CTM. You'll also learn about requirement strategies and planning with hierarchies.

This chapter introduces you to advanced CTM planning functions by leveraging the knowledge gained in the earlier chapters. Planning with requirement strategies is explained in detail. Supply chain planning processes within a plant are also introduced in this chapter.

6   Advanced Planning Techniques with CTM

CTM planning is mainly used for generating the multilocation constrained supply plan. In addition, CTM planning offers several advanced planning functions that you can use for cross-location planning and planning within a production plant. Planning with requirement strategies is also possible with CTM planning. The requirement strategies in SAP SCM define how the forecast is consumed by sales orders and distribution requirements and how the production is planned for the unconsumed forecast orders. Apart from the Make To Stock (MTS) requirement strategy, CTM planning can also be used for planning products with other requirement strategies.

Planning with the special procurement key Production in Alternative Location is used in CTM to plan for requirements in planning location and create the actual production in the production location. This special procurement is useful in planning scenarios where the production plant doesn't have any storage facility for the finished product. The distribution center (DC) is mainly responsible for planning the finished product. The DC and the production location represent either logical locations without any transport time or physical locations that are very close to each other and hence don't have any significant transport time relevant for planning.

CTM planning can be used to plan for the supply chain within a production plant modeled using storage location MRP areas. The storage locations in SAP SCM are defined as locations of type 1007 and are similar to other locations that can be used for supply chain planning. Using the special procurement key Stock Transfer from Plant to MRP Area, the SAP ERP application automatically creates the transport lanes in SAP SCM between the plant and the MRP area location. You can use these lanes in CTM for supply planning. You can use the Component Withdrawal in Another Location function to create the requirements of the planned order in a specific storage location MRP area without using the transport lanes across the MRP area storage location and the production plant.

You can use MTO planning without forecast in CTM to generate the supply plan according to a sales order in the MTO segment.

If you're working with several subcontractors, you'll want to use the procurement planning process with subcontracting scenario. In this form of procurement planning, the subcontractor is responsible for the production of the finished product, and the plant supplies the components. CTM planning can also be used to create the subcontracting purchase requisitions using the subcontracting transport lanes.

In addition, you can use Planning with Product Interchangeability in CTM to plan for simple discontinuation of products to consider phasing out old products. By using interchangeability master data for discontinuation, you can model the phase-out of certain products and introduce new products without changing existing definitions or master and transaction data. CTM planning will only use the supplies for the predecessor or discontinued products and create new supplies for the successor products.

CTM planning can also consider Form-Fit-Function (FFF) classes to group multiple products that are similar in form, fit, and function. In this case, the existing supply for each member of the FFF class is mutually interchangeable for the requirements but the new procurement is created only for the leading product of the FFF class. You'll use the FFF classes for supply planning when you have several products with different part numbers, but all of the products have the same attributes.

When you want to substitute products, you can use the Planning with ATP Substitution Rules function, which is also supported in CTM planning. By using substitution rules defined in the ATP rules, CTM can use the supply for the substitute products. You can also use a special planning process called down binning in CTM using the ATP substitution rules when the production process can use the substitution rules for generating optimal output quantity.

And, finally, aggregated planning using hierarchy in CTM is possible in SAP SCM 5.0 and is tightly integrated with the SAP Apparel and Footwear. By using aggregated planning, you can create constraint supply plans at the aggregate product level after inventory netting at the detailed product level. The aggregated supply plan can be disaggregated to the detail level before the transferring the data back to SAP ERP for order execution.

In the next section, you'll learn about the functions offered in CTM for planning with different requirement strategies that are available in SAP SCM.

6.1 CTM Planning with Requirement Strategies

SAP SCM offers several planning strategies for planning the products. We'll look at each of these in detail beginning with Demand Planning (DP), which is used in SAP SCM to generate the forecast or planned independent requirements (PIR) that form the basis for the supply and production planning in SNP and PP/DS. The requirement strategy defines how the forecast quantities in SAP APO DP are produced and how the demand forecast is consumed with the incoming sales orders.

The MTS production strategy is commonly used for planning when the production process is very consistent, and the production plan isn't influenced by the sales orders. With MTS, the PIR is the key requirement used for planning and for creation pegging relationships. With the MTO strategy, however, sales orders are used for requirements, not PIR. CTM planning can use both PIR and sales orders as requirements for planning, so you can plan using both the Make To Stock (MTS) and MTO strategies.

To really understand the CTM planning process for requirements strategy, it's important to understand the basic components of the requirement strategy shown in Figure 6.1. The requirement strategy in SAP SCM can be defined in SAP customization using the menu path IMG • ADVANCED PLANNING AND OPTIMIZATION • MASTER DATA • PRODUCT • SPECIFY REQUIREMENT STRATEGY.

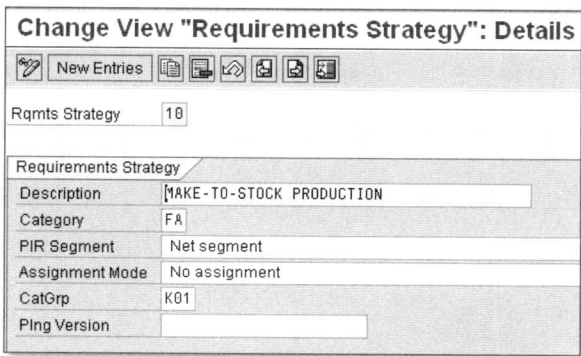

Figure 6.1 Requirements Strategy in SAP SCM

193

The requirement strategy in SAP SCM contains the following attributes:

- **PIR Segment**
  PIR Segment defines the planning segment in which PIR is created during the forecast release process from DP to SNP. In MTS planning, the forecast is created in the net segment 0. The planning segments 1 and 2 are used for the Planning Without Final Assembly strategy. The PIR segment is used in defining the peg area for the product location. The forecast order and the planned order are created in the peg area corresponding to the planning segment 1. The dependent requirements for the product are generated in the net segment 0.

- **Assignment Mode**
  The assignment mode determines how sales orders consume the forecast and whether final assembly is taken into account. No forecast consumption is carried out if the Assignment Mode 0 is selected.

- **CatGrp (category group)**
  CatGrp defines the ATP categories of the requirements in SAP SCM that can consume the forecast. You can select one or more categories in the category group.

The definition of the requirement strategy is mainly used for forecast consumption and requirement planning. The forecast consumption function is available as a generic function in SAP SCM and doesn't differ for CTM planning. The setting for the planning segment is used for CTM planning to determine the demands and creation of the supply in the respective planning segments. The requirement strategy defined in the customization is assigned to the product in the product master using the Proposed Strategy field available under the Demand tab.

SAP SCM delivers four standard requirement strategies (as described in the following sections):

- Make-to-Stock Production (10)
- Planning with Final Assembly (20)
- Planning Without Final Assembly (30)
- Planning with Planning Product (40)

6.1.1 Make-to-Stock Production (10)

You'll use the Make-to-Stock Production strategy if your sales orders don't influence production. The supply plan is mainly created with reference to the planned forecast orders. And because the sales orders don't influence the production, there's no consumption of the forecast by incoming sales orders. CTM planning for the MTS strategy is very straightforward because CTM simply selects all of the demands in the net segment and then creates the supplies in the net segment. You can apply this strategy for the products in SAP SCM using the Proposed Strategy setting of 10, and the corresponding strategy in SAP ERP is also strategy 10.

6.1.2 Planning with Final Assembly (20)

Planning with Final Assembly is used if you can accurately forecast production quantities for the final product. The net demand calculation for CTM planning takes into account both the forecast demand and the sales order. The sales orders can consume the forecast; as a result, the production quantity proposed by CTM will be according to the net demand. The advantage of this strategy is that you can react quickly to customer demand. The key element of this strategy is forecast consumption, which is executed outside the CTM planning run in SAP liveCache. The net demand is calculated in SAP liveCache, and the CTM planning uses only the net demand for planning. As a result, the planning process in CTM isn't influenced and follows the standard CTM planning process. You can apply this strategy for the products in SAP SCM using the Proposed Strategy setting of 20. The corresponding strategy in the SAP ERP is strategy 40.

Due to the multilevel planning logic used in CTM, the Planning at Assembly Level strategy can't be used in CTM. In this strategy, forecasts are generated for the assembly, and during planning of the finished products, dependent requirements and stock transport requirements can also be generated for the assembly. Using this strategy, the dependent requirements for the forecast consume the forecast for the assembly. This strategy is enabled using the Assembly Planning field in the product master for the Planning with Final Assembly requirement strategy.

When CTM is used for multilocation planning, the dependent requirements generated during the CTM assembly runs don't consume the forecast for the assembly. Remember that the forecast consumption is carried out in liveCache and not in the CTM engine. As a result, CTM can generate excess supply for the assembly when the planning results are saved in SAP liveCache. To overcome this limitation, you can re-execute CTM planning for the assembly to plan for the net demand generated after forecast consumption. This is possible only when you use the infinite planning mode in CTM.

6 | Advanced Planning Techniques with CTM

6.1.3 Planning Without Final Assembly (30)

The Planning Without Final Assembly strategy is used for the products if the main value-added process is final assembly. The planned order for final assembly itself depends on the sales orders. This strategy can be used to plan for the components before the sales orders are created to provide quicker response for fulfilling the sales order requirements. This strategy can be applied for the products in SAP SCM using the Proposed Strategy setting of 30. The corresponding strategy in SAP ERP is strategy 50. The forecast for the finished product is consumed by the forecast and triggers the production of the planned order for the finished product. The forecast order for the finished product is created in the special planning segment 1 and hence is segregated from other demands. Using the assignment mode Assign Customer Requirement to Planning Without Assembly, the sales orders can consume the forecast in planning segment 1.

CTM planning can be used for planning products with the Planning Without Final Assembly strategy. This strategy is used mainly for the products that are produced in-house, that is, products at the production plant. CTM doesn't plan for demands in planning segment 1 if the demands are created for the DC or a location where no production is allowed. The first step to fulfilling the demand in the planning segment 1 must be a planned order. Using this planning strategy, the forecasts are created in the planning segment 1. CTM selects the demands in planning segment 1. Demand aggregation in CTM can aggregate the demands in this planning segment. Note that the demand aggregation across the planning segments isn't possible. The demands in planning segment 1 and net segment 0 can't be aggregated. CTM demand prioritization is applied like normal demands and doesn't defer to the demands in planning segment 1. The demands are planned using the same sourcing logic as normal demands. The demand details can be displayed using the demand simulation list. The Planning Segment field can be used to display the planning segment assigned to the demand. The planning sequence for the product is shown in Figure 6.2. The forecast or the PIR is released in planning segment 1 based on the requirement strategy 30, which is used for the product in the production location. CTM uses the normal source determination procedure to select the in-house production alternative (PPM/PDS). The planned orders for the finished product is created in planning segment 1, but the dependent requirements for the components of the planned order are created in the net segment 0. The rest of the BOM or the supply chain is planned as usual in CTM.

CTM Planning with Requirement Strategies | 6.1

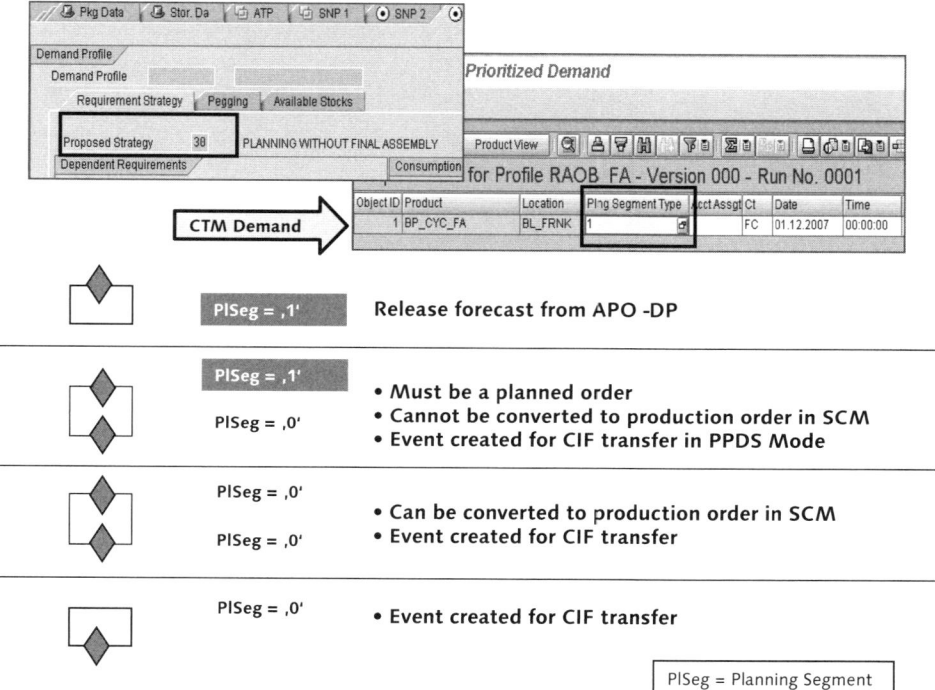

Figure 6.2 CTM Planning with Requirement Strategy 30

The planned order created for the finished product can't be converted to the production order because the production for the finished product is only triggered with the sales order. As shown in Figure 6.3, the Plng w/o Final Assem (Planning Without Final Assembly) flag is set for the planned orders created for the finished products. When attempting to convert these planned orders, the system checks the definition of conversion rules to check whether the conversion of the planned order is allowed. Normally, you'll allow conversion of the planned order created for the Planning Without Final Assembly strategy when the planned order is pegged to a sales order. When the SAP SCM system is integrated with the SAP ERP application for execution, the CTM-created planned orders are transferred to SAP ERP only when CTM planning uses PP/DS planning mode. In the SNP bucket-planning mode using CTM, the change pointers for the planned orders for the finished product aren't created. The planned orders and transfer orders for the rest of the supply chain are transferred to the SAP ERP application as usual.

6 | Advanced Planning Techniques with CTM

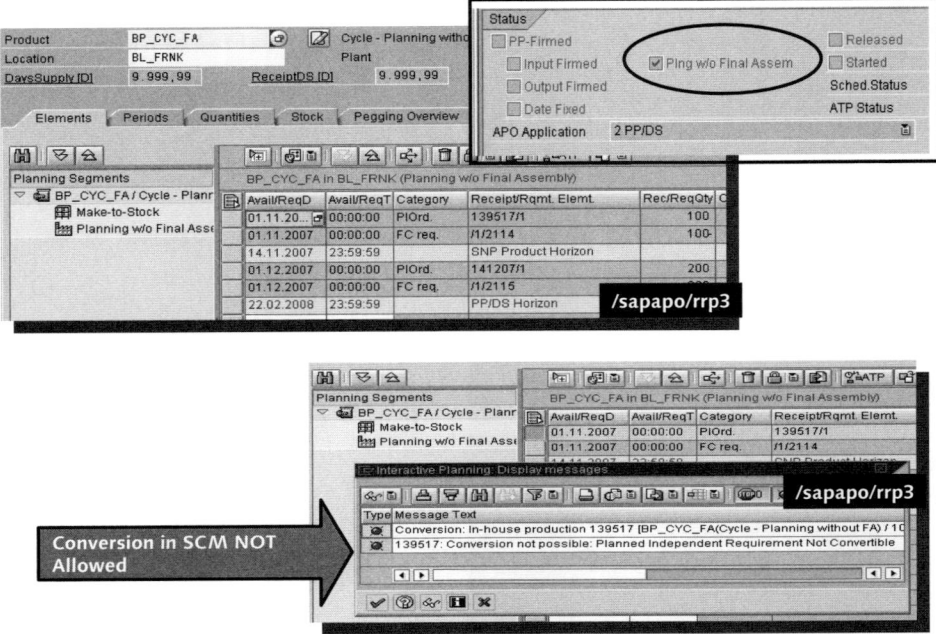

Figure 6.3 CTM Planned Orders Created for Strategy Planning Without Final Assembly

Note that strategy 30 isn't supported for the safety stock (SS) planning in CTM. The SS virtual demands in CTM are created always in net segment 0. The existing demands in planning segment 1 aren't considered for SS planning. Generally, SS planning with methods (SB, MB) must not be used. On the other hand, the SS planning for safety days of supply (SDS) is supported for strategy 30 and hence can be used in CTM planning for both SZ and MZ methods.

Table 6.1 shows the summary of the allowed functions for the Planning Without Final Assembly strategy in CTM planning using PP/DS or SNP mode.

CTM Planning Mode	Demand Selection	Order Conversion	SAP ERP Integration
SNP	YES	NO	NO
PP/DS	YES	NO	YES

Table 6.1 Allowed Functions for the Planning Without Final Assembly Strategy

CTM planning for the Planning Without Final Assembly strategy is supported in both SNP and PP/DS planning modes, but only the order created in the PP/DS mode can be published to SAP ERP.

6.1.4 Planning with Planning Product (40)

The Planning with Planning Product strategy is used to plan for groups of similar finished products that are represented by the planning product. This strategy ensures a rapid response to customer demand and is particularly useful for products that have a long manufacturing lead time. The planning product can be either a fictive entity that is never produced or a product that is actually produced. This strategy can be applied for the products in SAP SCM using the Proposed Strategy setting of 40. The corresponding strategy in SAP ERP is strategy 60. In the SAP ERP application, you have to define the planning product and assign the finished products to the planning product. Using the SAP standard function in CIF, the system creates the products in SAP SCM and groups the finished products and the planning product using the hierarchy definition. Using DP, the forecast or the PIR requirements are created for the planning product. The forecast for the planning product is consumed using the individual sales orders of the finished products. The net demand for the planning product is used for CTM planning to generate the constrained supply plan for the planning product. All of the relevant master data for planning must be maintained for the planning product during the CTM planning run. Any open supplies that exist for the finished products aren't available during the CTM planning of the planning product's demand. Similarly, the SS requirements for the finished products also don't influence the SS requirements for the planning product.

6.2 Make to Order Production with CTM

The MTO production process is used where the production process is based on sales orders. The planned orders are generated for specific sales orders and are linked to the sales orders. The sales orders in SAP SCM are created in the individual customer segments. Each individual customer segment is defined using the account ID, which is a combination of the sales order number, line item, and the logical SAP ERP application where the sales order is created. SAP SCM automatically creates a new peg area for each of the individual sales orders created in the customer segment. The planned orders created for the sales orders are also created

6 | Advanced Planning Techniques with CTM

in the customer segment to ensure that the planned orders aren't pegged to other requirements. The MTO sales orders can be selected for CTM planning similar to the normal demands. The MTO customer segment can be displayed using the demand simulation list in the CTM profile. The Acct Assgt (Account Assignment) field displays the customer segment of the sales order in the detail screen. The sales order in the MTO scenario can trigger production and create the planned order in the MTO segment. Demand functions such as demand aggregation can't be executed for the demands in different MTO customer segments because they belong to different peg areas. Demand prioritization, on the other hand, can be used for MTO sales orders similar to normal demands. During planning, the source selection for MTO demands that you use the same selection logic for MTO demands and normal demands. As you can see in Figure 6.4, the demands and the corresponding supplies are created in the MTO segment and can be displayed in the product view.

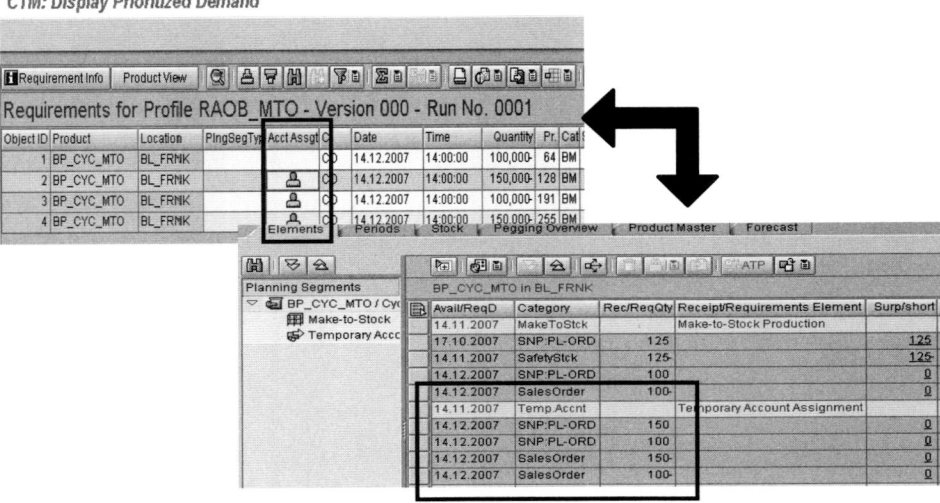

Figure 6.4 Make To Order Planning with CTM

The MTO planned order can be created with the dependent requirements also in the MTO segment. Using the Possible Individual Customer Requirement setting in the product master, CTM can create the dependent requirements and the supplies in the MTO segment. The MTO supplies for dependent requirements are assigned to the given sales order and are created with the lot-for-lot specification. You can also use the Always Collect Requirement option, and, in this case, CTM creates dependent and stock transfer requirements for the product in the MTO segment or the net segment 0. The requirements are covered from the storage location stock that is used for general purposes. If the storage location stock isn't sufficient, then CTM will create new orders using source determination (see Figure 6.5). If you use this option, the sales orders in different MTO segments can be fulfilled using the combined order for the dependent demands in the MTS segment.

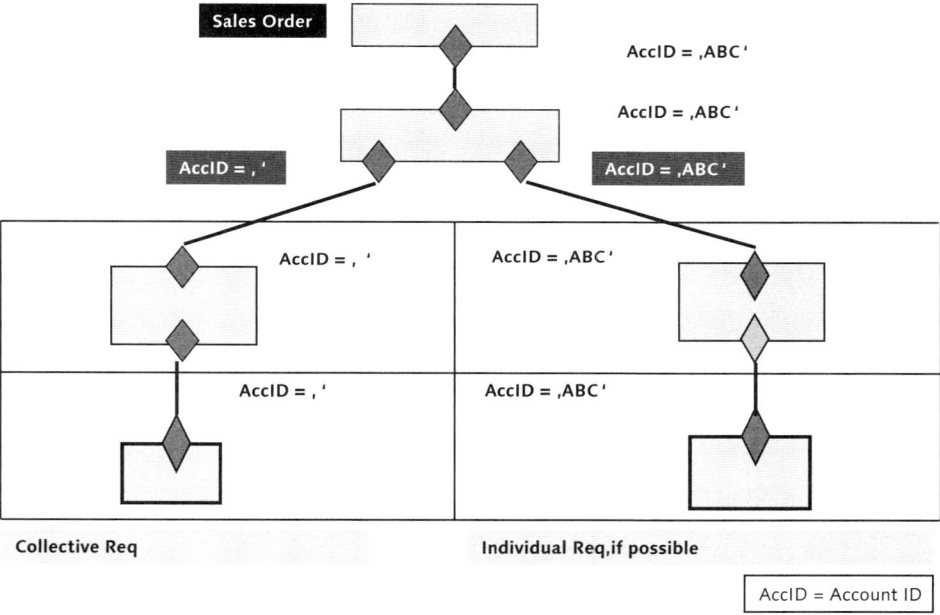

Figure 6.5 Collective and Individual Requirement Creation for MTO Planning in CTM

CTM planning for MTO sales orders can be used in both PP/DS and SNP planning modes. Planning with MTO sales orders is enabled by default in PP/DS planning mode, whereas in the SNP bucket planning mode, the MTO sales orders are selected for CTM planning using the planning parameter BUCKET_MAKE_TO_ORDER with Value 1 = X.

> **Note**
>
> CTM planning for the MTO sales orders in bucket planning mode is available using the planning parameter BUCKET_MAKE_TO_ORDER.
>
> For more details about this parameter, refer to SAP Note 996299.

6 | Advanced Planning Techniques with CTM

When you use CTM planning in the SNP bucket mode and the SNP planning book is used for display of the CTM planning results, you need to pay special attention to the display of the orders in the MTO segment and planning segment 1 used for planning without final assembly because in the capacity view, the MTO planned orders aren't considered. However, if you use the BAdI /SAPAPO/SDP_INTERACT and method GET_KEYF_SPECIALS, it's possible to display the orders in the SNP planning book from the MTO segment and planning segment 1. As of SAP SCM 4.0, orders or stocks can be displayed in interactive SNP planning, orders from forecasting without final assembly, or the sum of both segments. You can use the key figure functions 2006 and 2008 instead of the key figure semantics.

In addition, you can select the orders for display by implementing the BAdI method /SAPAPO/SDP_INTERACT → GET_KEYF_SPECIALS. The parameter CV_KEYF_SWITCH available in the BAdI can be set as shown here:

- 2 = Make-to-Order Production
- 3 = Make-to-Order Production + Forecast without Final Assembly
- 4 = Forecast without Final Assembly

When you set the parameter CV_KEYF_SWITCH to 3, the orders from the subcontracting planning segment as well as the orders from the MTO production planning segment are displayed in the key figure defined for the MTO production.

Table 6.2 shows the summary of the SAP SCM requirement strategies with respect to the SAP ERP strategies.

Requirement Strategy	SAP APO	SAP ERP
Make-To-Stock Production	10	10
Planning with Final Assembly	20	40
Planning at Assembly level	20 (Subassembly)	70
Planning Without Final Assembly	30	50
Planning with Planning Material	40	60
Make-to-Order Production	NA	20

Table 6.2 Summary of SAP SCM Requirement Strategies Available in CTM

6.3 Production in Alternative Location

The Production in Alternative Location strategy is a special form of planning available for in-house production. Using this special procurement function, you can define a planning location that is different from the production location. The planning location is used for planning the requirements for the finished products, and the production location is used for the actual production of the finished product. In the supply chain where the production and planning locations aren't geographically separated — so the transportation times aren't significant — you can use the Production in Alternative Location planning strategy. This form of planning doesn't consider any transport durations; however, so the advanced transportation planning tools such as deployment and TPVS (transportation planning and vehicle scheduling) can't be used with this planning strategy.

The Production in Alternative Location strategy is enabled in the SAP ERP application using the special procurement key 80 – Production in Alternative Plant, which is defined for the material in the SAP ERP material master. The special procurement key for the planning location contains the alternative plant or the production plant where the actual production is carried out. The production version is created in the production location. If you use the standard CIF, the system will generate the production alternatives (PPM/PDS) in the SAP SCM system as shown in Figure 6.6. The system generates two PPM/PDSs. One PPM/PDS is the normal PPM/PDS of type 002 and is created for the production planning at the production location. The second PPM/PDS is of type 006 and is created with the planning location and the production location. This special PPM/PDS of type 006 doesn't contain any plan but is based on the plan of the normal PPM/PDS. The validity of this PPM/PDS is also not restricted by the normal PPM/PDS. CTM planning can use both the production alternatives. When using the production alternative in the planning location, CTM will create the planned order for the finished product in the planning location and the dependent requirements and dependent orders in the production location. The order confirmation is then carried out in the production location while the goods receipt takes place in the planning location. For CTM to use the planning location PPM/PDS, the product must be defined for the planning location and must be included in the CTM master data selection.

6 | Advanced Planning Techniques with CTM

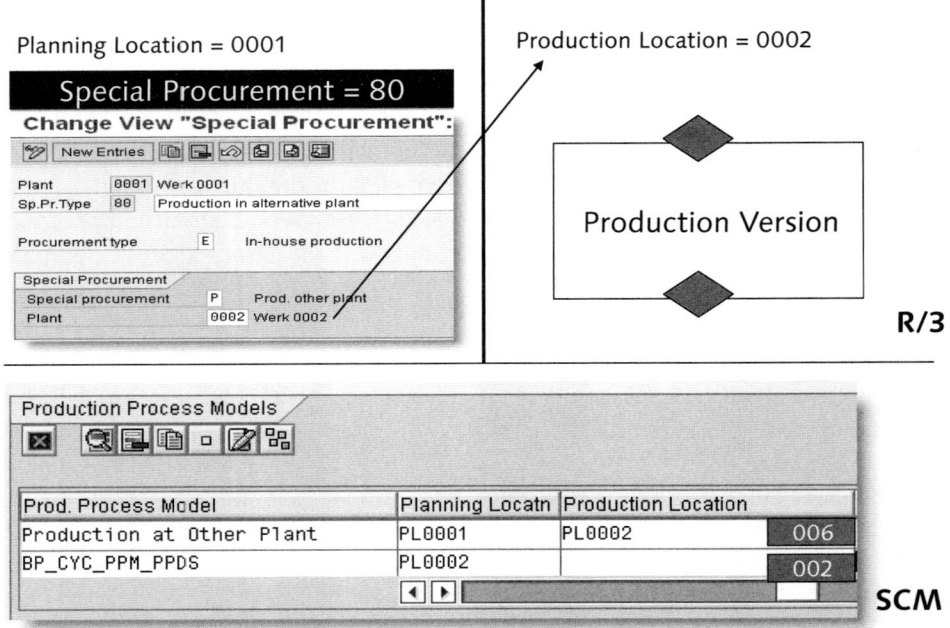

Figure 6.6 Master Data for Production in Alternative Location Strategy

With this planning strategy, the process is very simplified where no transport orders are created across the production and planning locations. This can also be implemented using the normal process where the production and planning locations are connected using the transport lanes. If you create a source of supply (SOS) — PPM — locally in the SAP APO system, you can manually enter the planning location and the production location in the SOS, which can be used for CTM planning.

During CTM planning for all of the requirements in the planning location, CTM will only select the source available in the planning location. CTM won't use PPM at the production location in case no transport lane is maintained between production location and planning location. Instead, CTM will use the normal procedure for source selection across the supply chain.

> **Note**
> Keep in mind that if any open supplies exist for the finished product at the production location, then CTM doesn't consider these supplies for the demands at the planning location.

Figure 6.7 shows the order scheduling used in CTM for the Production in Alternative Location strategy.

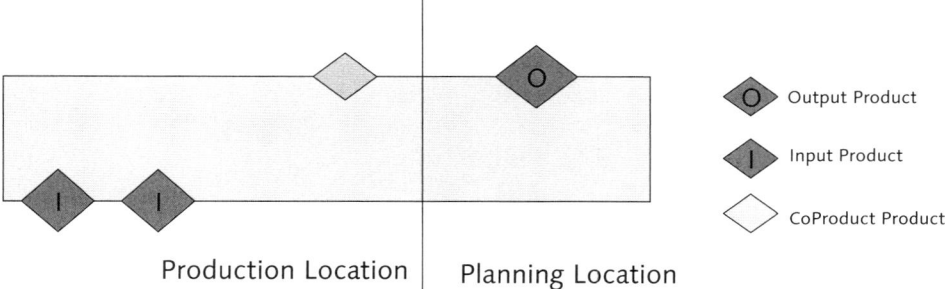

Figure 6.7 CTM Order Scheduling for Planning in Alternative Location

If the production process contains the co-products in PPM/PDS, then CTM will create co-product receipts in the production location. Additional CTM planning parameters, such as production horizon and GR processing time, are always considered from the planning location. The GR processing time is scheduled based on the handling resource and the receiving calendar in the planning location.

6.4 Supply Chain Planning in the Plant

CTM planning is predominantly used for cross-location supply chain planning. In SAP ERP and SCM applications, you can plan procurement processes within the plant. The plant is subdivided using the storage location MRP areas. The goods movement and the in-plant processes are executed using the storage location MRP areas. So by using the SAP standard interface (CIF) between SAP ERP and SAP SCM, the storage location MRP areas are automatically created in SAP SCM. These locations are similar to the other locations but are created with type 1007. The MRP area created for a plant can contain one or more storage locations. However, a storage location can't be assigned to more than one MRP area.

205

These locations in SAP SCM and CTM are used like normal locations in the planning process and can be used as source locations for both external procurement (transport lanes) and in-house production (PPM/PDS). For CTM planning using the MRP area locations, the products must be extended for the MRP location types. A supply chain model based on the storage location MRP areas in SAP ERP is very flexible because the organizational structure can be adjusted very easily by reassigning the storage locations to the MRP areas. The in-plant supply chain planning using MRP areas is also very flexible compared to using the plants. In Figure 6.8, you can see the basic structure of the MRP area storage location in the SAP ERP and SAP SCM applications.

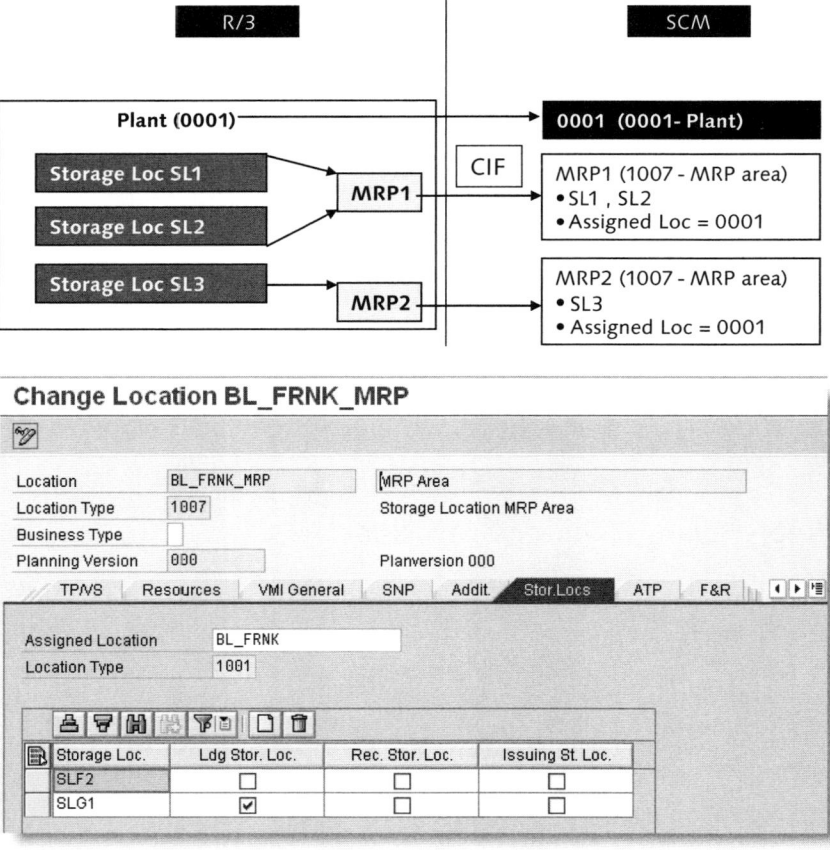

Figure 6.8 Storage Location MRP Area in SAP SCM

6.4 Supply Chain Planning in the Plant

In addition, planning for the supply chain inside the production plant is possible using storage location MRP areas. MRP area locations are similar to any locations in SAP SCM, and you have the flexibility to build the supply chain in SAP SCM using these locations and other standard locations. The stock transfer between two MRP areas can be created using transport lanes, which have to be created manually in SAP SCM. You could also use the special procurement key 45- Stock Transfer from Plant to MRP Area for a material in SAP ERP, in which case, a transportation lane is automatically created between the plant and the storage location MRP area when the material is transferred to SAP APO.

You can also use CTM planning to create the planned order in the storage location MRP area. For the component requirements, a stock transfer can be created from the plant to the storage location MRP area because the transport lane is available in SAP SCM. This is the normal process for CTM planning. In addition, you can use CTM planning to create component withdrawals directly in the storage location MRP areas and create the planned order in the plant. This process is described in detail in the next section.

6.4.1 Component Withdrawal in Another Location

In the production process, the finished product is produced in the plant, and the components are issued from a specific storage location. This process can be modeled in SAP APO using a transport lane between the plant and the storage location. Alternatively, you can use the storage location MRP area in CTM to create the component requirements and withdrawals directly in the storage location without using the transport lanes. For component withdrawals in the storage location MRP area, the issuing storage location must be maintained in the BOM and routing in SAP ERP. The corresponding PPM/PDS is created in SAP APO system using the storage location assigned to the components. The PPM/PDS is created in the production plant. During PPM/PDS usage in CTM planning, the input components are automatically created in the storage location MRP area locations.

As shown in the Figure 6.9, the PPM/PDS contains the reference to the storage location for the input components.

207

6 | Advanced Planning Techniques with CTM

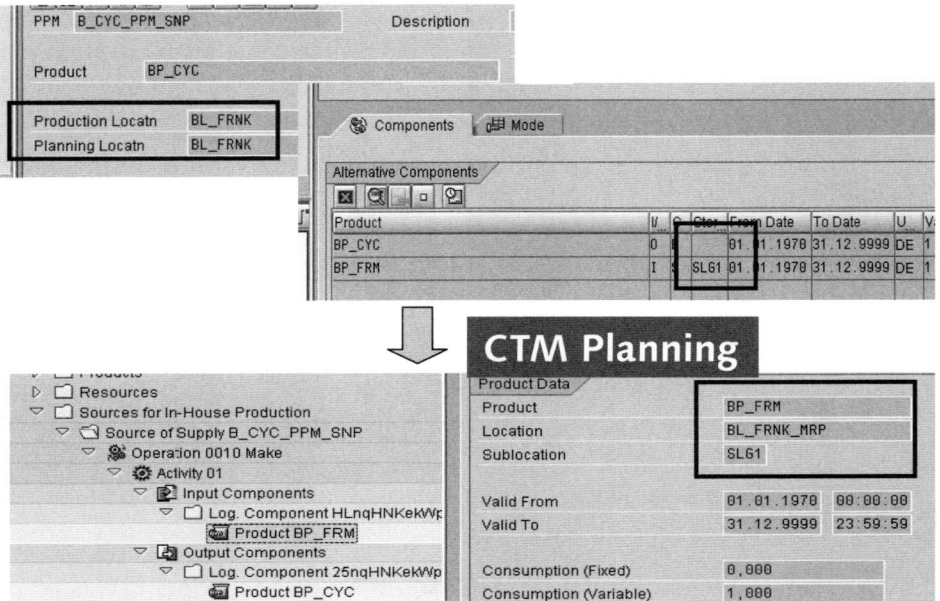

Figure 6.9 PPM Evaluation Using Storage Location MRP Area

During the CTM planning run, PPM is evaluated using the storage location and the production location to select the corresponding MRP area assigned to the plant. If no storage location MRP area is found, then the input components are planned directly in the production location. For CTM planning, the input product must be defined for the storage location MRP area and included in the CTM master data selection. As you can see in Figure 6.10, the planned order is created with CTM planning with output in the planning location and the input components in the storage location MRP area. There's no transport lane between the MRP area storage location and the production plant, so no transport duration is considered for planned order scheduling. During CTM order deletion, the storage area MRP location must also be included in the master data selection to delete the planned order successfully.

The use of the MRP location in CTM is very flexible and can be used for special planning requirements.

Subcontracting is another form of special procurement where the product is produced by an external supplier or vendor (subcontractor), as described in the next section.

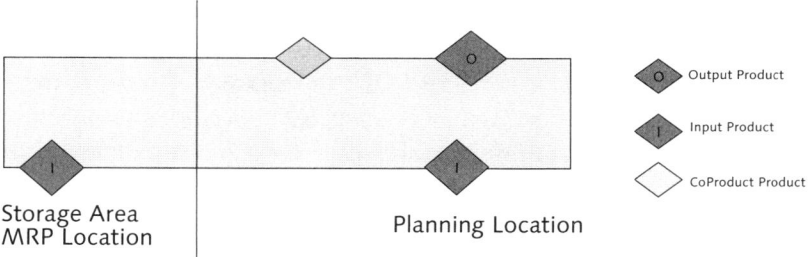

Figure 6.10 CTM Order Scheduling for Storage Location MRP Area

6.5 Subcontracting Planning with CTM

In subcontracting planning, the raw material required for production is supplied directly by the procuring plant or indirectly by the third-party supplier. Subcontracting planning in CTM can be used only if the subcontractor is modeled in SAP SCM. The source location that represents the subcontractor and the plant must have a transport lane of type Subcontracting. You also need to have the PPM/PDS maintained at the subcontractor location, but the location type of the subcontracting location isn't relevant for CTM planning. In SAP ERP, the subcontracting purchasing info record must be maintained with reference to the SAP ERP production version.

When you use the SAP standard interface (CIF), the master data relevant for CTM planning is automatically created. For example, the subcontracting transport lane and PPM/PDS in the subcontracting locations are automatically created in the SAP SCM system. So by using the customer exit APOCF012, it's possible to automatically create the product at the subcontracting location. Keep in mind that the transport lanes from the plant to the subcontractor for the raw material or the input components must be created manually in the SAP SCM system. This is required to plan for the input components in the procuring plant, which will be MRP relevant in the procuring plant. CTM planning is used to generate the subcontracting purchase requisition with reference to the planned order in the subcontracting location. It's also possible to use finite capacity planning at the subcontracting location if the appropriate capacity information is available. All of the follow-up processes, such as PO creation, transfer posting for the components, and GR for the finished product, are executed in SAP ERP.

6 | Advanced Planning Techniques with CTM

CTM planning for subcontracting scenario uses the subcontracting transport lanes and the PPM/PDS at the subcontractor location. As you see in Figure 6.11, the purchase requisition or the transfer order from the subcontractor to the plant is pegged to the subcontracting planned order. The key difference between the subcontracting transfer order and the normal transport order is that the subcontracting transfer order is always fixed pegged to the planned order.

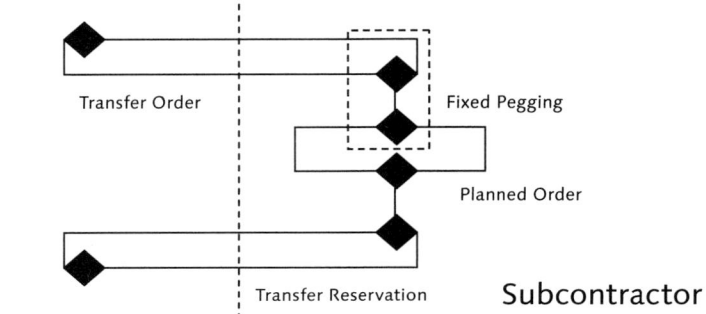

Figure 6.11 Subcontracting Purchase Requisition in CTM Planning

To publish the subcontracting transfer order to SAP ERP with suitable components successfully, the planned order is linked to the transfer order using a 1:1 relation. For example, for every planned order created in the subcontracting location, one transfer order is created. To create a single transfer order and planned order, the following restrictions are applied at the subcontractor location:

- Subcontractor stock is ignored for and demands are created for the subcontractor location.
- The procurement type for the products at the subcontractor location is always considered as type E – In-house Production.
- During CTM planning for the subcontractor location, no lot sizes are considered. If any subcontractor stock is available, then CTM won't use the stock for the dependent requirement at the subcontractor location.
- Due to the capacity constraint, if multiple planned orders are created, then individual transfer orders are created for each of the planned order.
- Quota split for in-house production at the subcontractor location is also ignored by the CTM planning run.

- The planned orders created in CTM are marked as "firmed" and hence aren't changeable in the SAP SCM system.
- When the stock transfer order is created in the SAP ERP application, the input components of the planned order are assigned as the components of the purchase requisitions and are visible for requirement planning.

By using CTM planning, you can create two level subcontracting scenarios when the components of the subcontracted finished products are also subcontracted to the same vendor as shown in Figure 6.12. To create the transfer order for the finished product and the components, the component products are created in the subcontractor location with procurement type F – External Procurement. As a result, the component requirements are fulfilled using the normal transfer order. A subcontracting transfer order is again created for the components that are fulfilled by the planned order. Please keep in mind that even though the procurement type is F – External Procurement for the component products, CTM will create a planned order. During CTM scheduling, a planned order is always created for dependent requirements created by a subcontracting transfer order irrespective of the procurement type.

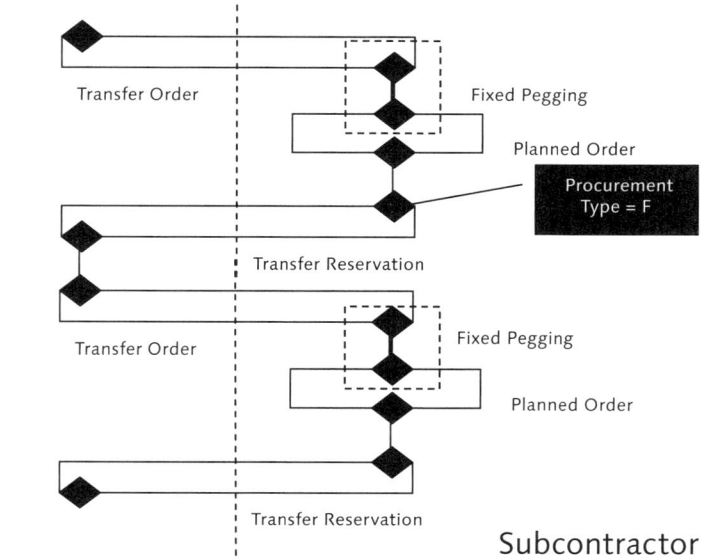

Figure 6.12 Two-Level Subcontracting Purchase Requisition in CTM Planning

When using a subcontracting transfer order with CTM, you must not use the Do Not Check Order Details option in the CTM profile for order deletion. Using this option, CTM will delete only the purchase requisition and not the associated subcontracting planned order. However, in the subcontracting scenario, both the transfer orders and the planned orders must be deleted and created simultaneously.

The subcontracting process with third-party provision can also be used in CTM planning. In this scenario, the input components aren't shipped to the procuring plant; instead, they are directly shipped to the subcontractor from a third-party supplier. For this process, you have to manually create a transport lane between the third-party supplier and the subcontractor. The CTM planning process creates the normal purchase requisitions at the subcontractor location, and during execution, the SAP ERP application creates the purchase requisition and the purchase order with the delivery address as the subcontractor location.

6.6 CTM Planning with Product Interchangeability

Product interchangeability is used in SAP SCM to plan for product replacement or product discontinuation. Product interchangeability master data in SAP SCM offers a very flexible user interface to define several interchangeability scenarios. There are several interchangeability relationships that can be maintained in the interchangeability master data as shown in Figure 6.13.

The interchangeability relationships are defined using the interchangeability group and can be defined using Transaction /INCMD/UI or using the SAP Easy Access menu ADVANCED PLANNING AND OPTIMIZATION • MASTER DATA • APPLICATION SPECIFIC MASTER DATA • PRODUCT AND LOCATION INTERCHANGEABILITY • MAINTAIN INTERCHANGEABILITY GROUP. Similar to other master data objects in SAP SCM, the interchangeability group must also be assigned to the supply chain model.

Two main scenarios can be modeled using the interchangeability master data that can be used for the CTM planning: supersession and FFF.

6.6 CTM Planning with Product Interchangeability

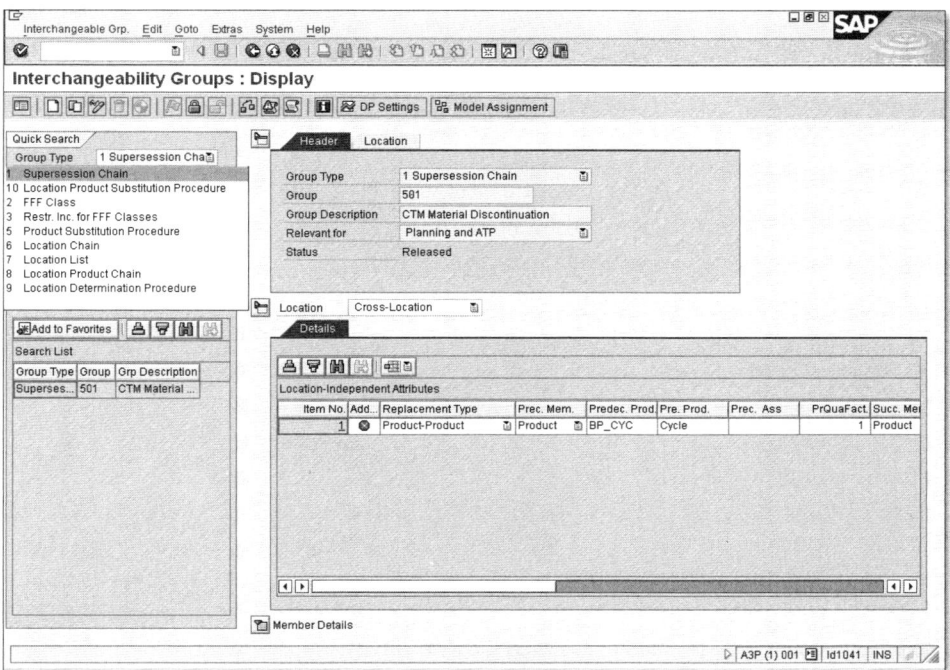

Figure 6.13 Interchangeability Group Definition for CTM Planning

6.6.1 Supersession

Supersession master data is used to model the product discontinuation or product replacement. The predecessor product can't be deleted because the product will be referred to in the existing master and transaction data. Using the interchangeability master data, you can define the supersession chain to define the production discontinuation relationship. CTM planning supports only the forward product discontinuation relationship where the successor product replaces the predecessor after a certain date. It's possible to define whether the existing supplies for the predecessor product can be used for the demand of the successor product using the Use-Up field of the supersession chain.

The following options can be used for the Use-Up field:

- **YES**
  Use all supplies of the preceding product without any date restriction.

- **NO**
  Do not use supplies of the preceding product.
- **RESTRICTED**
  Use all supplies of the preceding product with the date restriction maintained in Use-up date.

In addition, the attributes in Table 6.3 must be used for the supersession chain used in CTM material discontinuation planning.

Attribute	Value
Replacement Type	Product-Product
Preceding Member Type	Product
Succeeding Member Type	Product
Direction	Forward

Table 6.3 Attributes for the Supersession Chain

The supersession master data is used for all of the products selected in the CTM planning run. It's important to select both the predecessor product and successor product in the CTM master data selection to use the discontinuation relationship in the CTM planning. Using the CTM profile Product Interchangeability setting available in the Further Strategies tab, you can enable the use of discontinuation relationship in the CTM planning process. The discontinuation relationship can be displayed in the CTM master data check as shown in Figure 6.14.

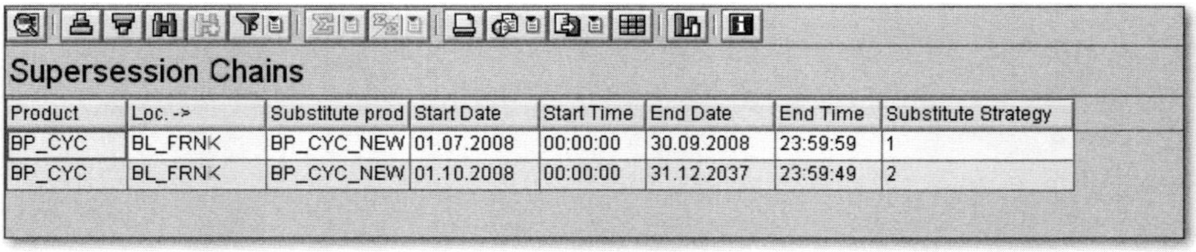
Supersession Chains

Product	Loc. ->	Substitute prod	Start Date	Start Time	End Date	End Time	Substitute Strategy
BP_CYC	BL_FRNK	BP_CYC_NEW	01.07.2008	00:00:00	30.09.2008	23:59:59	1
BP_CYC	BL_FRNK	BP_CYC_NEW	01.10.2008	00:00:00	31.12.2037	23:59:49	2

Figure 6.14 Material Discontinuation Relation in CTM Planning

The discontinuation relations defined in the master data is converted to a substitution rule based on the Use-up strategy. If the supply use-up of the predecessor product is allowed, then CTM will create two substitution rules based on the use-up date. Each of the rules is differentiated using the substitute strategy where 1 indicates no supply use-up, and 2 indicates supply use-up. The selected discontinuation rules are applied for all of the demands (normal demands and SS virtual demands) of the succeeding product that was selected for CTM planning.

Figure 6.15 shows the CTM scheduling logic and supply consumption when planning with the material discontinuation rule. Predecessor product A is discontinued and is succeeded by product B. The Use-up flag is used to indicate that the supplies for A can be used until the use-up date. For any demand for product A, CTM will check for the available supplies for product A from the planning start until the end of the use-up period. For the remaining quantity, CTM will create a substitution order to propagate the demand for the preceding product (A) to the succeeding product (B). The demand of B is fulfilled using the normal source selection process in CTM. Based on the capacity constraints, it's possible that the new supply for product B is created outside the validity period of the discontinuation rule. The complete supply tree generated for the demand is in Figure 6.15, which shows the substitution order used for creating the fixed pegging between the predecessor and the successor product.

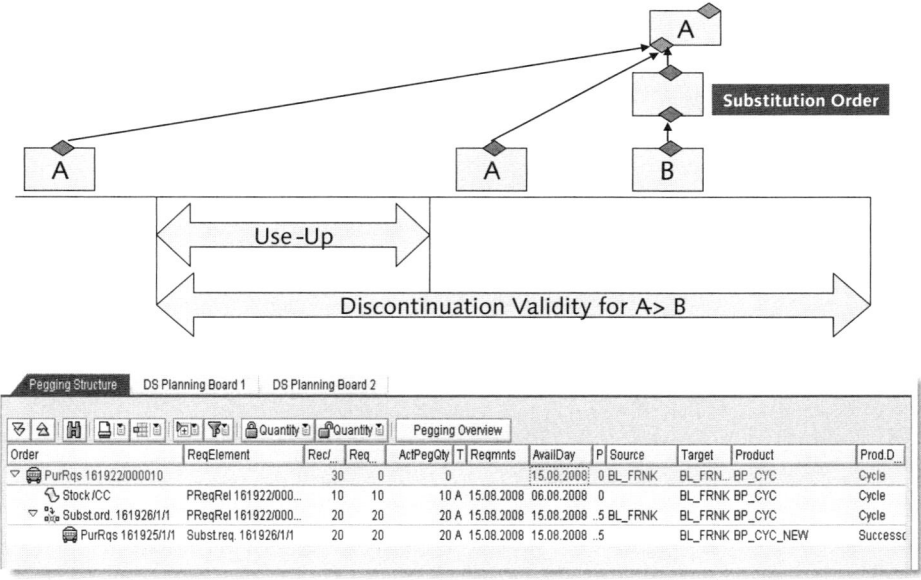

Figure 6.15 CTM Scheduling with Material Discontinuation Relationship

Additional functions in CTM also use the discontinuation rules in CTM. For example, the CTM master data generation function can be used to generate the depen-

6 | Advanced Planning Techniques with CTM

dent master data using the interchangeability groups. Similarly, the automatic parallel profile will use the interchangeability groups to generate the submodels for planning CTM in parallel.

6.6.2 Form-Fit-Function (FFF) Class

Form-Fit-Function (FFF) class is used in SAP SCM to group materials that have similar form, fit, and function. For example, the same material supplied by different vendors has different material numbers. In this case, each material is mutually replaceable. Each of the FFF classes contains one leading product, which is used for procurement or production when all of the supplies of the FFF class members are used completely. FFF classes can be defined using the same master data transaction as the supersession chain. FFF class is most commonly used in the discrete industries and can be defined in the SAP ERP application. In the SAP SCM system, the FFF class contains a location-independent collection of all similar products. An FFF subset must be created to assign the FFF class to a location. As shown in Figure 6.16, the FFF subset is created using the FFF class where the location is assigned. In the FFF subset, the leading product is also identified that must be part of the FFF subset. The FFF class must also be assigned to the model that is used for CTM planning.

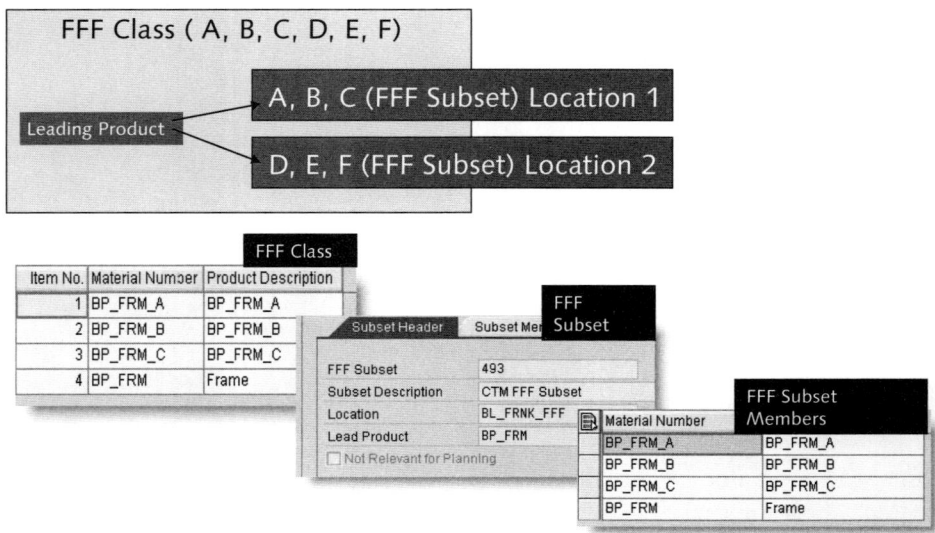

Figure 6.16 FFF Class Definition Used for CTM Planning

To use the FFF class in CTM planning, you can use the Use FFF Class setting available under the Further Strategies tab of the CTM profile. You must include the leading product of the FFF subset in the CTM master data selection. The CTM automatic master data selection function can be used to select all of the FFF subset products for CTM planning. If there are no inconsistencies in the FFF subset, then the FFF subset details can be displayed in the CTM master data check. CTM planning checks for FFF class definition during the source selection for the demand.

As shown in Figure 6.17, FFF Subset is defined for the four products. The product BP_FRM is defined as the leading product. During source selection for the demand for product BP_FRM, CTM will first check for existing supplies for the demand product. When no open supplies exist for the demand product, then the supplies for FFF subset members will be selected, which can lead to on-time demand fulfillment. If still some open quantity exists for the demand, then CTM will use the source selection (production or procurement) for the leading product. If all of the FFF subset members have supplies, then CTM will use the sequence given in the FFF subset to select the subset member for supply consumption.

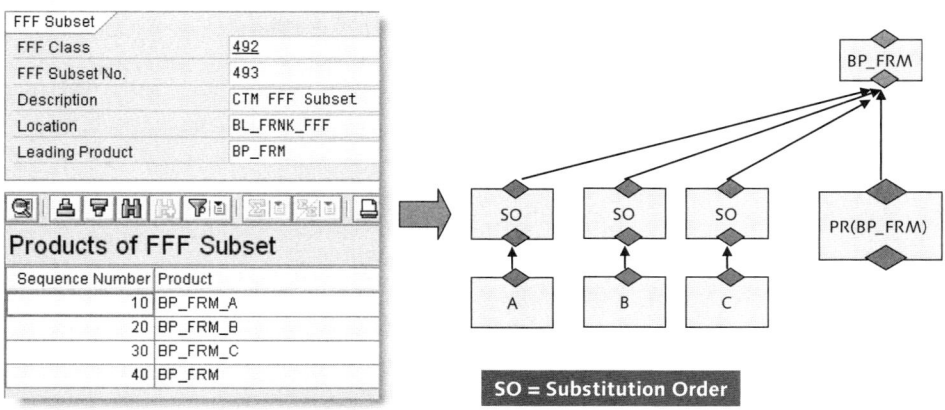

Figure 6.17 CTM Scheduling with FFF Class

It's important to emphasize the supply consumption logic when supply categorization is used in CTM. The supply categorization is applied locally for each member of the FFF subset and not globally across all FFF subset products. As shown in Figure 6.18, the search strategy is defined to use the 01 category supplies before 02 category supplies. CTM planning will first use the search strategy for the demand product, and during source determination ("**"), individual FFF member supplies are selected using the search strategy. As a result, it's possible that the category 02 supply of FFF subset member A is used before the category 01 supplies of FFF subset member B.

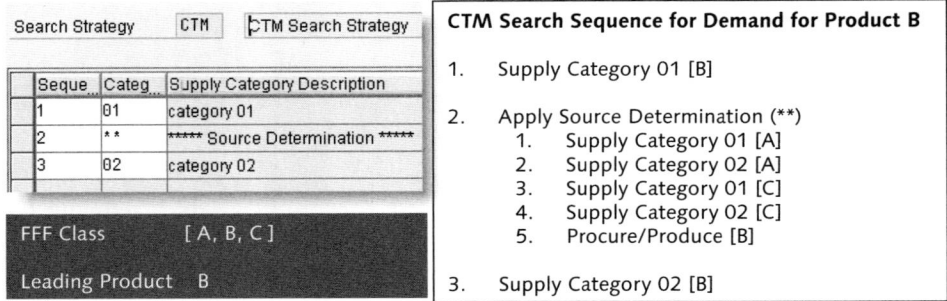

Figure 6.18 CTM Search Strategy When Using the FFF Class

6.7 CTM Planning with Substitution Rules

Substitution rules are used in CTM planning to fulfill the demand for a given product using the supply of the substitute product. The substitution rules can be maintained using the ATP rules or the interchangeability master data. Using the ATP rules for CTM planning can be very useful to generate an accurate supply plan that can be used for allocations in GATP. The ATP rules are maintained using the SAP APO Transaction /SAPAPO/RBA04 or using the SAP Easy Access menu ADVANCED PLANNING AND OPTIMIZATION • MASTER DATA • RULE MAINTENANCE • INTEGRATED RULE MAINTENANCE. The ATP rules are defined as inclusive rules, and the substitution procedures are assigned to the rule. You can define the substitutions in the ATP rules, or you can use the interchangeability master data function to define the substitution rules.

There are three types of substitution rules that can be used in CTM planning: product substitution, location substitution, and product location substitution as described in the following sections.

6.7.1 Product Substitution Procedure

The product substitution procedure is used to define location-independent substitution rules. For example, product A can be substituted by product B, whereas product A and B exist in different locations. This procedure can be used if there's no transport duration across the two locations that are relevant for planning. The substitution requirement is created in the source location, and the substitute receipt is created in the destination location without considering any transport duration or transport constraints.

6.7.2 Location Substitution Procedure

The location substitution procedure is used when all of the products can be substituted across two locations. Similar to the product substitution procedure, the substitution order is created for the source and destination products across two locations without considering the transport duration or transport constraints. CTM planning will search for supplies across the complete supply chain network using the transport lanes where all of the transport constraints are considered for planning. As a result, it isn't recommended to define the location substitution procedure. You can define the location substitution using the transport lane and the product location substitution.

6.7.3 Product Location Substitution Procedure

The product location substitution procedure is the most commonly used substitution procedure where the substitutions are defined for a specific product in a given location. You can define substitutions for a given product with multiple substitute products.

In addition to the substitute procedures, you can also define the calculation profile in the ATP rules. As shown in Figure 6.19, the Calculation Profile setting can be used to define demand-specific parameters that are available in the CTM global customization.

The use of ATP rules can be enabled in the CTM profile using the Rules setting in the Further strategies tab of the CTM profile.

6 Advanced Planning Techniques with CTM

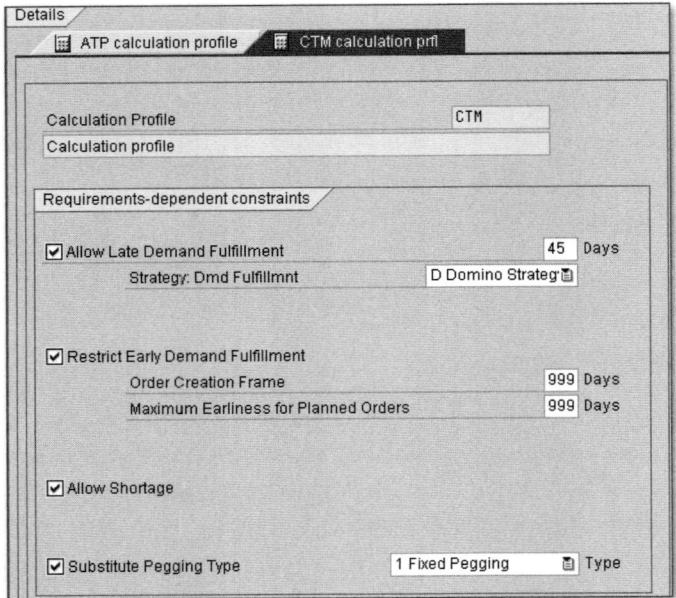

Figure 6.19 CTM Calculation Profile Assigned to the ATP Rules

There are four possible options for the CTM setting:

- **Do Not Apply Rules**
  No rules are used in the CTM profile.

- **Find and Use Rule According to Demand**
  With this option, substitution rules can be used in CTM for each demand based on the demand attributes. CTM uses the condition techniques available in SAP SCM to select the appropriate rule based on the sales order attributes. It's also possible to evaluate the rules using the descriptive characteristics assigned to the demands. As shown in Figure 6.20, for every demand selected in CTM planning, the ATP rules are selected using the condition techniques. The activation code is used to select different rule strategies for sales order, forecast, or dependent requirements. The rule evaluation function is very flexible and can be used to select specific rules for each of the CTM demands.

The rules evaluation function is primarily useful for ATP checks for the sales orders. Using the rules evaluation function in CTM planning for very large number of demands can have a negative impact on the overall performance. As a result, you shouldn't use this option for CTM planning.

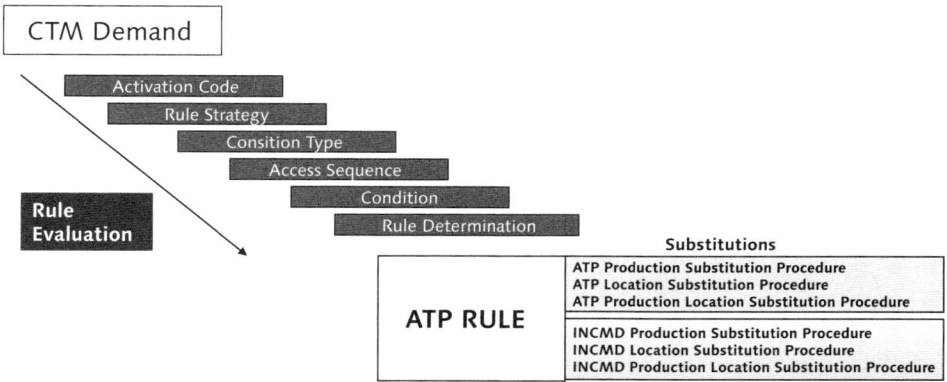

Figure 6.20 Rule Evaluation for CTM Demands

- **Use Specified Rule for Demand**
  This option is the most suitable method for using substitution rules in CTM planning for a very large number of demands. The ATP rules are defined with all of the substitution rules and explicitly used in the CTM profile. No rule evaluation function is used in this mode because the rule is predetermined and used in the CTM profile. This option is only available when the product location substitution procedure is used in the ATP rule.

- **Use First Found Rule for All Demands**
  Using this method, CTM evaluates the rules for the first demand only. The evaluated rule and the substitutions are used for all of the succeeding demands.

6.7.4 Production Substitution for Supply

Substitution rules that are selected for planning can be displayed in the demand details section of the CTM demand simulation list. Substitution rules can be used in CTM planning if both the original product and the substitute product are selected in the CTM master data selection. The validity dates assigned to the substitution rules are considered for CTM planning. The demand date is used to select the substitution rule. If there is more than one substitute product available for the original product, then the costs assigned to the substitution are used for prioritizing the substitutions. During the supply selection step of demand fulfillment, CTM will select the supply for all substitute products that are available in the substitute rules. It's important to understand that the substitution rules can be used only to use the supplies of the substitute product. It isn't possible to create any procurement or production for the substitute product using the substitution rules.

6 | Advanced Planning Techniques with CTM

6.7.5 Production Substitution for Production (Down Binning)

Substitution rules can be used in CTM planning for a special form of production called *down binning*. This form of production is mainly used in the high-tech industries where the production process can lead to production of output material with different attributes or quality. To define this output production, a quantity of co-products is used in the PPM/PDS. Using the substitution rules, it's possible to define if the co-products can be used to fulfill the demand of the main product. In CTM planning, during the planned order creation, CTM simultaneously includes generated co-products directly in the quantity conversion for covering the requirement.

Based on the substitution rules, the co-product supply is directly used in fulfilling the demand quantity. The net resource consumption is according to the demand quantity, which is fulfilled using the main product and co-products. The down binning process is shown in Figure 6.21. The PPM is defined with three output products: Q, Q1, and Q2. Q1 and Q2 represents the same product Q but with a different quality rating. Using the substitution rule products, Q1 and Q2 can be substituted for the demand of product Q. During the planned order creation, CTM will consider the allowed substitution rule to schedule the planned order with quantity 80, 10, 10 for the main product and the co-products. The net demand for the product Q is fulfilled using the main product and co-product output quantity. The resource consumption and input product I quantity is with respect to the output quantity of the main product Q.

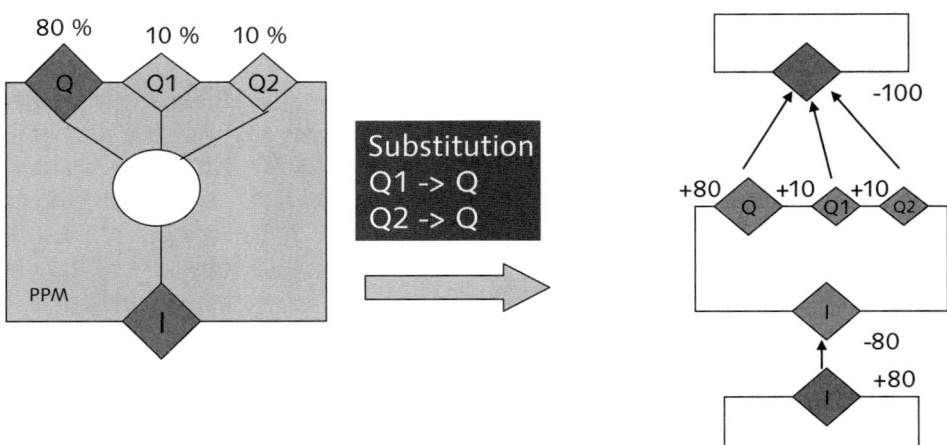

Figure 6.21 Down Binning Scenario Planning with Substitution Rules

6.8 Aggregated Planning with CTM

In CTM, you can carry out aggregated planning that takes hierarchy structures into account. You can execute an aggregated CTM planning run for capacity planning and source determination at the header location product level of a location product hierarchy. You can then use SNP disaggregation to disaggregate the planning result to the individual subproducts. With this type of planning, you achieve improved performance to execute CTM planning for a very large data volume.

When CTM is used in medium- to long-term planning horizons using the aggregated planning process, you can simplify the planning process by making the planning decisions at the header product level instead of the detail level. The hierarchy name used in the CTM planning must be maintained with reference to the hierarchy structure and must be used in the CTM profile. Aggregated planning in SAP SCM is tightly integrated with the SAP Apparel and Footwear industry solution with SAP SCM 5.0.

The SAP Apparel and Footwear product grids with multiple dimensions are converted automatically to the SAP SCM location product hierarchy. Using aggregated planning in CTM, you can create a constrained supply plan. SNP order disaggregation can be used to disaggregate the header level orders to the sublevel orders. Sublevel orders are grouped together using the order group number that is used for creating the orders items in the SAP Apparel and Footwear system for the product grid. Aggregated planning in CTM can be used for non-SAP Apparel and Footwear system also, but you have to create the order hierarchy manually in SAP SCM. You can use location product, resource, or PPM/PDS hierarchies in CTM planning. CTM planning is used to generate the supply plan at the aggregate level. The disaggregation of orders is executed using the central SNP disaggregation function that is also used to disaggregate the planning results from SNP Heuristics and SNP Optimizer.

> **Note**
>
> SAP SCM aggregated planning in SAP SCM 5.0 is only supported for SNP planning. As a result, CTM planning with hierarchies is only supported for SNP bucket mode. In the CTM profile, bucket-oriented planning and SNP order type are automatically selected for aggregated planning in CTM.

6.8.1 Hierarchy Definitions Used in CTM Planning

To use aggregated planning in CTM, you can maintain the following hierarchies for CTM planning:

- **Location product hierarchy**
  Location product hierarchy is used to assign several sublevel product locations to a header product location in a two-level hierarchy. You execute aggregated planning at the header location product level. A header location product is the header product of a location product hierarchy that you've generated from a location hierarchy and a product hierarchy. In this model, you create both header and sublevel products at the same location and combine them using the hierarchy definition. It's also possible to create a product location hierarchy where several sublevel locations are grouped under one header location. In this scenario, you'll assign the same product at both the header and the sublocations.

  The options in Table 6.4 are available for using the location product hierarchy in CTM planning.

Location Product Hierarchy		
Option 1	Header Product	Product Group – Location
	Subproduct	Product – Location
Option 2	Header Product	Product – Location Group
	Subproduct	Product – Location

Table 6.4 Location Product Hierarchy Options

You create all of the levels of these two-level hierarchies as standalone products and locations in the product and location master data. If you want to plan multiple locations of your network, the same header products should be defined in all locations. SNP disaggregation takes into account the rounding values and lot size parameters defined for the individual header and subproducts.

If you want to ensure that there are no remainders at the header product level during SNP disaggregation, the rounding values defined at the subproduct level must be the same within a location product hierarchy. The rounding value of the header product must be a multiple of the value at the subproduct level. In addition, the minimum lot size at the header level should be larger than or equal to the minimum lot size defined at the sublevel. The procurement type defined at the header product level should also be supported at the subproduct level. The same SNP production horizon, extended SNP production horizon, and SNP stock transfer horizon should be defined for all products of the location product hierarchy (including the header product).

▶ **Resource hierarchy**
When planning for resources on the aggregate level, it's possible to combine several sublevel resources to an aggregate resource using the resource hierarchy. You can use either bucket or mixed resources when planning with CTM using the resource hierarchy. During planning, CTM will ensure that the resource capacity of the header resource is consistent with the sublevel resource capacity. If you want to display the resource consumption at the header level and you're not using the same resources at the header and sublevel in the PPMs or PDS, you should create a resource hierarchy so that the resource consumption is displayed correctly. The resource hierarchy should be consistent with the PPM/PDS hierarchy used to consistently aggregate and disaggregate the planned orders across the header and sublevel resources.

▶ **PPM/PDS hierarchy**
The PPM/PDS hierarchy is mainly used during source determination of order disaggregation. The sublevel orders are created using the PPM/PDS hierarchy. Sources that aren't part of the hierarchy aren't used for order disaggregation. For CTM planning at the header product, the header product PPM/PDS are used. To disaggregate the order consistently, the PPM or PDS hierarchy should be consistent with the location product hierarchy.

Hierarchy structure as shown in Figure 6.22 is defined in the SAP SCM system using Transaction /SAPAPO/RELHSHOW or using the SAP Easy Access menu ADVANCED PLANNING AND OPTIMIZATION • MASTER DATA • HIERARCHY • MAINTAIN HIERARCHY.

The hierarchy structures defined in the master data can be used in the CTM profile either explicitly using the hierarchy names or with reference to the planning area. The standard planning book 9ASNPAGGR with data views SNPAGGR (1) and SNPAGGR (2) based on the standard planning area 9ASNP02 are delivered with SAP SCM 5.0. This planning area and planning book contain the key figures required for aggregated planning and the assignment of key figure attributes, such as the aggregation indicator and the key figure functions 9001 to 9026.

6 | Advanced Planning Techniques with CTM

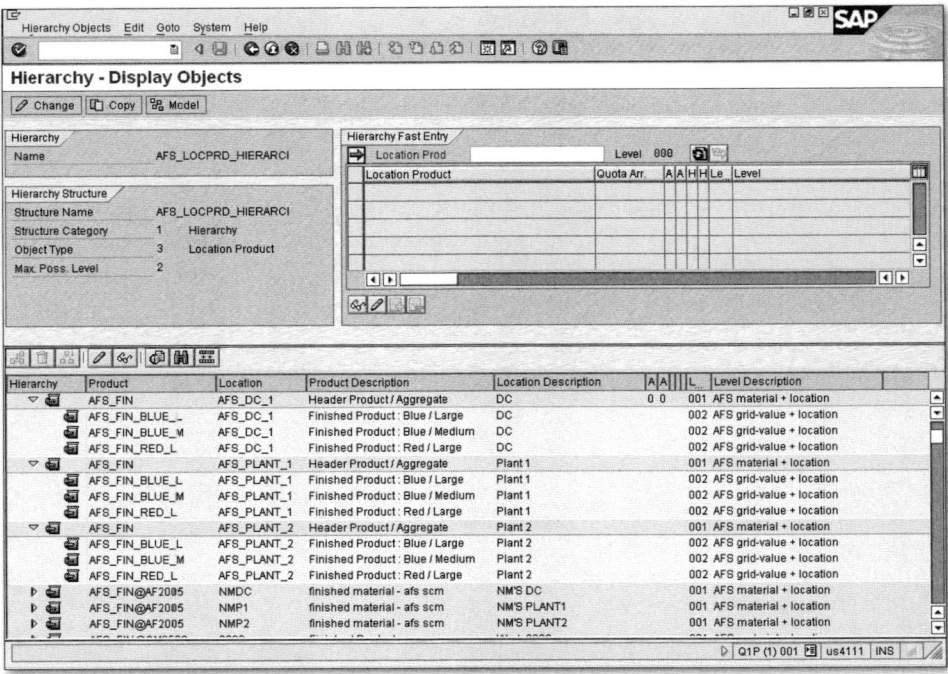

Figure 6.22 Hierarchy Structure Definition Used for CTM Planning

The aggregation indicator specifies whether the aggregated value or the normal value is calculated and displayed at the header location product level in a key figure. This indicator also controls whether the value is kept or deleted at the subproduct level after aggregation. For CTM planning, only the hierarchy name assigned to the planning area is sufficient. As shown in Figure 6.23, you can explicitly define the hierarchy names that are used for planning or you can use the Use Hierarchies from Planning Area setting. The planning area can be maintained in the CTM profile or defined in the CTM global customization.

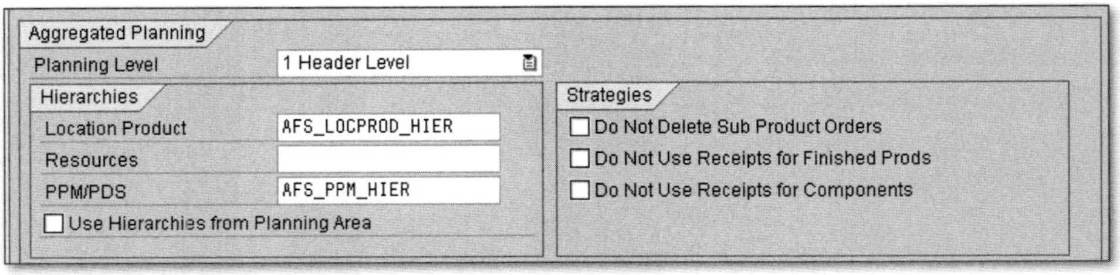

Figure 6.23 CTM Profile Settings for Aggregated Planning with Hierarchy

226

Aggregated planning in CTM can be executed at either the header level or sublevel. When planning at the header level, CTM selects only the header-level product locations, resources, and PPM/PDS. On the other hand, when planned at the sublevel, the hierarchies are evaluated to select the sublevel product locations, resources, and PPM/PDS for planning. The hierarchy definition must not combine products from header and sublevel. For example, it isn't possible to select the sublevel product in the supply chain or BOM of the header product when planning at the header level. Any such dependencies can be verified using the CTM master data check function. If the header and the sublevel products are combined using the hierarchy, the master data check will indicate this as an error, and CTM won't plan the respective products. The planning objects (locations, resources, and PPM/PDS) that are selected for CTM planning can be displayed using the CTM master data check function as shown in Figure 6.24

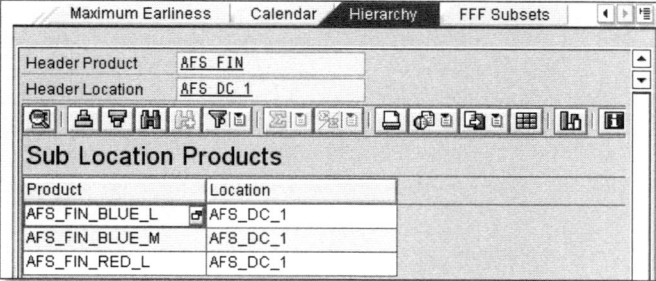

Figure 6.24 Hierarchy Display in CTM Master Data Check

6.8.2 Master Data Selection for Aggregated Planning in CTM

CTM planning can be used to plan for either header products or the subproducts of the hierarchy. The header and subproducts are created in SAP SCM as independent products and don't defer in terms of the master data attributes. In CTM master data selection, you can select both the header and sublevel products. In the CTM profile, if you use the hierarchy definition, then you can only select the header product of the hierarchy in the CTM master data selection. Based on the planning level, CTM will evaluate the hierarchy to select the appropriate products. For example, when planning at the header level, only header products, transport lanes, and PPM/PDS are selected for planning. On the other hand, when planning at the sublevel, only the sublevel products, lanes, and PPM/PDS are selected for planning. It isn't required to explicitly select the sublevel location products in the CTM master data selection.

6.8.3 Process Steps for Aggregated Planning in CTM

Aggregated planning with CTM is executed using several process steps. You perform the individual planning steps with your own CTM profiles with different settings. So that the master data remains the same for all process steps, you use the same master data selection in each CTM profile. You only include the header location products and the corresponding SOSs in the master data selection. Based on the location product hierarchy, CTM automatically considers the sublocation products during aggregated planning. Figure 6.25 provides the overview of the process steps that are required for order deletion, sublevel demand netting, header level demand aggregation and planning, and finally the disaggregation step.

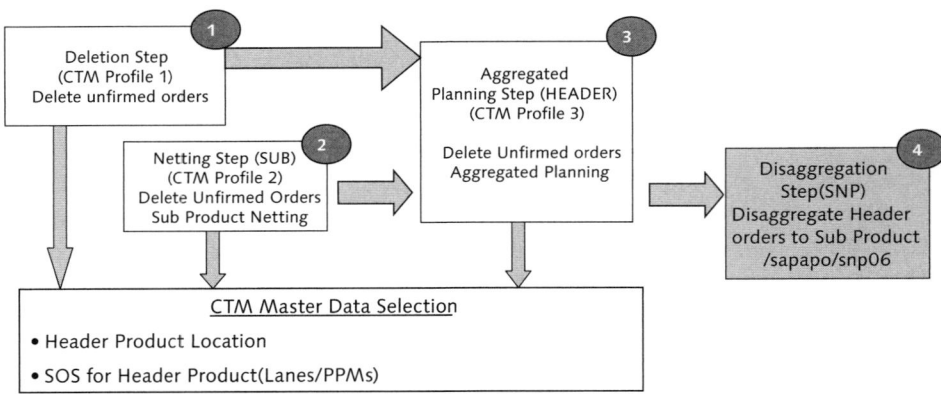

Figure 6.25 Process Steps for CTM Aggregated Planning

The following is an example of a process for aggregated planning with CTM. You perform each step with a different CTM profile.

- **STEP 1: Delete existing receipts and supplies.**
  During the regenerative planning with CTM, the first step is to delete all of the existing unfirmed orders. Before you start the actual CTM planning run, delete unfixed orders at the header location product level and at the sublocation product level in a separate planning run. To do so, use a CTM profile with the following planning strategies:

- Planning mode: Replan All Orders
- Delete mode: Delete Orders That Are Not Firm

- **STEP 2: Net sublevel supply and demand.**
  The second step in aggregated planning is to net the existing demands and supplies at the subproduct level as shown. This is to ensure that only the net open demand is planned for the header product. You carry out a single-level or multilevel assignment of existing receipts and supplies at the sublocation product level in a separate CTM run. An assignment at the sublocation product level can prevent a surplus or a lack of stock when you disaggregate the planning results at the sublocation product level at a later time. In the CTM profile, you select the Sublevel setting as the planning level for aggregated planning. In this process step, only the existing supplies across the supply chain are used for demand netting, and no new orders must be created. If you're using netting across locations, the transfer order must be created. Figure 6.26 shows the CTM netting results at the subproduct level.

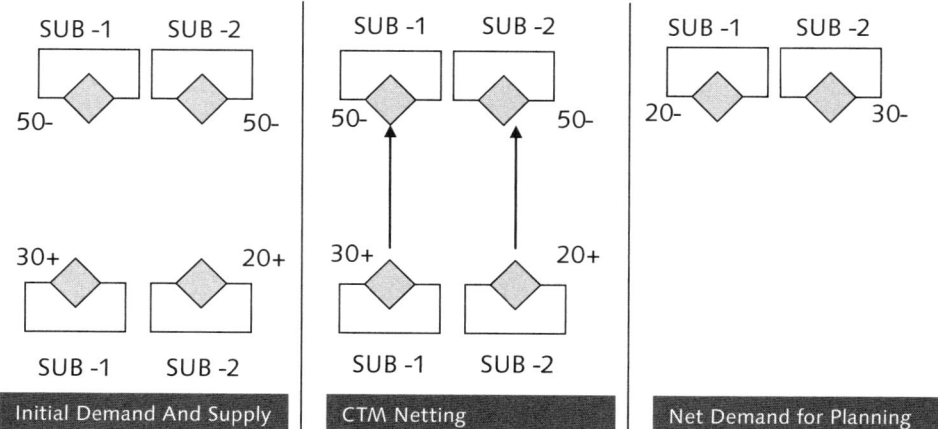

Figure 6.26 CTM Demand Netting at Subproduct Level

Two subproducts SUB-1 and SUB-2 are assigned to the header product HEAD. Using the supply demand netting at the subproduct level, the existing demands and supplies are netted using the fixed pegging between the demand and supply elements. In the CTM profile under the Basic Settings tab you'll exclude the procurement alternatives PPM/PDS and External Procurement. This will ensure that CTM doesn't generate any new planned orders or purchase requisitions. As a result only existing supplies are used for demand fulfillment. The net open demand at the subproduct level is used for aggregation and supply planning at the header level.

- **STEP 3: Aggregate and plan demands at the header level.**
  In this CTM planning step, the system aggregates the demands and receipts from the sublocation product level to the header location product level using the hierarchy definition. Aggregation with hierarchy can be followed by aggregation by time buckets. The net demand at the sublevel is selected and aggregated to the header level. It's recommended that you use the same UOM for the sublevel product and the header-level product. If you choose to use a different UOM, then CTM will use the standard UOM conversion process to convert the sublevel demand and quantities to the header level. To retain the planning results (transfer order, fixed pegging) from the netting step, you have to use the CTM profile with the following planning strategies:

  - Planning Mode: Orders Without Fixed Pegging
  - Delete Mode: Do Not Delete Any Orders

The system generates planning for the header location product using the aggregated demand. The aggregated demand in CTM is a virtual demand and is only generated during the CTM planning run. The aggregated demand isn't persistently stored in SAP liveCache. The aggregated demand can be displayed in the CTM demand simulation list. In the demand details section, you can display the actual sublevel demands that are used for demand aggregation as shown in Figure 6.27.

The aggregated demand is planned like normal demands and can be used for time-based aggregation and demand prioritization. All of the attributes that are relevant for the demand prioritization must be maintained for the header product. For example, the material priority from the individual sublevel products isn't considered for the aggregated demand. You have to maintain the material priority for the header product. The production horizon, GR/GI times, and resource consumption must be maintained for the header product. CTM will create the constrained supply plan for the aggregated demand while considering the same source determination and supply consumption rules as used for normal demands as shown in Figure 6.27.

Aggregated Planning with CTM | **6.8**

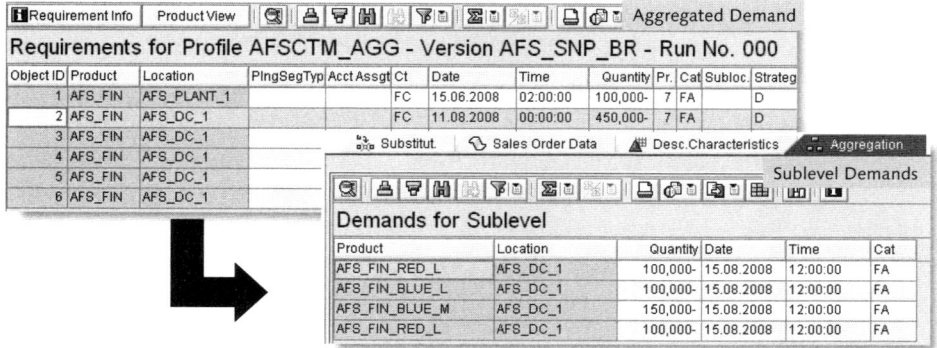

Figure 6.27 CTM Demand Aggregation Using Hierarchy

The supply created for the CTM aggregated virtual demand can't be pegged to the aggregated demand because the aggregated demand doesn't exist in SAP liveCache. CTM planning results can be displayed using the SNP planning book, which is designed to show both the aggregated demand and supply using appropriate key figures. It's possible to create fixed pegging for the dependent demands and supplies that are created for the aggregated demands.

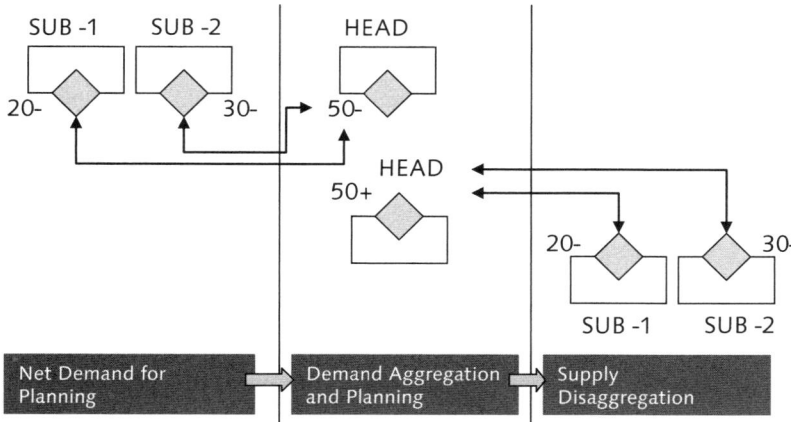

Figure 6.28 CTM Aggregated Planning and Disaggregation Steps

The supply corresponding to the aggregated demand is disaggregated to the subproduct level using several disaggregation techniques as shown in Figure 6.28

231

If you specified a resource hierarchy in addition to the location product hierarchy, CTM also takes capacity restrictions into account during planning.

- **STEP 4: Disaggregate aggregated planning data**

    CTM planning results at the aggregate product level can be disaggregated to the subproduct level. You can execute this function within aggregated planning in SNP. It disaggregates the results of CTM planning that you have performed at the header location product level of a location product hierarchy, to the level of the individual subproducts. You can use the disaggregation function interactively in the SNP planning book or in background mode using Transaction / SAPAPO/SNP06. This is shown in Figure 6.29. This function can be started using the SAP Easy Access menu ADVANCED PLANNING AND OPTIMIZATION • SUPPLY NETWORK PLANNING • PLANNING • SNP IN BACKGROUND • SNP DISAGGREGATION.

SNP disaggregation disaggregates the planning result saved in the distribution receipt (planned), distribution demand (planned), production (planned), or dependent demand key figures, to the individual subproducts. The aggregated value for the header location product is displayed in the aggregated distribution receipt or aggregated distribution demand (Planned) key figures and in the aggregated production (Planned) or aggregated dependent demand key figures after disaggregation in interactive SNP.

The disaggregated value for the individual subproducts is again displayed in the nonaggregated key figures, such as distribution receipt (planned), and so on when you select the individual subproduct. If you display the detail view of the aggregated key figures by right-clicking, you'll see a list of orders that the system created for the subproducts of the header product. You can change this order data. SNP disaggregation is necessary to transfer orders to an SAP ERP application. To transfer the disaggregated planning results successfully to the SAP Apparel and Footwear system, you have to use the order group numbers for the CTM created order. Order group creation can be enabled in CTM planning with the Use Order Group setting under the Technical Settings tab in the CTM profile.

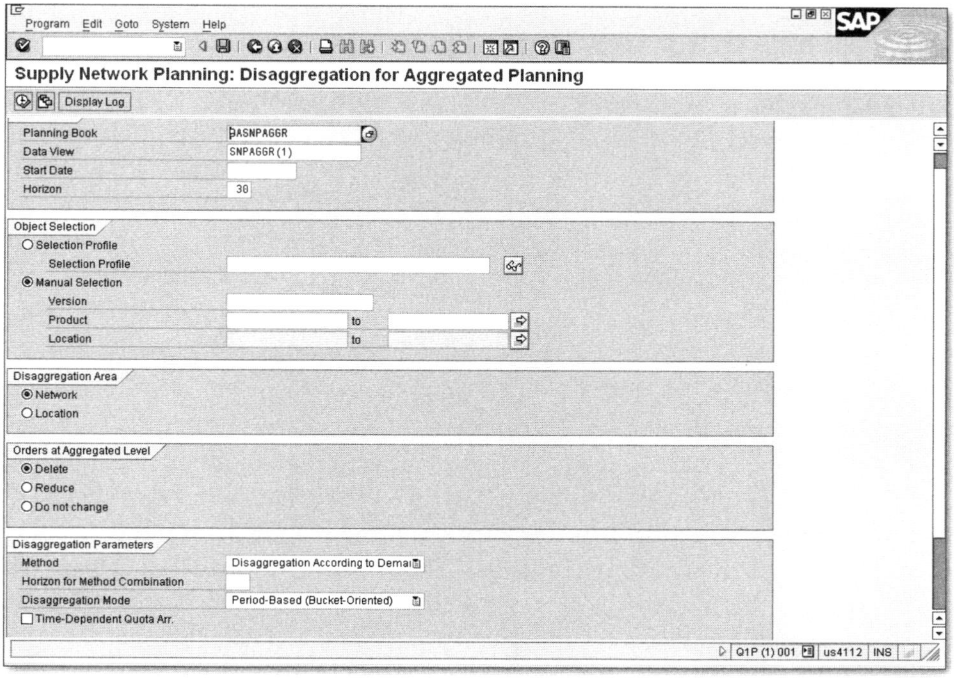

6.8 Aggregated Planning with CTM

Figure 6.29 SNP Order Disaggregation

Disaggregation Methods

You can choose between two disaggregation methods or combine both methods.

- **Disaggregation according to demands**
  Values are disaggregated from the header product level to the subproduct level according to fair share distribution or push distribution principles that are also used by deployment. With fair share distribution, if demand exceeds supply, the system distributes the supply evenly over the individual subproducts according to their demand. With push distribution, the procedure is similar but is used when supply exceeds demand. SNP disaggregation determines disaggregation demand; in other words, the demand of the subproducts, based on the NETDM auxiliary key figure or a user-defined auxiliary key figure. The system calculates the net demand saved in the NETDM key figure at the subproduct level using the net demand (disaggregation) macro, while taking the stock level changes into account. It ignores the demand from earlier periods (shown in the

supply shortage key figure) and only considers the demand starting with the period containing the value to be disaggregated.

- **Disaggregation according to quota arrangements**
Values are disaggregated from the header product level to the subproduct level according to quota arrangements that you have defined for the subproducts. You define these quota arrangements either as time-independent in the master data of the product hierarchy or location product hierarchy, or time-dependent in a time-series key figure. You specify the time-series key figure in the disaggregation settings. You can either use an existing (not yet used) key figure of your planning area, or create a new key figure and assign it to your planning area and planning book.

- **Method combination**
You can also select the Disaggregation According to Quota Arrangements option from the Method field and specify a horizon. The system performs disaggregation according to demands for orders within the horizon, and disaggregation according to quota arrangements for orders outside the horizon. This is useful, for example, if you have more exact demand information for a time frame in the near future than for a later time frame.

In addition to the disaggregation methods, you can choose between period- or order-based disaggregation modes. The disaggregation function can be executed at a single location or across the network.

- **Network disaggregation**
The value stored at the header product level is automatically disaggregated at all locations in the distribution network where the chosen header product and subproducts exist.

- **Location disaggregation**
The value stored at the header product level is only disaggregated at the selected locations for the selected products.

If you've determined the low-level codes before executing network or location disaggregation, the system automatically processes the locations in a specific sequence so that it can correctly determine the disaggregation demand. The system begins with the final location of the supply chain where the demand exists at subproduct level (a DC, for example).

▶ **Delete orders at the header level**
During order disaggregation, you can configure how you want the system to proceed after disaggregation with the orders at the header location product level. This refers to the values saved in the distribution receipt or distribution demand (planned) and production (planned) or dependent demand key figures. You can specify that the system deletes, reduces, or doesn't change the orders. In the production environment, it's highly recommended to note the following:

▶ **Delete**
The system deletes the orders at the header product level (the values saved in the distribution receipt or distribution demand (planned), and production (planned) or dependent demand key figures.

▶ **Reduce**
The system reduces the orders at the header product level by the total of disaggregated orders at the subproduct level in the respective period. There might be a remainder if you've defined different rounding values or minimum lot sizes for the subproducts and header product in the product master data. This remainder is then displayed in the distribution receipt or planned distribution demand and planned production or dependent demand key figures in interactive planning.

▶ **Do Not Change**
The values saved in the distribution receipt or planned distribution demand and planned production or dependent demand key figures are retained. The system takes these values into account when it calculates the total receipt/demand, thus calculating them twice. This can cause problems when the data is processed further in other locations. The system deletes or reduces the orders in the disaggregation horizon. You should mainly use the option of retaining the orders for simulation purposes.

6.8.4 Aggregated Planning with Safety Stock

Safety stock (SS) planning for the header product can be executed during the CTM planning. The SS planning data can be maintained at the header product, or you can maintain the SS method and the SS values at the subproduct. Using the setting in the hierarchy definition, you can aggregate the subproduct SS values to the header product (see Figure 6.30).

6 | Advanced Planning Techniques with CTM

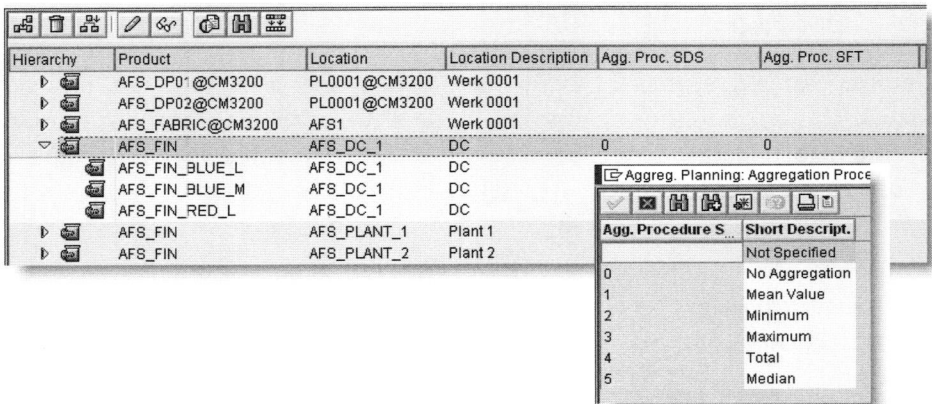

Figure 6.30 Safety Stock Aggregation Modes in Hierarchy

You can define the SS data as either time independent in the location product master data or time dependent in interactive SNP. In the master data of the location product hierarchy, you can define at the header location product level that the system automatically aggregates the data from the sublocation product level to the header location product level using the Aggregated SDS and Aggregated SFT fields. Various procedures are available for aggregation, such as average and total. So that the time-dependent data can be automatically aggregated, it has to be saved in time-series key figures in SAP liveCache. Aggregation is only temporary, meaning the aggregated data isn't saved permanently. The SS method defined for the header product must be used for all of the sublevel products.

Two-phase SS planning for the header product isn't supported in CTM because it isn't possible to create fixed pegging between the demands at the subproduct level and supply created at the header product level. For SS planning, you should use single-phase SS planning in CTM using the Do Not Plan Demands and Consider Supply Shortage settings.

> **Limitation of Aggregated Planning in CTM**
>
> CTM aggregated planning is a flexible planning tool for planning with hierarchies. The aggregated planning function in SAP SCM is supported only for the SNP bucket mode, so the following restrictions must be considered before using aggregated planning in CTM:
>
> ▶ Only two-level product location hierarchies are supported by CTM.
> ▶ The aggregated planning function is only possible in the SNP bucket-planning scenario. Order types should also be of type SNP.

- Interactive processes, such as changing, creating, and deleting an aggregated order, aren't possible in CTM. They can only be performed with SNP interactive planning.
- Descriptive characteristics for subproducts can't be used for aggregation, so they aren't used in CTM demand prioritization.

Because SNP disaggregation doesn't support the following scenarios, we recommend that you don't use them in aggregated planning with CTM either:

- Product interchangeability and CTM planning with rules
- Subcontracting
- MTO production
- Planning without final assembly

6.9 CTM Planning in Distribution Networks

CTM planning can be used for supply demand matching in the distribution network. In a distribution network, all of the DCs can supply each other. As a result, the supply chain isn't a linear network, but materials can be transported across locations. As shown in Figure 6.31, the distribution network consists of three warehouses, and each one can be a source location. The demand also can be placed across any location of the network.

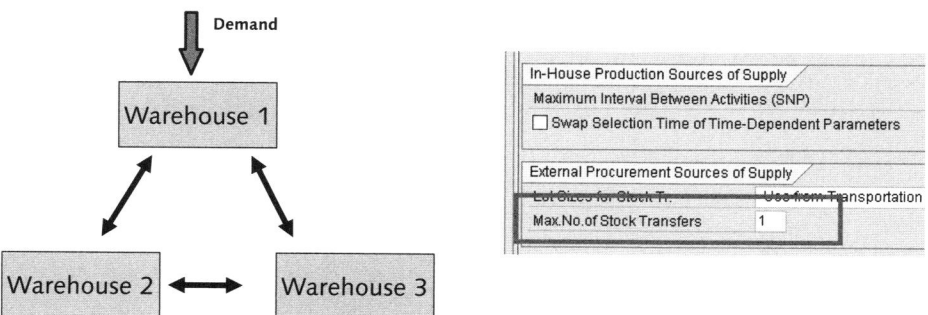

Figure 6.31 Maximum Transports for Distribution Planning in CTM

Due to the multilevel planning logic in CTM, the search tree starts from the demand location, and all possible source locations are used for supply selection.

The following search tree is generated for the demand in Warehouse1:

Transport (WH2 → WH1)

Transport (WH1 → WH2) (Error due to cyclic transport)

Transport (WH3 → WH2)

Transport (WH2 → WH3) (Error due to cyclic transport)

Transport (WH1 → WH3) (Error due to cyclic transport)

Transport (WH3 → WH1)

In extreme cases, the number of search points will be 3*2 = 6 per demand.

For a distribution network with 10 DCs, the maximum search points generated are 3,628,800 (10*9*8*7*6*5*4*3*2*1).

As shown in the preceding example, due to the large number of search points that are generated during the CTM planning process, demand processing can take a significant amount of time. To reduce the CTM search points, you can use the Max. No. of Stock Transfers (maximum number of stock transfers) parameter (refer to Figure 6.31) to define successive transport orders than can be created for a given demand. By using this parameter, CTM won't search for multiple transports.

The following search points are generated by CTM using the Max.No. of Stock Transfers parameter with a value of 1:

Transport (WH2 → WH1)

Transport (WH3 → WH1)

6.10 Summary

You can use CTM planning for implementing advanced planning methods using requirement strategies. You now understand the master data and the order data used for supply chain planning within a plant. Subcontracting planning methods in CTM was also explained in detail. You can now use the aggregated planning function in CTM using the location product hierarchy structure.

In the next chapter, the technical details of the CTM planning process are explained.

In this chapter, you'll learn the technical details about the CTM engine in order to analyze and optimize the CTM planning run. You'll also learn about the parallel processing methods and customer exits available in CTM planning.

7   Technical Details of CTM Planning

A successful implementation of the CTM supply planning process requires a careful analysis of the requirements and a clear understanding of the CTM planning engine algorithm. To ensure that the CTM planning process using the CTM engine is configured optimally for the best performance and supportability, it's important to understand the key process steps and interfaces that are used by the CTM planning engine. CTM application logs are available to identify and analyze the bottlenecks in key process steps with respect to the overall runtimes of the CTM panning process. There are several best practices described later in the chapter that must be used to achieve the optimal performance of the CTM planning run. The CTM planning run using the parallel profile is supported from SAP SCM 5.0. This can be used to optimally use the available system resources during CTM planning. Sizing considerations for the CTM planning is also described. CTM planning offers several user exits and BAdIs to extend the CTM functionality to meet specific requirements. Detailed description is provided for all of the BAdIs and user exits later in this chapter. CTM variable planning parameters can be used to enable specialized planning functions. This chapter provides a list of all variable planning parameters available in SAP SCM 5.0. The last section of this chapter describes the commonly faced issues with CTM planning.

7.1   CTM Planning Performance Optimization

A CTM complete planning run consists of four steps as shown in Figure 7.1. Each step can contribute significantly to the overall runtime of the planning process.

To evaluate each process step of the planning run, it's important to enable application log creation for the CTM planning run. The CTM application log can be cre-

7 | Technical Details of CTM Planning

ated using the Save CTM Messages setting available in the Technical Settings tab of the CTM profile. The planning application logs can be displayed for the CTM run using Transaction /SAPAPO/CTMAPLOG or using the SAP Easy Access menu path Advanced Planning and Optimization • Supply Chain Planning • Multilevel Supply and Demand Matching • Capable To Match • Reporting • Application Log.

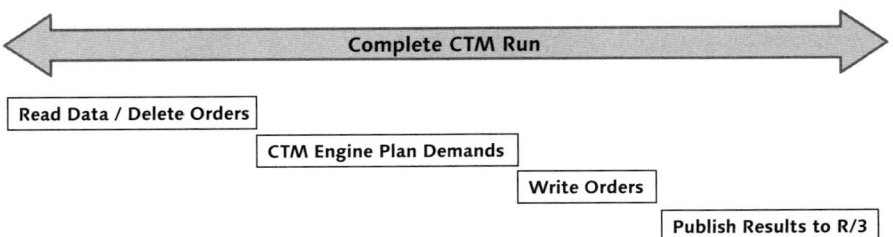

Figure 7.1 CTM Planning Steps

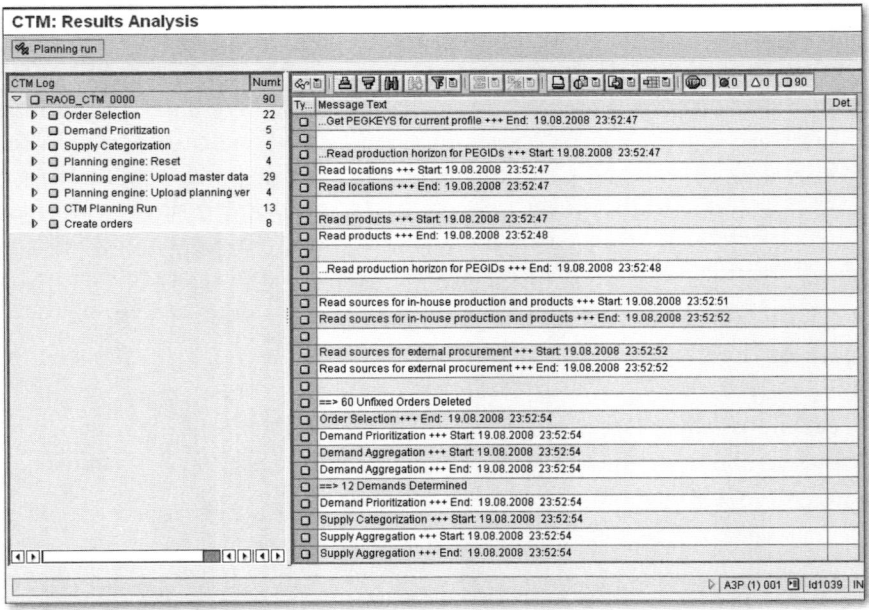

Figure 7.2 CTM Application Log

The CTM application log shown in Figure 7.2 is the most important tool, which can be used for top-down performance analysis. Detailed messages are created for each of the steps. The number of objects selected for planning and the planning results are listed in the application log. You can identify the overall runtimes and

240

the runtimes for each of the planning steps. For example, you can determine if the overall runtime for data selection is optimal or if the main bottleneck is the CTM engine planning run.

Using the application log, you can identify the total time required for order selection, demand prioritization, supply categorization, product location selection, transport lane selection, PPM/PDS selection, CTM engine planning runtimes, and order creation in SAP liveCache. The number of planning objects selected for planning can also be displayed in the CTM application log.

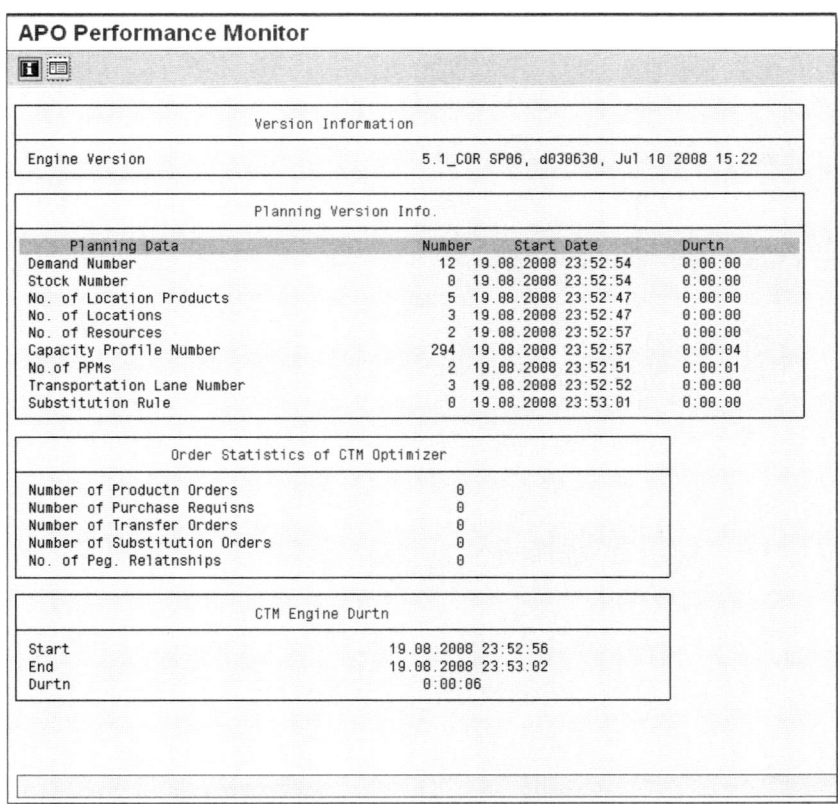

Figure 7.3 SAP SCM Performance Monitor Data for CTM Planning

Another important tool available in SAP SCM to identify the overall performance of the CTM run is the SAP SCM Performance Monitor. This function can be invoked using Transaction /SAPAPO/CTMPERFMON. Figure 7.3 shows the performance results for one of the CTM planning runs. Using Performance Monitor, you can identify the total duration for each of the steps and the number of objects used for planning. The Performance Monitor log can also be used to determine the CTM engine version.

Based on the planning process and overall system configuration, the overall runtime and performance can be influenced by each of the planning steps. The factors that can influence the four planning steps are described in detail in the following sections.

7.1.1 STEP 1: Read Data and Delete Order

Step 1 of the CTM regenerative planning is used for deleting all of the firmed orders and to read firmed orders. The firmed orders are converted to CTM demands and supplies. During CTM re-planning mode, CTM planning first selects the data from SAP liveCache for order deletion. After the orders are deleted from SAP liveCache, the remaining orders are selected again for planning. By default, the order selection for deletion selects all of the details associated with the orders. For example, input nodes, output nodes, order pegging, and so on. To avoid selecting order details, you should use the Do not Check Order Details setting along with the End Planning Run After Order Selection setting available under the Technical Settings tab of the CTM profile. Because these are profile-specific settings, it's recommended to create a separate CTM profile for order deletion using these settings. As shown in Figure 7.4, it's recommended to use two separate planning profiles for CTM planning. The first profile is used for order deletion, and the second profile is used for order selection and planning.

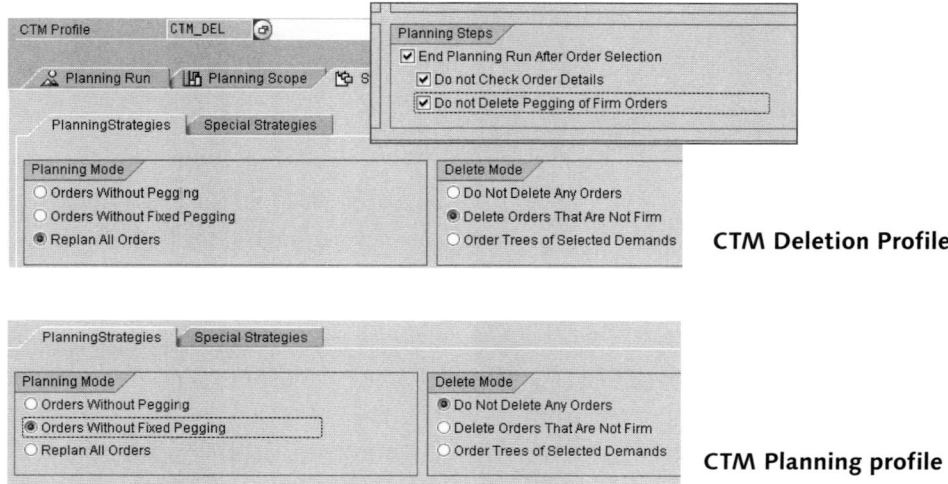

Figure 7.4 CTM Profiles for Optimal Order Deletion and Planning

Using a separate profile for order deletion, you can use fast deletion options in the CTM profile. The order deletion is executed much faster. You can also use the parallel processing profile to optimally use the available system resources during order deletion. This deletion profile skips the default checks required for order deletion. For example, the pegging information and input and output nodes aren't read. Firmed orders aren't deleted. The system will read all orders for all location/products that belong to the master data selection. Every unfirmed order for a location product that is in the selection will be deleted if it has an input or output node in the master data selection. The fast deletion profile must not be used if you're using the Subcontracting planning scenario. Using the fast deletion method, only the purchase requisition assigned to the subcontracting planned order is deleted because the subcontracting planned order is a firmed order. The subcontracting purchase requisition and planned order must always be created and deleted simultaneously. The second profile is used for planning the open demands and supplies. To select only the open demands, you can use the Orders Without Fixed Pegging and Do Not Delete Any Orders options for the planning and deletion mode in the CTM profile.

Similar to other planning tools in SAP SCM, CTM also uses SAP liveCache COM functions to read the order data from the SAP liveCache. SAP liveCache and application routines provide very fast access to the order data. The order data selection using SAP liveCache application routines can be optimized using package sizes available in the CTM global customization. By using the Package Size for Order Selection setting available in CTM global customization, CTM will select the order data from SAP liveCache using smaller packages. The package size for order selection is used to select the orders from SAP liveCache and represents the number of product locations or peg areas that can be used to select orders from SAP liveCache. This can improve the overall performance of the order data selection. A very low or high package size can negatively influence the overall performance of the order data selection. In addition to the deletion profile and package size for order selection, the following parameters can also improve the overall performance of the order data selection:

▶ During order data selection, by default, the dynamic pegging relationships are calculated by SAP liveCache. During regenerative planning, the dynamic pegging relationships aren't relevant for planning. The calculation and reading of this data can take a significant amount of time during the order selection. You can exclude the reading of dynamic pegging by SAP liveCache for order selection using the CTM variable planning parameter FIX_PEG_LC with Value1 = X (see SAP Note 1076350 for more details).

- Order data in SAP liveCache consists of additional attributes that aren't relevant for CTM planning. You can exclude the reading of additional attributes of orders that aren't relevant for CTM planning using CTM planning parameter EXCLUDE_ LC with Value1 = X (see SAP Note 1056215 for more details).

- Order data selection from SAP liveCache can be much faster by using the latest COM routines in SAP SCM 5.0. You can enable data selection using new functions by using CTM planning parameter FAST_READ with Value1 = X (see SAP Note 1070611 for more details).

- When the Make To Order (MTO) planning scenario is used in the SAP SCM application, it creates peg areas for each of the MTO sales orders in the customer system. Over time, the peg areas aren't relevant for planning and hence must be deleted using the SAP standard report for peg area deletion /SAPAPO/ DM_PEGKEY_REORG (see SAP Notes 390151, 693767).

The data selected for planning is converted into CTM demands and CTM supplies. The selected demands, supplies, and SC Model data (product locations, transport lanes, and PPM/PDS) are uploaded to the CTM engine for planning and generating the supply plan. To reduce the number of demands and supplies uploaded to the CTM engine for planning, you should use demand and supply aggregation. As described in Chapter 3, time-based aggregation can be used to group multiple demands or supplies for planning. The use of time-based aggregation must be carefully evaluated for your business requirements.

The selected demands and supplies are temporarily saved in the SAP SCM database using the Tables /SAPAPO/CTMDEM and /SAPAPO/CTMSUP. The saved demands and supplies are selected by the CTM engine for planning using the RFC interface. In certain planning scenarios where a large number of demands and supplies are selected for planning, saving the data in database tables can be very performance intensive. Using the Only Hold in Active Mode option available in the CTM global customization, it's possible to save the demand and supply data in the SAP SCM application sever memory rather than saving it in the database. This can improve the performance of the CTM demand and supply selection step but would require additional memory for the SAP SCM application server. The performance gain versus the cost of additional memory must be carefully evaluated when using this setting in the CTM global customization.

In STEP 1, after all of the master and transactional data is prepared, the CTM planning engine is started using the RFC communication.

7.1.2 STEP 2: CTM Engine Planning for Demands

The CTM engine receives the planning data and generates the supply plan for the selected demands. The CTM engine is a C++ based scheduling and planning engine. It's based on RFC server implementation to communicate with the SAP SCM server. To identify and analyze the performance of the CTM engine, it's important to understand the CTM planning algorithm described in Chapter 4. It's also important to check the technical configuration of the CTM engine interface and optimization server configuration.

Setting Up the RFC Connection for the CTM Engine

The connection to the CTM engine is established using the RFC connection definition in Transaction SM59. SAP delivers the standard connections for CTM and other planning tools in SAP SCM. The default connection name, OPTSERVER_CTM01, is used for the CTM engine. To enable communication between the SAP SCM server and the CTM engine, the gateway service and the gateway host must be also assigned to the RFC connection. Figure 7.5 shows the typical RFC connection definition used for the CTM engine. The CTM engine is a precompiled C++ engine named as CTMSVR.EXE, which is executed on the Windows-based 32/64-bit optimization server. The CTM engine isn't supported for the UNIX-based systems.

It's possible to define multiple RFC connections in the SAP SCM system for the CTM engine. You define multiple RFC definitions to connect multiple optimization servers to the SAP SCM server. This is mainly useful if you want to execute multiple CTM runs in parallel without causing any CPU bottlenecks in the optimization server because the CTM engine planning is a highly CPU-intensive process.

7 | Technical Details of CTM Planning

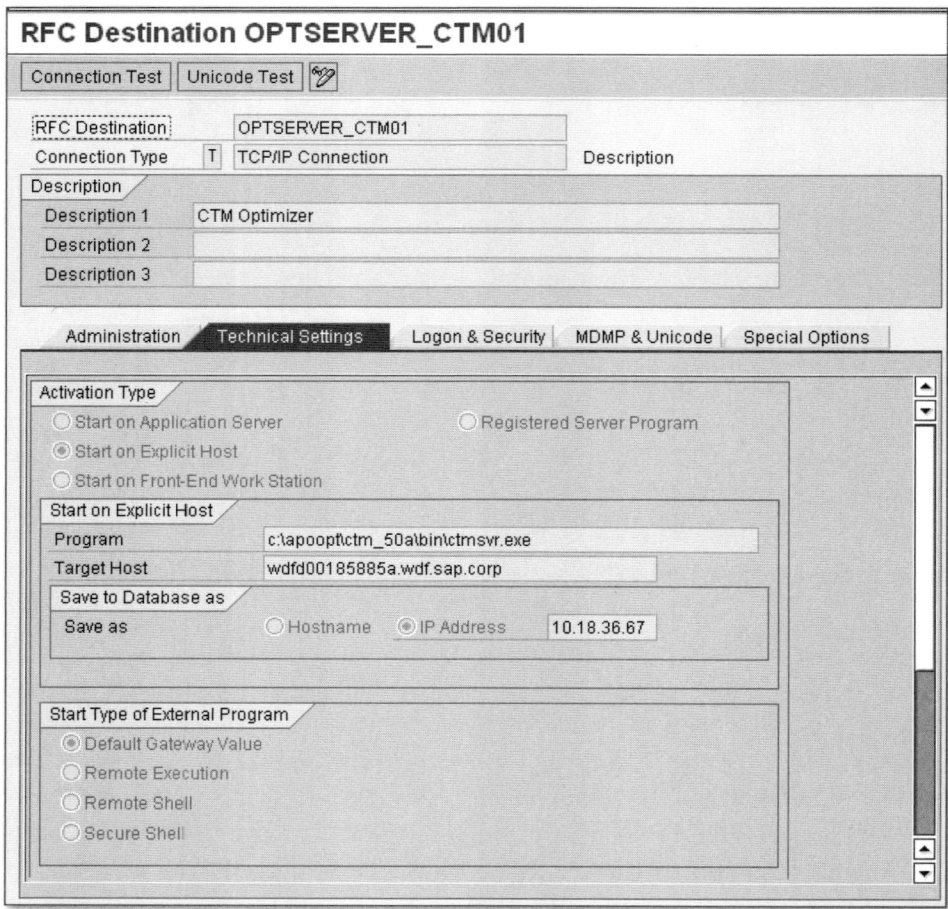

Figure 7.5 RFC Connection Definition for CTM Engine from SAP SCM Server

SAP SCM offers a central optimization server management function and customizations to define additional parameters for the RFC connections. Using the customization Table /sapapo/optsvr available under customization SAP SCM IMPLEMENTATION GUIDE • ADVANCED PLANNING AND OPTIMIZATION • BASIS SETTING • OPTIMIZATION • BASIC FUNCTIONS • MAINTAIN MASTER DATA FOR OPTIMIZATION SERVER. Figure 7.6 shows the CTM optimization server configuration.

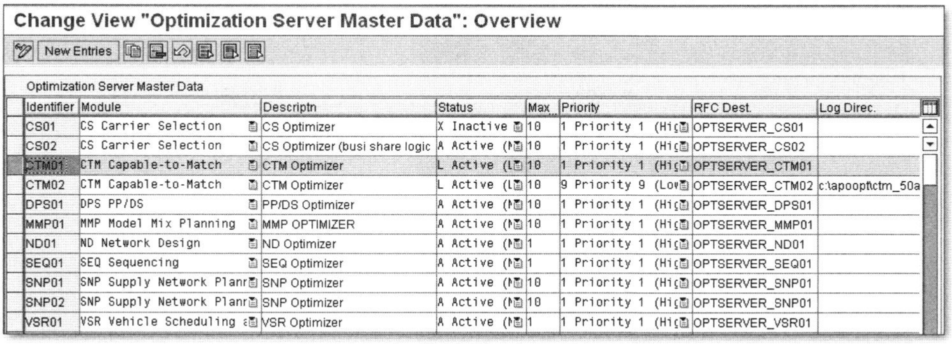

Change View "Optimization Server Master Data": Overview

New Entries

Optimization Server Master Data

Identifier	Module	Descriptn	Status	Max	Priority	RFC Dest.	Log Direc.
CS01	CS Carrier Selection	CS Optimizer	X Inactive	10	1 Priority 1 (Hig	OPTSERVER_CS01	
CS02	CS Carrier Selection	CS Optimizer (busi share logic	A Active (N	10	1 Priority 1 (Hig	OPTSERVER_CS02	
CTM01	CTM Capable-to-Match	CTM Optimizer	L Active (L	10	1 Priority 1 (Hig	OPTSERVER_CTM01	
CTM02	CTM Capable-to-Match	CTM Optimizer	L Active (L	10	9 Priority 9 (Low	OPTSERVER_CTM02	c:\apoopt\ctm_50a
DPS01	DPS PP/DS	PP/DS Optimizer	A Active (N	10	1 Priority 1 (Hig	OPTSERVER_DPS01	
MMP01	MMP Model Mix Planning	MMP OPTIMIZER	A Active (N	10	1 Priority 1 (Hig	OPTSERVER_MMP01	
ND01	ND Network Design	ND Optimizer	A Active (N	1	1 Priority 1 (Hig	OPTSERVER_ND01	
SEQ01	SEQ Sequencing	SEQ Optimizer	A Active (N	1	1 Priority 1 (Hig	OPTSERVER_SEQ01	
SNP01	SNP Supply Network Planr	SNP Optimizer	A Active (N	10	1 Priority 1 (Hig	OPTSERVER_SNP01	
SNP02	SNP Supply Network Planr	SNP Optimizer	A Active (N	10	1 Priority 1 (Hig	OPTSERVER_SNP01	
VSR01	VSR Vehicle Scheduling a	VSR Optimizer	A Active (N	1	1 Priority 1 (Hig	OPTSERVER_VSR01	

Figure 7.6 CTM Optimization Server Configuration

In the master data for the optimization server, you can specify which standard optimizers are available for SAP APO, in which position they are, and how they should be accessed. In each row, information for precisely one optimizer is maintained. Table 7.1 lists the attributes that can be maintained for each of the RFC connections used for CTM planning.

Attribute	Description
Identifier	Exact description of the optimization program (optimization for CTM, PP/DS, SNP, ND) that is on an optimization server.
Module	Module in SAP APO that provides optimization servers. You can choose among CTM, DPS (PP/DS), SNP, and ND.
Short text	Description of the optimizer.
Status	**Inactive:** The optimizer is inactive and can't be started. **Active (normal situation):** The optimizer is active. **Active (logging switched on):** The optimizer is active, and a log file is written during an optimization run.
Max. users	Maximum number of users that can work simultaneously with the optimizer

Table 7.1 Attributes for RFC Connections

Attribute	Description
Priority	Specifies the priority with which an optimization server is chosen if several optimization servers are available. If two optimization servers have the same priority, then the one on which there are the fewer active users is chosen. **Possible values:** 1 (highest priority) to 9 (lowest priority)
RFC destination	Logical destination for calling up the optimization server. Entry must be made when installing an optimization server in the table for the RFC destinations (Transaction SM59).
Log file index	Each optimizer can save log files to the hard drive if its status field is set to L. The CTM optimizer saves its log data to the complete index path entered here (e.g., c:\apoopt\ctm\log).

Table 7.1 Attributes for RFC Connections (Cont.)

Using the configuration setting for the RFC connection and optimization server, CTM planning can start the CTM engine. The system will automatically select the optimization server based on the server attributes such as priority and maximum number of users. To explicitly select the optimization server for CTM planning, you can use the Optimization Server ID setting available in the Technical Settings tab of the CTM profile. The CTM profile will only select the optimization server defined in the CTM profile.

CTM Engine Trace Generation

CTM planning generates the supply plan for the selected demands using the master data model and the CTM planning strategies. The planning results generated by the CTM engine in the form of planned orders, transport orders, and purchase requisitions are saved in SAP liveCache. To identify and analyze the performance of the CTM planning engine, it's important to enable the CTM engine trace for the optimization server using the status L. As shown in Figure 7.7, in the CTM profile, you can select the relevant data for trace output.

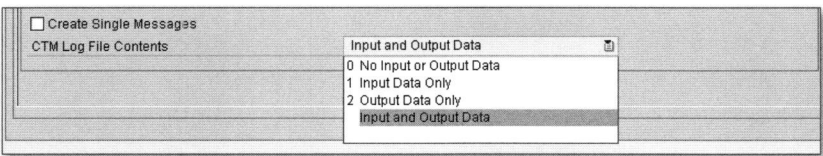

Figure 7.7 CTM Engine Trace Options in the CTM profile

Four options are available for selecting the CTM engine trace file contents:

- **No Input or Output Data**
  The CTM engine only selects the optimization server configuration data (memory and CPU), RFC interface, and performance counters (peak memory and CPU time) in the trace file.

- **Input Data Only**
  The CTM engine selects the input data (demands, supplies, master data, CTM planning parameters), optimization server configuration data (memory and CPU), RFC interface, and performance counters (peak memory and CPU time) in the trace file.

- **Output Data Only**
  The CTM engine selects the output data (supply tree, order data), optimization server configuration data (memory and CPU), RFC interface, and performance counters (peak memory and CPU time) in the trace file.

- **Input and Output Data**
  The CTM engine selects the input data (demands, supplies, master data, CTM planning parameters), output data (supply tree, order data), optimization server configuration data (memory and CPU), RFC interface, and performance counters (peak memory and CPU time) in the trace file.

For better performance, you should use the Input Data Only option in the productive system because large amounts of data are generated by the CTM engine. Generating the trace for all of the input and output data is very performance intensive and can negatively impact the overall performance of the CTM planning run. Additionally, with SAP SCM 5.0, tracing of CTM engine input and output data can lead to severe performance problems. In the production environment when large datasets are used for CTM planning, engine logging must be switched off. To generate the trace file with input data for root cause analysis of any planning errors, you can use the following CTM control parameter to generate the CTM input data file. This CTM variable planning parameter doesn't cause any severe performance issues during CTM engine tracing.

> **Note**
>
> Parameter Name = CTM_MG
> Value1   = bWriteInputToFile
> Value2   = true

7 | Technical Details of CTM Planning

> The following conditions must be satisfied to use this planning parameter:
> - CTM optimization server status must be set as Active (Logging Enabled).
> - CTM profile settings for log file contents must be set as No Input and Output Data.
> - The CTM profile must be set with the variable control parameter given at the beginning of this box.
> - With these settings, the CTM input data file is generated under the gateway log directory of the optimization server.
> - The CTM input data file format is ctm<date>_<time>_<pid>.in.
>
> Refer to SAP Note 1073902 for more details about the parameter.

CTM Engine Trace Evaluation

The CTM engine trace is used to identify and analyze the overall performance of the CTM engine. The trace file contains all of the planning data, optimization server environment, and output data generated during the planning run. The trace file can be displayed using Transaction /SAPAPO/OPT11 or using the SAP Easy Access menu path ADVANCED PLANNING AND OPTIMIZATION • SUPPLY CHAIN PLANNING • MULTILEVEL SUPPLY AND DEMAND MATCHING • CAPABLE TO MATCH • REPORTING • OPTIMIZER LOG DATA. Figure 7.8 shows the key sections of the CTM engine trace file.

Section 1 of the trace file displays the CTM engine version. It's important to use the latest CTM engine version available in the SAP Service Marketplace. The CTM engine is downward compatible so you can use the latest CTM engine without using the latest SAP SCM support pack levels.

Section 2 contains the optimization server environment parameters. For example, number and type of CPUs, total and available memory, and the free disk space available. This information is useful to identify any hardware bottlenecks that can influence the performance of the CTM planning engine.

Section 3 displays the master and transaction data used by the CTM planning engine. CTM planning parameters used for planning are also listed in this section. This section is very useful for analysis by the support teams because it provides a snapshot of the data available at the time of the CTM planning run. All of the data in the trace file is displayed using the SAP SCM internal GUIDs, so it isn't very user friendly. Understanding the trace data requires deep technical knowledge of the SAP SCM system and the SAP SCM data model.

CTM Planning Performance Optimization | 7.1

```
<i> 16:33:03 optsvr_main.cpp(609)  'SuperVisor'  * SAP APO CTM Engine [CTM/ctmsvr]
<i> 16:33:03 optsvr_main.cpp(610)  'SuperVisor'  * Copyright @ SAP AG 1993-2008
<i> 16:33:03 optsvr_main.cpp(611)  'SuperVisor'  *
<i> 16:33:03 optsvr_main.cpp(612)  'SuperVisor'  * Version       : 5.1_COR SP06, d030630, Jul 10 2008 15:22:43
<i> 16:33:03 optsvr_main.cpp(613)  'SuperVisor'  * Platform      : ntamd64/x64
<i> 16:33:03 optsvr_main.cpp(614)  'SuperVisor'  * Interface     : 2.0
<i> 16:33:03 optsvr_main.cpp(615)  'SuperVisor'  * Build date    : Jul 10 2008 15:22:43 [1215696163]
<i> 16:33:03 optsvr_main.cpp(616)  'SuperVisor'  * Build machine : WDFD00183867A
<i> 16:33:03 optsvr_main.cpp(617)  'SuperVisor'  * Latest change : d030630                              1
```

```
<i> 16:33:03 core_sysinfo.cpp(377)  'SuperVisor' * Memory information:
<i> 16:33:03 core_sysinfo.cpp(377)  'SuperVisor' *   physical memory: 4093 MB total, 3142 MB available [76% free]
<i> 16:33:03 core_sysinfo.cpp(377)  'SuperVisor' *   page file      : 5876 MB total, 5318 MB available [90% free]
<i> 16:33:03 core_sysinfo.cpp(377)  'SuperVisor' *   virtual memory : 8388607 MB total, 8388550 MB available [99% free]
<i> 16:33:03 core_sysinfo.cpp(377)  'SuperVisor' *
<i> 16:33:03 core_sysinfo.cpp(326)  'SuperVisor' *
<i> 16:33:03 core_sysinfo.cpp(326)  'SuperVisor' * CPU#0:
<i> 16:33:03 core_sysinfo.cpp(326)  'SuperVisor' *   Identifier: EM64T Family 6 Model 15 Stepping 6
<i> 16:33:03 core_sysinfo.cpp(326)  'SuperVisor' *   estim. MHz: 2394
<i> 16:33:03 core_sysinfo.cpp(326)  'SuperVisor' *   Name      : Intel(R) Core(TM)2 CPU          6600  @ 2.4  2
<i> 16:33:03 core_sysinfo.cpp(326)  'SuperVisor' *   Vendor    : GenuineIntel
```

```
// TABLE ET_COMPALTLOC
// TRPID                  AMATID                 MATID                  SUBLOC LOCID
// STRING                 STRING                 STRING                 STRING STRING
   MenEI16CPspX00002X56VG 5enEI16CPspX00002X56VG P5nqHNKekWpX00002X56VW        mrjqHNKekWpX00002X56VW
   MenEI16CPspX00002X56VG 5unEI16CPspX00002X56VG HLnqHNKekWpX00002X56VW        mrjqHNKekWpX00002X56VW
//
// TABLE ET_DEMAND
// PRFLID  DEMID DEMCAT PRIO MATID                  LOCID                  ACCID PLSEC QUANTITY DUEDATE       ATPCAT ATP
   HIP SHIPPACK PEGGINGTYPE SUBSTKEY OBJID  CHARACTERISTICS CHARSTRCNT CLASSID NOSUBST EXPL_EXPLAIN
// STRING  INT   STRING INT  STRING                 STRING                 STRING STRING STRING  STRING               NT
   STRING      INT         STRING  STRING STRING        INT        INT     STRING STRING
   RAOB_CTM 1    FC     21   25nqHNKekWpX00002X56VW wLjqHNKekWpX00002X56VW       0    -10.000  200808161200       3
   0.000       1                                                 1          0
```

```
<0>
<0> (10/12) [10] Demand 25nqHNKekWpX00002X56VW   (56)
<0> ----------------------------------------
<0> in-time satisfaction (without TDS)
<0> ----------------------------------------
<0> [D] (18, 0, 0) [1218888000]  |?10|
<0>    [SOS] 19 Supply, cat 00 MIC: -9223372036854775808
<2>    [SOS] 25nqHNKekWpX00002X56VW
<0>       <-[(0, 9223372036854775807), (0, 1218888000)]  |?10|
<0> [D]  ||0|
<0>    [SOS] 46 Transport MIC: -9223372036854775808
<2>    [SOS] wOPEI5T7PcpX00002X56VG
<0>       <-[(1219190400, 9223372036854775807), (1219190400, 1218888000)]  |?10|    4
<2> EST is behind due date
<0> [D]  ||0|
```

```
bSuccess#true
tracefile#ctm.RAOB_CTM.0000_0001.20080820163303.log

<2> 16:33:05 optsvr_main.cpp(1144)  'SuperVisor' performance counters:
ImageName                     ctmsvr
   6: Processor Time          625000#[0s]
 142: User Time               468750#[0s]
 144: Privileged Time         156250#[0s]
 172: Virtual Bytes Peak      68988928#[67372K]
 174: Virtual Bytes           68988928#[67372K]
  28: Page Faults             4390
 178: Working Set Peak        16883712#[16488K]
 180: Working Set             16875520#[16480K]
 182: Page File Bytes Peak    15314944#[14956K]
 184: Page File Bytes         15306752#[14948K]                                5
 186: Private Bytes           15306752#[14948K]
```

Figure 7.8 CTM Engine Trace details

251

7 | Technical Details of CTM Planning

Section 4 displays the complete search tree generated for each of the demands planned by the CTM engine. If a large model contains several locations and BOMs, the search tree can be very large and complex. Mainly expert support teams must analyze the CTM search tree. Likewise, users who use the SAP SCM tools, such as SAP SCM Alert Monitor and interactive planning books, should analyze the CTM planning results

Section 5 provides a summary of the CTM planning results, both technical and functional. Table 7.2 shows the summary listed in the CTM trace file.

Summary	Description
Planning Results	▶ Number of demands planned ▶ Demands satisfied completely in time ▶ Demands satisfied partially in time ▶ Demands satisfied completely but late ▶ Demands satisfied partially but late ▶ Demands not satisfied
Engine Performance Counter	▶ Net CPU Time ▶ Gross CPU Time ▶ Peak Memory used by CTM engine ▶ Peak Virtual Memory used by CTM engine

Table 7.2 Summary Listed in the CTM Trace File

Using the CTM engine trace, it's possible to identify any hardware bottlenecks on the optimization server.

The CTM planning engine performance is also influenced by the CTM planning parameters and the attributes used for the master data selected for planning. Lot sizes can have significant impact on the overall performance of the CTM run. Using very small lot sizes can lead to a large number of orders, thus increasing the overall planning and order creation time. On the other hand, using very large lot sizes can improve the performance but would not be suitable for business users. Additionally, planning in time-continuous mode can be performance intensive when the resources are planned finitely. If the model contains several planning alternatives (modes, PPMs, lanes, and means of transport), then CTM would evaluate all possible alternatives to find an in-time solution for the demand quantity. Because CTM uses the heuristics-based planning approach, CTM will use all of the alternatives to evaluate the complete supply chain network. Constraints detected using the first alternative aren't propagated when planning with the second alternative or other demands. This can lead to long runtimes for the CTM engine. Late demand handling modes can also lead to an overall increase in the planning runtimes. You should select the late demand frame (LDF) as small as required by the business instead of the default value of 999 days.

To ensure that the CTM engine isn't using an extraordinarily long time for planning individual demands, you should use the Maximum Scheduling Time per Demand parameter for the CTM demands. This parameter can be maintained under the Technical Settings tab of the CTM profile. This parameter is maintained as a number of seconds and defines the maximum time that the CTM engine will use for generating the supply for a given demand. After the maximum scheduling time is elapsed, CTM will save the current results and switch to the next demand in the demand list. You can use a value of 3-5 seconds. All of the demands that could not be satisfied due to the maximum scheduling time limit are displayed in the CTM application log.

7.1.3 STEP 3: Write the CTM Planning Result in liveCache

By default, the CTM planning engine plans for all of the demands in the synchronous planning mode and then saves the complete supply plan in SAP live-Cache. This can lead to high memory requirements for the CTM engine. To reduce the overall runtime and the memory requirement of the CTM planning run, you should use the asynchronous planning mode. In the asynchronous planning mode, the CTM engines process itself contains two threads. The first thread will plan the demands in smaller packages. The planning result for the first package is saved in SAP liveCache using a parallel process by the second thread. Using asynchronous planning mode, the complete CTM process and order writing can be performed in parallel as shown in Figure 7.9.

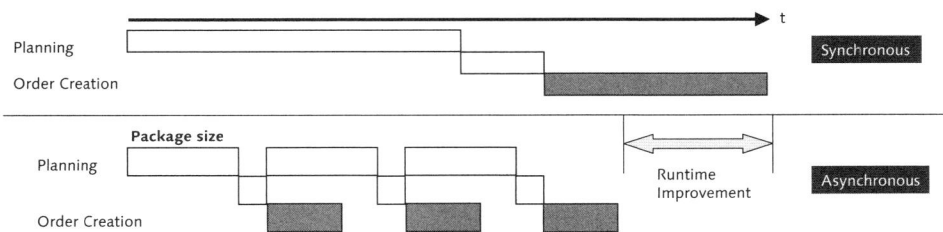

Figure 7.9 Synchronous and Asynchronous CTM Planning Mode

7 | Technical Details of CTM Planning

The packet size for demands selected for planning is maintained in the CTM global customization using the Packet Size setting. To use the Packet Size parameter, you must enable the Asynchronous liveCache Upd parameter as shown in Figure 7.10. The planning results generated by the CTM engine consist of planned orders, transport orders, purchase requisitions, and fixed pegging links. The orders are saved in SAP liveCache using the COM functions similar to order selection functions. To optimally save the planning results in SAP liveCache, you should use the package size for creating orders and pegging relationships.

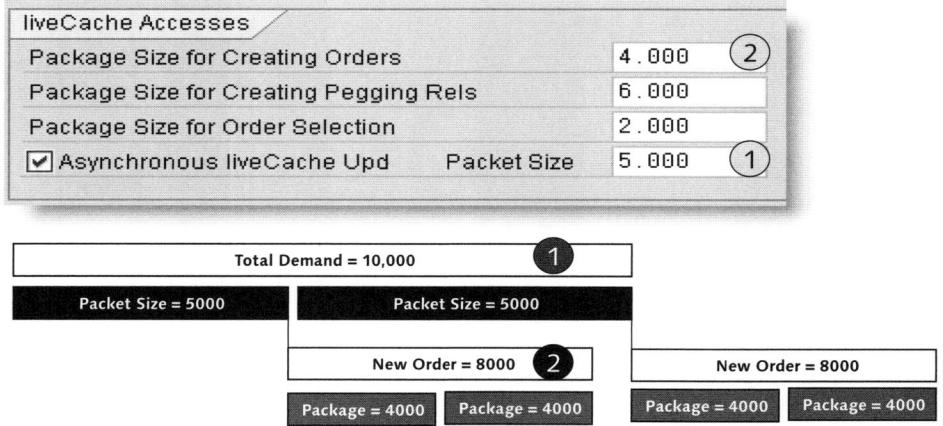

Figure 7.10 Package Size for Order Selection and CTM Demand Planning

Figure 7.10 also shows the package sizes available in CTM global customization for order creation. The Package Size for Creating Orders parameter defines the maximum number of orders that can be saved in SAP liveCache in a single package. This is applied for each individual order type (planned orders, transport orders, purchase requisitions, and substitution orders). Similarly, the fixed pegging links can also be created in SAP liveCache in smaller packages.

Note that incorrect package sizes can have a negative influence on the overall CTM runtimes. Too small package sizes will result in a lot of very small packages being transferred to SAP liveCache, where the transfer of package administration data becomes the biggest part of response time and a performance bottleneck occurs. In extreme cases, the Asynchronous liveCache update can then be slower than the synchronous one, where only one huge package is sent. Too big package sizes will result in few but very big packages, which can in extreme cases result in just one package and be the same as with Synchronous liveCache update. Optimal package size can be determined during volume testing of the CTM planning process.

7.1.4 STEP 4: Publish CTM Results to SAP ERP

The planning results created by CTM can be transferred to the SAP ERP system using the SAP CIF. CIF uses the change pointers to select the order relevant for publications to SAP ERP. The change pointers contain the key identifiers for the order data created by CTM and other planning tools in SAP SCM. CTM planning results can be published to the SAP ERP system when planning is executed in the active version 000. The CTM profile offers three options for creating the change pointers as shown in Figure 7.11.

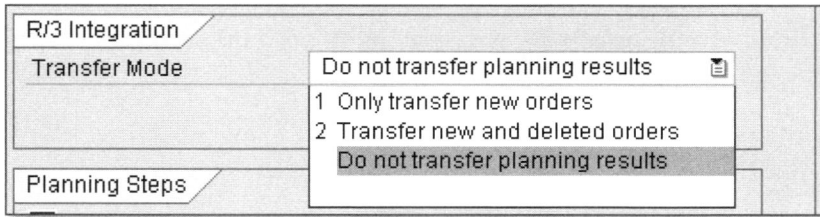

Figure 7.11 CTM Options for Order Publication to SAP ERP

- Only transfer new orders
- Transfer new and deleted orders
- Do not transfer planning results
- To ensure that the planning results are consistently published to the SAP ERP system, you should use the Transfer new and deleted orders option. If you use the Only transfer new orders option, then you shouldn't delete orders in SAP SCM using the CTM planning process because this can create inconsistencies across SAP SCM and the SAP ERP system.

The CTM planning process only creates the change pointers for the new and deleted orders. The actual processing of the change pointers is carried out by CIF. Three options are available to select the processing type of the change pointers:

7 | Technical Details of CTM Planning

▶ **Do not collect changes**
The planning results are published to SAP ERP as soon as they have been saved in SAP APO.

▶ **Collect changes**
The planning results are first collected and then transferred to SAP ERP at a later time using the report /SAPAPO/RDMCPPROCESS.

▶ **Default**
Publication occurs according to the settings made in customizing for SNP or PP/DS. The standard setting for SNP is Collect changes; for PP/DS, it's Do not collect changes.

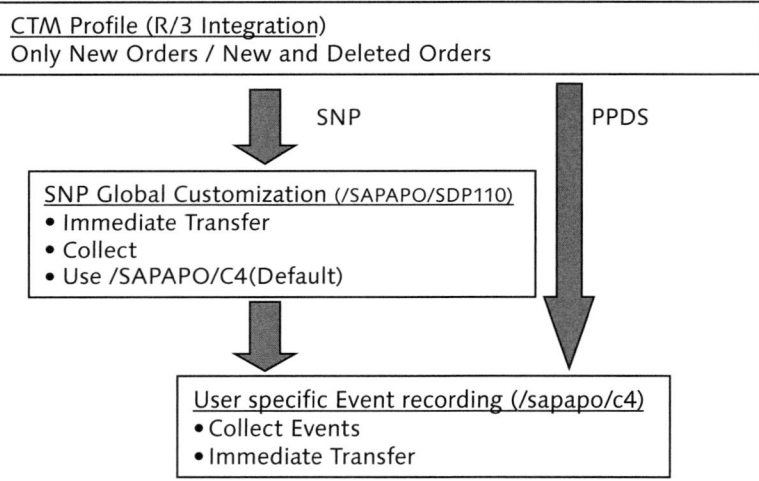

Figure 7.12 Customization for Publication of CTM Planning Results

▶ The processing type for CTM-created orders is selected based on the CTM planning type. As shown in Figure 7.12, in SNP planning mode, the processing type is selected from the SNP global customization (Transaction /SAPAPO/SDP110). In PP/DS planning mode, the processing type is selected from the PP/DS global customization (Transaction /SAPAPO/C4).

For optimal performance during CTM planning, you should use the Collect changes option for the processing type of the orders.

7.2 Using Parallel Processing for CTM Planning

Automatic parallel processing in CTM planning is supported from SAP SCM 5.0. In the earlier SAP SCM releases, parallel CTM planning was manual. For example, you can create independent master data selections and CTM profiles to plan the demands in parallel. The manual master data selection process is prone to data selection data errors. For complex SC Models, it isn't feasible to identify the independent SC Models. Creating multiple master data selections and CTM profiles increases the overall system administration efforts. Manual parallel model selection also doesn't ensure that the SAP SCM resources are optimally used for planning. Automatic parallel processing in CTM can be used to significantly improve CTM performance during planning. With automatic parallel processing, CTM distributes the complete SC Model into several smaller submodels and executes CTM planning for the submodels in parallel. Each submodel contains a specific number of location products, including their sources of supply (SOS). The complete supply chain network of a finished product is evaluated and assigned to a submodel. The submodel generation considers the following dependencies:

- Input and output products of a source of supply (PPM/PDS)
- Product in source location and target location of an external procurement or transport lane
- All products of a supersession chain
- All products of a Form-Fit-Function (FFF) subset

If the SC Model contains common production, handling, and transport resources, the system will select all of the products using the same resources in the same submodel. If you use infinite planning mode, then resource dependencies can be excluded during automatic submodel generation. Three options are available to influence the submodel generation using resources:

- **Do not consider any resources**
  Automatic submodel generation doesn't consider any resource-related dependencies.
- **Consider finite resources**
  Automatic submodel generation considers dependent products linked by finite resources.

7 | Technical Details of CTM Planning

- **Consider all resources**
  Automatic submodel generation considers dependent products linked by all resources.

- During parallel processing, the system doesn't consider the application of rules in CTM planning. In addition, the system doesn't support the simulation of supplies and demands during parallel processing.

- The complete planning process using automatic parallel processing is shown in Figure 7.13. Using the automatic parallel profile settings, CTM will generate independent submodels. Each submodel is planned independently considering the availability of the system resources in the SAP SCM system. The application log contains the details of each of the submodels selected for planning.

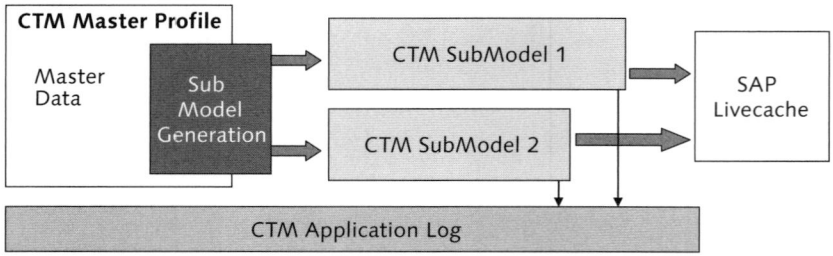

Figure 7.13 Automatic Parallel Processing and CTM Planning

- To use the automatic parallel processing in CTM planning, you have to define the parallel processing profile (see Figure 7.14). The parallel processing profile can be defined using Transaction /SAPAPO/CTMPAR or using the SAP Easy Access menu path ADVANCED PLANNING AND OPTIMIZATION • SUPPLY CHAIN PLANNING • MULTILEVEL SUPPLY AND DEMAND MATCHING • ENVIRONMENT • PARALLEL PROCESSING • DEFINE PARALLEL PROCESSING PROFILE.

- In the parallel processing profile, you specify how many submodels CTM is allowed to generate. The more submodels you allow, the better the performance of the CTM planning run. An improvement in performance, however, depends on the parallel processing capacity of the application server, optimization server, and SAP liveCache.

7.2 Using Parallel Processing for CTM Planning

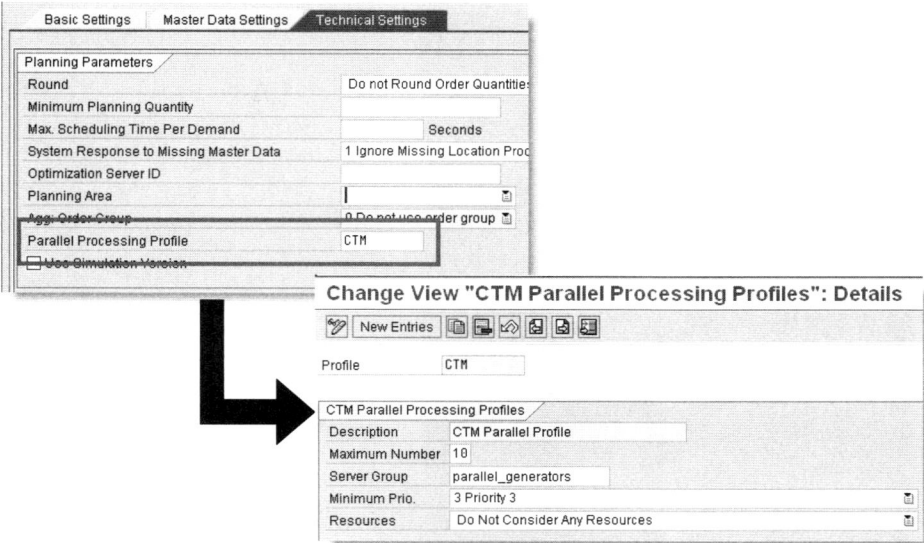

Figure 7.14 Using CTM Parallel Processing Profile

The attributes in Table 7.3 must be defined for the parallel processing profile used in CTM planning.

Parameter	Description
Maximum Number	Defines the maximum number of submodels created for the main model. This parameter must be set accordingly to the available system resources.
Server Group	Defines a group of application servers dedicated for CTM parallel processing.
Minimum Priority	Defines the minimum priority of the CTM optimization server connections that can be used for planning.
Resources	Defines whether the submodel generation must consider resource dependencies.

Table 7.3 Parallel Processing Profile Attributes

▶ The parallel processing profile must be assigned to the CTM profile using the Parallel Processing Profile setting available under the Technical Settings tab of the CTM profile.

7.3 CTM Planning Business Add-Ins

To modify the input and output data used for CTM planning, several BAdIs and user exits are available in CTM. Figure 7.15 shows the complete planning process and the enhancement points available for each step of the planning process. The BAdIs can be used to change the master data, demands and supplies, and the planning results generated during the CTM planning run. The CTM engine itself doesn't offer any customer exits for influencing the CTM engine algorithm.

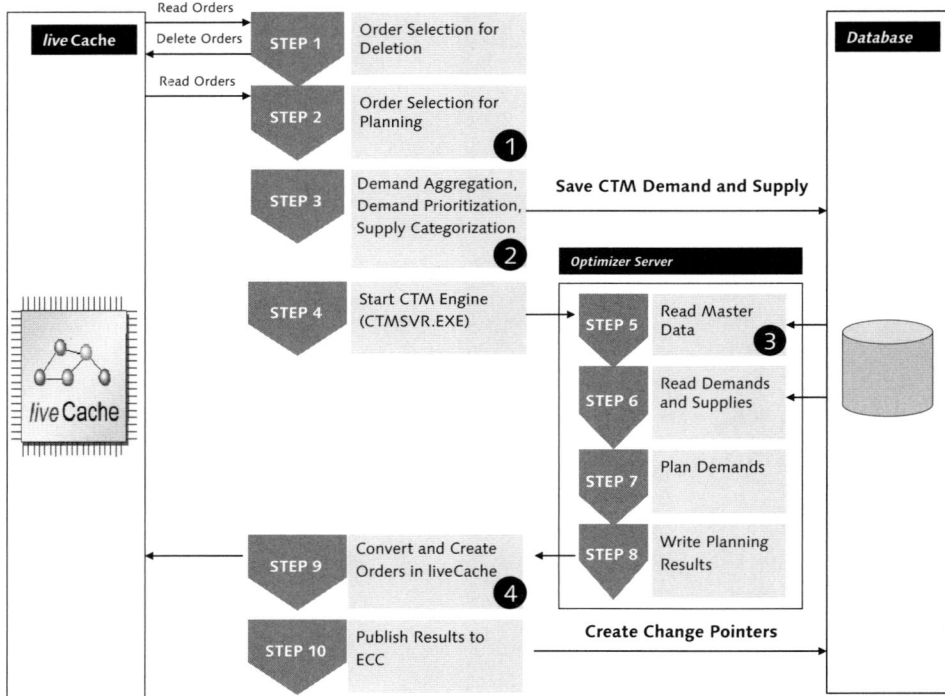

Figure 7.15 CTM BAdIs and User Exits

Table 7.4 lists the BAdIs available for CTM planning.

CTM demands that are selected for planning can be modified in the user exit APOBO020. The user exit can be used for defining custom prioritization of CTM demands. In the user exit, you can modify the demand attribute DEMID based in custom sort logic. The CTM engine will plan the demands using the sort sequence of the DEMID field.

Step	Business Add-In Name	Description
1	/SAPAPO/CTM_MATLOC /SAPAPO/CTM_MCHECK	Product location attributes used for CTM planning can be modified using this BAdI.
2	/SAPAPO/CTM_SUPPLY	Supplies used for CTM planning can be modified using this BAdI.
3	/SAPAPO/CTM_PLPAR /SAPAPO/CTM_RESOURCE /SAPAPO/CTM_SOSEXT /SAPAPO/CTM_SOSINT /SAPAPO/CTM_SUBST	Master data (resources, transport lanes, PPM/PDS, and substitution rules) attributes used for CTM planning can be modified using this BAdI.
4	/SAPAPO/CTM_ORDERS	CTM engine planning results before saving to SAP liveCache can be modified using this BAdI.

Table 7.4 CTM Planning BAdIs

Note

Refer to SAP Note 450794 for more details about the interface and usage of the user exit APOBO020 in CTM demand prioritization.

7.4 Summary

In this chapter, you learned about the technical details of the CTM engine. Now you know the settings required for creating the RFC connection for the CTM engine. You learned the structure of the CTM application log and CTM engine trace files, which you can use to analyze the CTM planning process. Now you understand the planning steps of the CTM planning process and can optimize each of the process steps for optimal performance. The automatic parallel processing of the CTM planning run available in SAP SCM 5.0 was also introduced to you in this chapter. This chapter contains a list of customer exits and BAdIs that are directly available in the CTM planning process.

Glossary

aggregated planning Supply Network Planning (SNP) and the Capable-to-Match (CTM) method where planning is performed at the level of a header location product, and the planning results are then disaggregated to the level of subproducts of the location product hierarchy. The demand values of the subproducts are first aggregated in the demand key figures for the header location product.

Alert Monitor A component that handles common exceptions and problems for the SCM applications Advanced Planner and Optimizer (APO), Inventory Collaboration Hub (ICH), and Fulfillment Coordination (FC). The Alert Monitor uses event triggers and alarm conditions established during planning and scheduling to automatically identify problems in the supply chain. It monitors factors such as material, capacity, transportation, and storage constraints, as well as metrics such as delivery performance, cost flow, and throughput. In essence, the Alert Monitor is a tool used by planners to monitor the state of plans in the system, and the actual alerts serve as guidelines for re-planning.

bill of materials (BOM) A complete, structured list of the components that make up a product or an assembly. The list contains the description, the quantity, and unit of measure. The components are known as BOM items. In the SAP system, BOMs can form different objects and manage object-related data. You can maintain material BOM, document structure BOM, equipment BOM, document BOM, equipment BOM, and sales order BOM.

bucket A time period such as a day or week that can used for planning in SNP and CTM.

Capable-to-Match (CTM) An advanced supply chain management function in SAP APO that complements SAP APO SNP's multi-site supply chain planning strategies. The CTM engine performs a quick check of production capacities and transportation capabilities. CTM grades and works out multisite production processes using time-dependent process parameters such as yield and process times. To exploit production capabilities to the maximum, the capacity check is performed down to the operational level. Planning strategies control the sequence of supply consumption and the multilevel BOM explosion.

constraint Constraints are restrictions, conditions that have to be fulfilled in production to enable the execution of the master production schedule, such as availability of the necessary components or work centers with sufficient capacity.

constraint-based planning A form of production planning based on the assumption that the whole production process is determined by certain bottlenecks. Possible bottlenecks that have a crucial influence on production are resources with low capacity and raw materials that are only available in limited quantities. The bottlenecks are planned in constraint-based planning with special attention. A resource with low capacity is planned with priority. Planning of all remaining resources is dependent on the planning results of this work center.

disaggregation Function by which a key figure value on a high level is automatically broken down to the detailed level. For example, if you forecast demand in a particular region, the system instantly splits up this number among the different sales channels, product families, brands, products, customers, and so on, in this region. This ensures a consistent planning approach throughout your organization. Key figure values are stored at the lowest level of detail. If you use aggregates, the data is also stored on the aggregate levels. You set the disaggregation type of a key figure in S&DP administration.

distribution requirement planning A function that allows the optimization of inventory replenishment at warehouses in a multilevel distribution network. Stock outs and shipping costs can be reduced without an increase in overall stock levels.

down binning Down binning scenarios, often found in the high-tech industries (e.g., in the semi-conductor business), can be supported using rules. For instance, you can specify substitutions that the system can use so that a product of higher quality can be used to fulfill the demand for a lower-quality product to meet the customer demand and maintain service levels.

explanation tool Function for CTM-based planning that the user can use to have the system explain two significant exceptional situations within the CTM run, that is, late or nonfulfillment of the demand quantities. The function displays possible causes of the exceptional situations in the log for the CTM run.

InfoCube An InfoCube describes a self-contained dataset (from the reporting view), for example, for Demand Planning (DP). This dataset can be evaluated with the BEx query. An InfoCube is a set of relational tables that are created in accordance with the star schema: a large fact table in the center, with several dimension tables surrounding it.

interchangeability group Groups together products for interchangeability purposes. The types of interchangeability groups available are supersession chain, FFF class, restricted interchangeability for FFF classes, and product substitution procedure.

lot size Lot for material is used as a quantity to be produced or to be procured. Additionally, in CTM planning, the lot size is also used as a criterion for selecting the production process model or for selecting PPM BOMs and routings.

pegging Procedure in production planning and detailed scheduling (PP/DS) that establishes the relationship between receipt elements and requirements elements of a product within a location. Using pegging, the corresponding receipt elements are assigned to the requirements. Two types of pegging are available in SAP SCM. With fixed pegging, the assignment of a receipt element to a requirements element remains fixed during planning. With dynamic pegging, the assignment of receipt elements to requirements elements can change depending on the planning situation.

pegging area Combination of product, location, account assignment object, and planning version. A requirements, stock, or receipt element is in a specific pegging area. Only stock and receipt elements that lie within the same pegging area can be assigned to a requirements element. The stock and receipts of a pegging area can only therefore cover the requirements from the same pegging area. The pegging area is identical to the planning segment in SAP R/3, with the exception of the planning version. In SAP APO, the term "planning segment" is often used as a synonym for "pegging area."

plan   A plan describes location-independent work processes and components involved in the manufacture of a product or co-products on a nonorder-specific basis. Key elements of a plan include the following:

- The work steps (activities) necessary to manufacture the product
- The resources needed to carry out the activities
- The temporal relationships between the activities
- The components needed to manufacture the product

To determine which plan is used to manufacture a product, a production process model (PPM) is generated for the plan. The bill of materials (BOM) and the routing (or the recipe) from the R/3 or SAP ERP application correspond to the plan in SAP APO. To avoid confusion, in this context, the "plan" is also often referred to more precisely as the "PPM plan."

Plan Monitor   A tool in the SAP SCM system that evaluates the accuracy of a production plan or detailed production line schedule. The Plan Monitor is used for evaluating production key figures, key figures pertaining to characteristics, and other figures derived from calculations based on formulas. The key figures are evaluated by a points system that results in a total score. The results can be displayed in a grid or in an aggregated or detailed format.

planned delivery time   The number of days required to procure the material through external procurement. In CTM planning, the planned delivery time is considered from the planning start day or the current day. No purchase requisitions can be created or deleted inside the planned delivery time.

planned independent requirement (PIR)   A planned requirement quantity for a finished product in a period of time. It isn't based on sales orders. PIRs are used in CTM as demand elements for prioritization and planning.

planning area   Central data structure of Demand Planning (DP) and Supply Network Planning (SNP). The planning area is created as part of the DP/SNP setup. A planning book is based on a planning area. The end user is aware of the planning book, not the planning area. The SAP liveCache objects on which data is actually saved are based on the planning area, not the planning book. The planning area specifies the following elements:

- Unit of measure in which data is planned
- Currency in which data is planned (optional)
- Currency conversion type for viewing planning data in other currencies (optional)
- Storage buckets profile that determines the buckets in which data is stored in this planning area
- Aggregate levels on which data can be stored in addition to the lowest level of detail to enhance performance
- Key figures that are used in this planning area
- Settings that determine how each key figure is disaggregated, aggregated, and saved
- The assignment of key figures to aggregates

SNP comes with predefined planning areas.

planning book   Defines the content and layout of the interactive planning screen. You use planning books in Demand Planning (DP) and Supply Network Planning (SNP). They allow you to design the screen to suit individual planning tasks. A planning book is based on a planning area. There is no limit on the

265

number of planning books you can have for a planning area.

In the planning book, you define the following elements:

- Key figures and other rows
- Characteristics

Functions and applications that can be accessed directly from this planning book:

- User-specific planning horizons
- User-specific views on the planning book, including initial column, number of grids, and accessibility of the view for other users (there is no limit on the number of views you can have within one planning book)

You can configure these and further elements of the interactive planning screen (such as the position of columns and rows, the use of colors and icons in rows, the visibility or not of rows, the appearance of the graphic, and macros) by using the context menus in interactive design mode.

SNP comes with two standard books:

- 9ASNP94 for traditional SNP
- 9ASOP for SAP Sales and Operations Planning (SAP SOP)

You can use these books as a basis for creating your own planning books by using the standard views as templates.

production data structure (PDS) Structure that contains the master data for planning in SAP APO. PDSs are differentiated by the source of the generation data. PDS data can be generated from iPPE data (product structure, process structure, factory layout) or from R/3 data (classic master data such as BOM, routing, and recipe). In both cases, the production version provides the basis for generating the PDS. In addition, the PDS is also maintained for individual applications Demand Planning (DP), Supply Network Planning (SNP), Capable-to-Match (CTM), production planning/detailed scheduling (PP/DS). The PDS is used as a source of supply (SOS) in SAP APO. In CTM planning, the SNP PDS can be used for bucket planning and CTM PDS for PP/DS planning. The main difference between the CTM and PP/DS PDS is that the CTM PDS is much simpler and doesn't contain all of the attributes that are available in PP/DS PDS, which is mainly used for detailed scheduling in PP/DS.

production horizon Period in which no new sales orders may be scheduled because the sales orders that have already been released are produced in this period. The production horizon serves to protect the planned production. Therefore, new sales orders can only be scheduled outside this horizon; that is, their start dates must lie outside this horizon. The production horizon is a part of the time-series horizon and precedes the checking horizon.

production planning and detailed scheduling (PP/DS) A module in SAP APO that enables the production within a plant to be planned while, at the same time, taking product and capacity constraints into account. The aim of this module is to increase throughput and to reduce product stock. This results in a feasible master production schedule.

production planning run Execution of background planning with heuristics or planning functions. In a production planning run, you can execute different kinds of planning successively, for example, first planning according to MRP logic for selected products, and then sequence optimization on the relevant bottleneck resources.

production process model (PPM) A production process model (PPM) describes when a plan can be used to manufacture a product. A location and a lot size interval are defined in the PPM as validity criteria. The temporal validity is adopted from the output product. The production version from SAP R/3 corresponds to the PPM in SAP APO.

resource A machine, person, facility, warehouse, means of transportation, or other asset with a limited capacity that fulfills a particular function in the supply chain. In SAP APO, the following resources can be modeled:

- **Resources whose capacity is determined by working time data:** The capacity of these resources is continuously available during working hours. There are single-activity resources, on which only one activity can be processed at any one time, and multi-activity resources, on which several activities can be processed simultaneously. Single-activity resources and multi-activity resources are used for scheduling in the SAP APO components Capable-to-Match (CTM) and production planning and detailed scheduling (PP/DS), in which production dates of orders and operations are scheduled in seconds.
- **Bucket resources**: Capacities are defined by quantities (e.g., transport or warehouse capacities) or by daily rates (e.g., production rates). Bucket resources are used for scheduling in Supply Network Planning (SNP). The most detailed scheduling that can be done is on a daily basis.

resource category The classification of the use of a resource (e.g., for production or for transport).

resource consumption Capacity of a resource that is required for carrying out an activity. An activity that is carried out on a multi-activity resource can have variable resource consumption, depending on the quantity to be produced. A single-activity resource can only process one activity at a time; it has a capacity of 1. An activity that is carried out on a single-activity resource, therefore, has a fixed resource consumption of 1.

resource type Determines how resource planning is to be controlled, that is, which attributes are available for planning.

The following resource types exist:

- Single resource types
- Multiresource types
- Bucket resource types
- Line resource types
- Transportation resource types
- Mixed resource types
- Vehicle resource types

Example: Single resource types can be set up. Multiresource types and bucket resource types can't be set up. All resource types are available to all applications, but an application can't necessarily use all resource types. In CTM planning, single, multi, mixed, bucket, and transportation resources are supported for planning.

safety stock (SS) The quantity of stock that is always available in the warehouse to fulfill unexpectedly high demand or that can be used in production if there are time delays.

scheduling agreement An outline agreement against which materials are procured at a series of predefined points in time over a certain period.

source determination Method that determines feasible sources of supply based on application-specific data. It uses a number of different criteria, such as quota arrangements, procurement priorities, or costs, as a basis for producing a ranked list of sources, from which

Glossary

the desired source is then chosen. In interactive planning, the source is chosen from this ranked list by the user; in automatic planning, the system chooses (using a heuristic, for instance). In the case of third-party order processing, source determination determines a source location (supplier) based on valid contracts or scheduling agreements. The goods are then sent from the supplier to the destination location (customer).

stock transfer horizon CTM doesn't create stock transfer orders inside this horizon and can be maintained for each product and location.

supply category Grouping of all receipts and supplies available for Capable-to-Match planning (CTM) according to various criteria. Supply categories form the basis of the CTM search strategy. You use the CTM search strategy to specify the sequence in which the individual supply categories are to be used to cover demands.

supply chain A sequence of operations and centers through which supplies move from the source of supply to the final customer or point of use. The supply chain starts with the extraction of raw materials or origination of raw concepts for services. Each link in the chain processes the material or the concept or supports processing. The supply chain extends from the raw material extraction or raw concept through many processes to the sale of the final products, goods, or services to the consumer.

Supply Chain Cockpit (SCC) One of the planning applications of the SAP Advanced Planner and Optimizer (SAP APO). The Supply Chain Cockpit (SCC) is a graphical instrument panel for modeling, navigating, and controlling the supply chain. It acts as a top-planning layer through which the user can oversee other planning areas within an enterprise, including demand, manufacturing, distribution, and transportation.

Supply Network Planning (SNP) A module in the SAP Advanced Planner and Optimizer (SAP APO) that enables organizations to determine sourcing, production plans, distribution plans, and purchasing plans. The system draws on the data universally available in SAP liveCache to optimize such plans based on optimization algorithms and heuristic approaches that enable the planner to define rules and inventory policies.

Vendor Managed Inventory (VMI) VMI scenario describes how vendors can plan material requirements in the customer's company. Vendors can only offer this service if they have access to stock figures and sales data at the customer. In R/3, you can implement VMI from a vendor point of view and from a customer point of view. VMI would typically be used when the manufacturer of consumer products plans the replenishments of the products at a retailer. You can use VMI functions independently of each other and also in different contexts.

The Author

Balaji Gaddam completed his Masters in Engineering from Madras Institute of Technology, Chennai, India in 1996 where he received the Gold Medal for academic excellence. After graduation, he joined Ramco Systems as a systems analyst. At Ramco systems, he was responsible for the design and development of the Purchase Planning solution for MIGROS, the biggest retailer in Switzerland.

After the successful implementation of the purchase planning solution at MIGROS and spending two years in Switzerland, he returned to India and joined SAP Labs India as a developer in 1999.

Since joining SAP Labs, Balaji has worked mainly in the Logistics and Supply Chain Management solutions. He was part of the Strategic Development project for Diamler Chrsyler and was responsible for the design and development of new functions in the R/3 MM module. In 2001, Balaji moved to Walldorf, Germany and joined SAP Ag as a developer and was responsible for the design and development of some of the key functions of the Capable-to-Match solution from release APO 2.0 until SCM 5.0.

Balaji moved to the United States and currently leads the SCM Center of Expertise (COE) team based in Newtown Square Philadelphia. Over the years, Balaji has worked with and provided expert services to large corporations in the United States and other regions. He worked with Freescale Semiconductors, Nike, Amgen, Monsanto, Panasonic, Fonterra, Microsoft, Merck Pharmaceuticals, and other large and mid-sized corporations during the project blueprinting and implementation phase.

If you have questions regarding SAP SCM or CTM, or if you want to provide feedback on this book, you can contact the author via the following:

Email: *balaji.rao.gaddam@sap.com*

Index

A

Aggregated planning, 223
Airline strategy, 131
ATP rules, 57
Automatic master data selection, 40

B

Bucket planning mode, 68
Bucket resources, 49

C

Capable to Match (CTM), 16
Capable-to-Match planning, 21
Capacity planning, 66
Component Withdrawal in Another Location, 207
Constant safety stock planning, 166
CTM application log, 239
CTM BAdI, 260
CTM demand and supply attributes, 72
CTM engine trace, 248
CTM engine trace evaluation, 250
CTM order scheduling, 115
CTM planning engine, 27, 101
CTM planning parameters, 31
CTM planning steps, 242
CTM search strategy for source selection, 97
CTM source of supply selection, 107
CTM supply selection, 106
CTM time stream, 65

D

Decision criteria for source selection, 106
Deletion modes, 61
DEMAGGBYLOTSIZE, 79
Demand aggregation, 76
Demand prioritization, 82
Demand selection horizon, 136
Depth first strategy, 103
Descriptive characteristics (DCs), 89
Domino strategy, 130
Down binning, 222
Dynamic data selection, 40
Dynamic pegging, 60

E

Explanation profile, 143
External procurement relationships, 50

F

Fixed pegging, 60
Form-Fit-Function (FFF) class, 216

G

Global-ATP (GATP), 16

I

Interval planning, 172

L

LANE_NOSOURCE_IGNORE, 52
Late demand frame, 131
Late demand scheduling, 132
Late demand strategies, 68
Late demand strategy, 130
Location, 46
Location product hierarchy, 224

Index

M

Make-to-Order (MTO), 199
Make-to-Stock Production, 194
Master data check function, 42
Master data selection identifier, 38
Maximum Earliness, 139
Maximum Earliness for Planned Orders, 138
MBDAT_TZ, 86
Minimum build, 188
Mixed resources, 49
Model consistency check profile, 43

N

Net change planning, 63, 64

P

Parallel processing, 257
Pegging type, 70
PIR Segment, 194
Planning modes in CTM, 61
Planning strategy, 64
Planning with Final Assembly, 195
Planning Without Final Assembly, 196
Planning with Planning Product strategy, 199
PP/DS time-continuous planning mode, 35
PPM/PDS hierarchy, 225
Procurement processes within the plant, 205
Procurement type, 108
Product interchangeability, 57, 212
Production data structure, 53
Production in alternative location, 203
Production planning and detailed scheduling (PP/DS), 16
Production process model, 53
Product location, 47
Publish CTM results to SAP ERP, 255

R

Regenerative planning, 63
Requirements strategy, 193
Resource hierarchy, 225
Resources, 48
Resource utilization, 125
Result indicator, 147

S

Safety days of supply, 159
Safety lead time, 179
Safety stock planning, 157
SAP Advanced Planner and Optimizer (SAP APO), 15
SAP APO Demand Planning (DP), 15
SAP APO Supply Network Planning (SNP), 18
SAP liveCache, 26
SAP Supply Network Collaboration, 18
Scheduling direction, 69
Scheduling of planned order, 116
Scheduling purchase requisitions, 129
Scheduling stock transfer order, 126
Scheduling substitution order, 129
SNP Deployment, 16
SNP Heuristics, 20, 35
SNP Optimizer, 20, 35
Sort sequence, 84
Source selection with inbound quota, 110
Static data selection, 40
Storage location MRP area, 207
Store Transport and Prod. at Destination Location, 185
Subcontracting planning, 209
Substitution rule, 218
Supersession, 213
Supply aggregation, 90
Supply categorization, 92
Supply chain coordination, 17
Supply Chain Event Management (SCEM), 17
Supply Chain Management (SCM), 13

Supply distribution, 25
supply distribution (SD), 187
Supply Network Planning (SNP), 15

T

Time-continuous planning mode, 67
Time-continuous resource, 48
Time-phased safety stock, 168
Transactional data selection, 58

Transportation planning/vehicle scheduling (TP/VS), 16
Transport Load Builder (TLB), 16
Transport Receipts Elements Individually, 186

U

Unscheduled break, 125

www.sap-press.com

Teaches how to identify and assess key figures for your sales processes in SD

Provides step-by-step instructions for creating customer and material oriented analysis

Contains practical tips on how to create effective, useful data and analysis

Susanne Hess, Stefanie Lenz, Jochen Scheibler

Sales and Distribution Controlling with SAP NetWeaver BI

This book teaches users how to define, evaluate, and report key figures for sales and distribution controlling in SD (SAP ERP 6.0) using SAP NetWeaver BI 7.0. It starts with an overview of essential key figures in SD controlling and explains their business background. From there, it details the sales processes, and provides an overview of how raw data is created. Users learn how to map key figures for business controlling in a business warehouse, and how to use key figures in various analysis tools.

approx. 250 pp., 68,– Euro / US$ 85
ISBN 978-1-59229-266-0, March 2009

>> www.sap-press.de/2019

www.sap-press.com

Introduces readers to the ins-and-outs of SAP DMS

Addresses all uses and details of Document Management

Provides real-world examples and practical

Up-to-date for ERP 6.0

Eric Stajda

Effective Document Management with SAP DMS

This essentials guide is a complete and practical resource to SAP Document Management System. It teaches project managers, functional users, and consultants everything they need to know to understand, configure, and use SAP DMS, and provides step-by-step instructions and real-world scenarios. This is a must-have book for anyone interested in learning about and creating an efficient, effective document management system using SAP.

202 pp., 2009, 68,– Euro / US$ 85
ISBN 978-1-59229-240-0

>> www.sap-press.de/1936

www.sap-press.com

Teaches how to integrate cProjects and RPM to provide a high-level visibility over the entire project portfolio

Provides functionality and integration details for cProjects and RPM with SAP Project System

Includes real-world customer examples throughout

Up-to-date for cProjects 4.5 and RPM 4.5

Stefan Glatzmaier, Michael Sokollek

Project Portfolio Management with SAP RPM and cProjects

SAP PRESS Essentials 49

This essentials guide introduces and teaches users how to integrate and use project portfolio management with SAP to support their business processes. The book focuses on cProjects and SAP RPM, as well as the integration with SAP Project System. With real-life examples, this book uses examples to illustrate specific solution options and projects. The main chapters are based on the actual business processes in an enterprise and contain industry-specific recommendations. The book is based on the latest releases, and is a must-have addition to any SAP library.

355 pp., 2009, 68,– Euro / US$ 85
ISBN 978-1-59229-224-0

>> www.sap-press.de/1838

www.sap-press.com

Learn how to use E-Procurement effectively with other SAP components, including MM and Financials

Explore the implementation processes to ensure an effective implementation

Find out how to optimize your procurement processes, reduce ordering costs, decentralize purchase orders, and more

Up-to-date for SAP ERP 6.0

Eduard Gerhardt, Kai Krüger, Oliver Schipp

Efficient E-Procurement with SAP

SAP PRESS Essentials 47

This book describes how to carry out procurement processes and map these processes in the SAP system, using the E-Procurement solution. Readers will learn which SAP tool is best suited for which requirement in purchasing and procurement, and which usage options these tools provide. Above all, readers will get to know how they can use E-Procurement in order to optimize their own procurement processes, reduce ordering costs, decentralize purchase orders, and reduce the Purchasing department workload.

201 pp., 2008, 68,– Euro / US$ 85
ISBN 978-1-59229-209-7

>> www.sap-press.de/1789

www.sap-press.com

Master real-life business processes and the structuring of plant maintenance technical systems

Discover tips and tricks for implementing daily operations

Explore interfaces, reporting, and new EAM technologies – MAM, RFID, Enterprise SOA, NetWeaver Portal, and more

Karl Liebstückel

SAP Enterprise Asset Management

This is a must-have guide for anyone interested in learning about the implementation and customization of SAP EAM. Consultants, managers, and administrators will learn about the plant maintenance process, how to evaluate which processes work best for them, and then go on to review the actual configuration steps of these processes. This book includes practical tips and best practices for implementation projects. The companion DVD contains examples, practice tests, presentations, and more. This book is up-to-date for SAP ERP 6.0.

552 pp., 2008, with CD, 69,95 Euro / US$ 69.95
ISBN 978-1-59229-150-2

>> www.sap-press.de/1528

www.sap-press.com

Improve supply chain efficiency using non-standard SNC scenarios

Discover practical solutions for enhancing SNC

Learn from customizing examples, tips, and techniques to configure or extend the capabilities of SNC

Christian Butzlaff, Thomas Heinzel, Frank Thome

Non-Standard Scenarios for SAP Supply Network Collaboration

SAP PRESS Essentials 43

This Essentials is a detailed guide for those needing unique and new scenarios to maximize their SNC solution. Based on SAP SNC 5.1, it focuses on insightful, new information usually only available from highly experienced consultants or SAP development, such as enhanced business scenarios, and notification and authorization enhancements. The book begins with a concise review of SNC, its architecture, and standard scenarios, and then quickly moves on to the non-standard scenarios and other techniques for enhancing and customizing SAP SNC.

213 pp., 2009, 68,– Euro / US$ 85
ISBN 978-1-59229-195-3

>> www.sap-press.de/1741

www.sap-press.com

Discover what Logistics with SAP is all about and whether its right for your organization

Learn how this powerful, time-tested tool can improve your supply chain and transportation processes to save you money

Explore the major components, including procurement, inventory management,

Martin Murray

Discover Logistics with SAP ERP

With this reader-friendly book, anyone new to SAP or considering implementing it will discover the fundamental capabilities and uses of the Logistics components. You'll learn what's available, and how it works to help you determine if Logistics with SAP is the right tool for your organization. This book is written in a clear, practical style, and uses real-world examples, case studies, and insightful tips to give you a complete overview of the SAP logistics offerings.

385 pp., 2009, 39,95 Euro / US$ 39.95
ISBN 978-1-59229-230-1

>> www.sap-press.de/1851

Interested in reading more?

Please visit our Web site for all
new book releases from SAP PRESS.

www.sap-press.com